Negotiated governance
and public policy in Ireland

Manchester University Press

D1057754

To 'Babs' Merrill

Thanking you

Negotiated governance and public policy in Ireland

George Taylor

Manchester University Press

Manchester and New York

distributed exclusively in the USA by Palgrave

Published by Manchester University Press
Oxford Road, Manchester M13 9NR, UK
and Room 400, 175 Fifth Avenue, New York, NY 10010, USA
www.manchesteruniversitypress.co.uk

Distributed exclusively in the USA by
Palgrave, 175 Fifth Avenue, New York,
NY 10010, USA

Distributed exclusively in Canada by
UBC Press, University of British Columbia, 2029 West Mall,
Vancouver, BC, Canada V6T 1Z2

British Library Cataloguing-in-Publication Data
A catalogue record for this book is available from the British Library

Library of Congress Cataloging-in-Publication Data applied for

ISBN   0 7190 6998 X *hardback*
EAN   978 0 7190 6998 7
ISBN   0 7190 6999 8 *paperback*
EAN   978 0 7190 6999 4

First published 2005

13 12 11 10 09 08 07 06 05   10 9 8 7 6 5 4 3 2 1

Typeset
by Northern Phototypesetting Co Ltd, Bolton
Printed in Great Britain
by Biddles Ltd, King's Lynn

Contents

List of tables

Acknowledgements

In any academic work I have completed it would be remiss of me not to acknowledge the enduring influence of Dave Marsh. That he continues to provide a sounding board for ideas as well as intellectual stimulus is something for which I am extremely grateful. That such engagement is possible while having a great craic over a few beers simply makes me fortunate. I would also like to take the opportunity to thank Cathi Murphy and Avril Horan, postgraduates of mine who stimulated my interest initially in environmental politics and later Irish public policy.

In a work of this length the assistance of librarians is invaluable. I would like to thank the librarians at NUIG and in particular Eileen Maloney and Laurie Greenfield. Although it is a cliché that 'you may well remember good teachers but you never forget great ones', it is one worth repeating. Educated at an 'average comp' I was indeed lucky to have been taught by some very good teachers that include: Nigel Pickles, Martin Warren, Andy Snart, Mrs Beckett and John Foley. However, my deepest gratitude goes to Barbara Merrill, a truly exceptional teacher, to whom this book is dedicated.

Abbreviations

ALMPS	active labour market policies
AMCSS	Association of Management of Catholic Secondary Schools
ASTI	Association of Secondary Teachers in Ireland
BATNEEC	best available technology not entailing excessive cost
BTWA	Back to Work Allowance
C&AG	comptroller and auditor general
CAAI	Clare Alliance Against Incineration
CAP	Common Agricultural Policy
CE	Community Employment
CEDP	Community Employment Development Programme
CFYPS	Control Farmyard Pollution Scheme
CHIU	Conference of the Heads of Irish Universities
CPSMA	Catholic Primary School Managers' Association
DACG	Department of Arts, Culture and the Gaeltacht
DAFF	Department of Agriculture, Food and Forestry
DoE	Department of Education
EIA	Environmental Impact Assessment
EIS	Environmental Impact Statement
EPA	Environmental Protection Agency
ESRI	Economic and Social Research Institute
FÁS	Training and Employment Authority
FIS	Family Income Support
HEA	Higher Education Authority
HR	Human resources
IBEC	Irish Business and Employers' Confederation
ICTU	Irish Congress of Trade Unions
IDA	Industrial Development Authority
IFA	Irish Farmers' Association
IIRS	Institute for Industrial Research and Standards

IMF	International Monetary Fund
INOU	Irish National Organisation for the Unemployed
INTO	Irish National Teachers Organisation
IPC	integrated pollution control
IRN	*Industrial Relations News*
IRR	Income replacement ratio
KWS	Keynesian welfare state
LES	Local employment service
LRC	Labour Relations Commission
NAP	National Action Plan
NESC	National Economic and Social Council
NESF	National Economic and Social Forum
NPM	New public management
NTMA	National Treasury Management Agency
NU	National Understandings
NWA	National Wage Agreements
OECD	Organisation for Economic Co-operation and Development
OPRD	Operational Programme for Rural Development
PCW	Programme for Competitiveness and Work
PD	Progressive Democrats
PESP	Programme for Economic and Social Progress
PNER	Programme for National Economic Recovery
PPF	Programme for Prosperity and Fairness
PR	Proportional representation
PRSA	Personal Retirement Savings Account
PRSI	Pay Related Social Insurance
PR-STV	Proportional representation – single transferable vote
REPS	Rural Environmental Protection Scheme
RTE	Radio Telefís Éireann
SAC	Special Area of Conservation
SES	Social Employment Scheme
SIPTU	Services, Industrial, Professional and Technical Union
SMI	Strategic Management Initiative
TD	Teachta Dála (parliamentary representative, often referred to as 'Deputy')
TLAC	Top Level Appointments Committee
TUI	Teachers' Union of Ireland
UA	Unemployment assistance
YPP	Youth Progression Programme

Words in Irish

An Bord Pleanála	planning authority
An Foras Forbatha	development agency
Coillte	state-owned forestry company
Dáil (Eireann)	Lower House of Parliament (Leinster House)
Fianna Fáil	largest political party in Ireland – usually translated as 'soldiers of Destiny'
Fine Gael	second largest political party in Ireland
gardai	Police force
Seanad	Upper House of Parliament
Tánaiste	deputy prime minister
Taoiseach	prime minister
Teagasc	Research body for agriculture

Introduction

Amid the clamour to celebrate the bewildering economic success of the Celtic Tiger, it almost seems perverse to record that as recently as the late 1980s political historians such as J. J. Lee were castigating Ireland's economic performance, attributing failure to the lack of an indigenous entrepreneurial spirit. For Ireland to prosper, what was required in his considered opinion (and it was an opinion held by many) was the creation of an entrepreneurial cadre capable of dismantling the lumbering Irish state (Lee, 1989). Impressive though the turnaround has been it is perhaps all the more remarkable for its surprising durability, a fact confirmed in the lavish praise which often emanates from EU officials who look idolatrously upon the stratospheric levels of growth achieved in Ireland.

For many political scientists and neo-liberal economists, such a reversal in the fortunes of the Irish polity was all the more puzzling because it occurred against the backdrop of a period dominated by a succession of macro-political bargaining agreements. Critics of such organised political intermediation contend that these political structures are incompatible with global capitalism and are little more than a hindrance to economic restructuring (see Goldthorpe, 1984; Lash and Urry, 1987; Streeck, 1992; Gobeyn, 1993). And yet, there can be little doubt that despite the constraints these agreements allegedly impose, the Irish state has effected a decisive break with the trappings of an age of state-led modernisation, symbolised in the rise and later ignominious fall from grace of Team Aer Lingus, part of the Irish state-owned company Aer Lingus which was involved in international aircraft maintenance at Dublin airport. If the 1980s were about such projects, then the 1990s were about creating the free market conditions in which investment from the information-rich, high-technology multinational companies could flourish.

The pessimism which prevailed among political historians at the beginning of the 1990s has since been replaced by an overwhelming political ebullience encapsulated, if not altogether explained, in the concept of our times: the Celtic Tiger. Though detailed definitions are few and far between, what remains incontrovertible is that if its leitmotif is flexibility then its flagship is the US IT multinational Intel. It often appears that little is required in the way of an excuse for Radio Telefís Éireann (RTE) news to haul before us the mesmeric image of Intel workers wearing 'space suits'. As a global leader in a field of cutting-edge technology the company not only acts as an icon of this new era, but serves as a barometer for the well-being of the Irish economy, reinforcing impressively the magnitude of change.

It is a commonplace to suggest that phrases such as 'the Celtic Tiger' assume such prominence (and widespread acceptance) because they somehow resonate with our experience of everyday life. In this way it is argued that individuals interpret the Celtic Tiger in terms of their experience of the information age with its extended use of the tools of the global economy: mobile phones, PCs, modems, cable TV, multimedia packages and the internet. And yet the term also captures a level of dynamism previously not associated with the Irish polity, reinforcing the impression that the Irish state has embarked upon a (successful) venture to develop a new political architecture, one which befits its status as an emerging, cosmopolitan European nation. In this vibrant and more confident polity it seems that we are all surfers now (Taylor, 2002b).[1]

As a phrase, however, 'the Celtic Tiger' remains all the more quixotic because definitions have thus far proven elusive. There are those who may dispute its constituent elements but few would deny that it appears to possess that most ethereal of qualities: the ability to act as a prism through which our disparate, individual experiences of the contemporary Irish polity are refracted and made intelligible. On the one hand, it is capable of pervading the currency of the mundane aspects of everyday life, confirming our intuitive sense of change: from the transformation of the workplace experience to conversations which express dismay at either escalating house prices or the time we have spent in Dublin's gridlock. On the other hand, it has found considerable favour in political and media circles, where it has rendered intelligible the almost incomprehensible: a period of unprecedented economic growth unimaginable at the start of the 1990s.

That references to the Celtic Tiger abound hardly requires comment. However, more often than not the term does little more than relieve us of the onerous task of providing a thorough explanation of contemporary events (Taylor, 2002b). Amid the enthusiasm for embracing all that is 'particularly Irish' in this political and economic project, it is hardly surprising to find that there are few dissenting voices. Indeed, even among the more vocal supporters of the Celtic Tiger it is rare to publicise or challenge other, more contentious elements of this new age: the uncertainty of employment tenure, the inescapable increase in poverty during a period of economic boom, or (and let us speak in hushed tones at this point) the emergence of a potential underclass in Irish society. Certainly, where the dissenters surface, they run the risk of being charged with that most heinous of Irish crimes, begrudgery.

And yet, almost perversely, it is precisely at this point that we can locate the appeal of the term 'Celtic Tiger' for both Irish academe and elements of the media. For it is not so much that it expresses anything uniquely Irish or indeed Celtic. Rather, its allure rests on something it is definitely not. It is definitely not Thatcherism. The ease with which the Celtic Tiger metaphor has been subsumed into the Irish political psyche rests on the fact that, in some intangible fashion, it confers upon an economic strategy a social democratic ethos (or at least its proponents hope it does) capable of securing a place at the table of the global economic leaders without enduring the divisions that have riven British society. It is this transformation, or at least an exploration of its first tentative stages, which forms the central preoccupation of this book.

It should surprise few of those who endured the long periods of high structural unemployment in the recent past to see the issue of economic growth figure so prominently in political discourse. Almost imperceptibly, however, attention has focused increasingly upon the need for change within the political structures of the Irish polity. Certainly, the political scandals which enveloped a succession of Irish governments in the 1990s did little to assuage the concerns of its citizenry about the suitability of its political structures or indeed much of its personnel. Political discourse is now replete with demands for greater political transparency, enhanced political participation, and the construction of political institutions capable of accelerating the momentum towards a flexible economy while retaining a democratic impulse to reduce social exclusion. For the spin doctors of this era the quest is now under way to forge a new political shell, one capable of embracing the disparate political views of modern Ireland.[2]

To this end a concern with the relationship between the state, the market and the maintenance of social order forms a significant theme throughout this book. There has always been a temptation to present the market as the principal mechanism for allocating resources (and therefore the site of conflict) and the state as the 'regulator' of that activity. This simple dichotomy presents us with at least two problems. First, the tendency to view the state and the market as the sole regulative mechanisms ignores the important functions performed by other institutions. Second, there is also a discernible tendency to downplay the role of institutions outside of

the market. This book therefore examines the plethora of new forms of regulation which have emerged in which the state 'sanctions', 'reinforces' or
lends authority to policy outcomes (Lange and Regini, 1989). As such, it
examines the changing nature of state–civil society relations in Ireland, a
project which demands more than the simple reiteration of the legislative
developments or policy changes which have taken place (although this is
undertaken in each chapter). Rather, the book seeks to situate such change
within the overall context of a new and developing form of governance in
Ireland.

One of the more significant features of this new form of governance is
the pre-eminence of a flexible and innovative pattern of accumulation. For
those such as Jessop, the move to a new global economic order will be signified by a shift to polyvalent skilled workers and an increased demand for
niche products. In addition, new forms of flexible production and organisation will emerge. Under the Conservative governments of the UK or New
Zealand this project took a deliberately neo-liberal slant. It set about cir-
cumventing the power of trade unions and openly challenged the Fordist
wage relation (Jessop, 1994, p. 20). A political platform was constructed
that sought to replace the labyrinthine bureaucratic structures of the Keynesian welfare state (KWS) with self-regulating markets, a move expected
to stimulate a new entrepreneurial spirit. Although privatisation and liber-
alisation were the most prominent legacies of this period, successive governments were also active in attempts to produce flexible labour markets
and a welfare state that would support a low-wage economy. In essence,
then, Thatcherism represented a systematic rejection of the post-war settlement that had, in some form or other, embraced the ideal of social partnership (Jessop, 1994, p. 30).

By the end of the 1980s, Irish political historians such as J. J. Lee were
echoing such sentiments when they attributed the principal failing of Irish
capitalism to its inability to create an entrepreneurial spirit (Lee, 1989). A
decade of discontent with state-led modernisation had culminated in
demands to protect the habitat of Ireland's most endangered species: the
elusive entrepreneur (Taylor, 1993). While political debate in media circles
was often reduced to little more than discussions about the benefits of
either reductions in taxation or increases in welfare provision, the central
issues remain more complex and deep-rooted. This book suggests that the
Irish state has been occupied with an altogether more important political
project, one designed to engineer a form of governance capable of meeting
the demand for the level of economic growth associated with other major
European countries while ensuring at least a modicum of social inclusion.

To most economists the principal features of this change are usually
identified in the transformation of company structures and/or the adop-

tion of new flexible working practices. There can be little doubt that change in this sphere has taken place. However, if we are to comprehend more fully the dynamics that underpin the Celtic Tiger, then it is important to acknowledge the changing nature of political institutions and their effect upon the direction of Irish society. This book argues that Irish political institutions have altered radically in response to the pressures of competing in the global economy. Moreover, the determination to restructure the country's institutional apparatus should not be viewed as simply another belated attempt to modernise, but forms part of a wider programme of establishing a new consensus around the drive towards a flexible economy. If this project is to be successful then political as well as economic change will be crucial.

In contrast to the neo-liberal form of disengagement to be found in either New Zealand, the USA or the UK, Ireland has pursued a neo-corporatist approach which has been proactive (and at least partially successful) in pursuing a programme of restructuring. In line with the prime objective of remaining competitive in the new global economic order, the Irish state has initiated a reordering of both the productive side of the economy and its attendant political institutions. This has involved a fundamental shift in the nature of governance, since economic management has not been left solely to the market or to the state. In addition, while a more general process of 'hollowing out the state' has taken place, the neo-corporatist form of economic management has increasingly sought to restructure along lines more suited to the new global market. The onus has shifted firmly away from macro-level demand-side considerations to a restructuring of the supply side or micro-level of the economy. In the wider areas of public policy an increased diffusion of responsibilities for the construction, direction and implementation of policy among different political actors has complemented this.

If we are to grasp the changing nature of state–civil society relations in Ireland it remains crucial that we examine the plurality of actors involved in the policy process. It is a process always understood as dynamic and open to political disagreement. Indeed, if we are to comprehend this emerging governance, and consequently establish its more salient features, then it remains imperative we examine the political struggles that shape the context in which a political discourse is constructed and challenged.

All too often within contemporary political debate, explanation, interpretation or, in the case of politicians and civil servants, justification is sought immediately. Given the preponderance of spin doctors and political advisers it should surprise few that we rely increasingly upon sound bites or opinion polls to capture the 'onset of crisis'. The temptation is to attribute change to a particular incident, despite the fact that significant political protest rarely manifests itself over a single issue. More often than not, political protest involves a build-up of grievances and objections that bear fruit at a later date. It may well be that particular flash-points serve to condense political discontent. They certainly attract the gaze of the media. However, a more rigorous explanation of events such as those involving Ryanair in 1999 or the taxi drivers in 2000 demand a more searching examination of the forces of development and the strategies of actors over a longer period of time.[3]

If we follow this line of thought then we need to acknowledge that what is not in dispute among commentators on Irish politics is that the origins of its current economic largesse can be traced back to 1987. However, before we can begin to explore the importance of this as a turning point, and by implication the trajectory of the social and political project which has been undertaken since, we need to examine at both an empirical and an analytical level the dynamic(s) of a moment of social and political crisis.

This is an area of social and political thought that has of late attracted a considerable amount of attention. Here, one of the more influential analytical expositions of crisis theory is to be found in the work of Colin Hay (1999). The starting point for his exposition of crisis lies in the observation that, within much of the literature surrounding both marxist and radical theories of the state, there has been a tendency to posit a separation of the material and the discursive within the process of crisis formation (see Hay, 1999, p. 319; see also Taylor, 1995). Dissatisfied with this dichotomy, Hay suggests that that if we are to provide a satisfactory account of the nature of crisis (at both the analytical and empirical levels) then we need to recognise that the material and ideational are inextricably interwoven.

From the outset he draws an important distinction between the state as a dynamic system and the state as an inertial system. The former is presented as a dynamic body possessing the capacity to manage change proactively through reflexive, strategic and decisive self-transformation. In contrast, the latter tends to evolve through unreflexive adaptation (Hay, 1999, p. 320). It is the characteristics of an inertial state that interest Hay most, largely because it more accurately corresponds to a capitalist state that is an 'amorphous complex of agencies with ill-defined boundaries, performing a variety of not very distinctive functions' (Schmitter, 1985, cited in Hay, 1999, p. 320).

Given the range of organisational practices, rules of conduct and social mores within any part of the state it can, at best, display only 'a partial and latent unity' (Hay, 1999, p. 320). Thus, while Hay is willing to concede that there may be an element of central co-ordination, the state is unified largely as a result of the constraints and conditions imposed by the 'legacies of former state projects'.[4] If these are themes familiar to state action in a period of stability or consensus, then how do we begin to define a period of crisis?

Here there are at least two further elements of Hay's view of crises that are useful. The first draws upon Block's work (1987) and suggests that it is possible to distinguish between decisive forms of intervention as intentional action and *tipping points*, where relatively minor interventions are made.[5] The second element aims to draw a distinction between structural crisis and conjunctural crisis. In the case of the latter, and following Offe, Hay suggests that the mode of political rationality will influence the search for a response within the pre-existing structure of the state. However, in a structural crisis a radical shift in political rationality takes place, one that seeks a resolution in the restructuring of the system altogether (Hay, 1999, p. 328).

Within this view of crisis it is possible to suggest that the 'degree of systemic failure conditions different responses by the state', that a conjunctural crisis implies the deployment of management failure responses which may achieve (albeit temporarily) system stability. However, should these symptoms persist then there will be an accumulation of contradictions and steering problems which will 'precipitate a fully fledged condition of state and economic failure' (Hay, 1999, p. 331).

In Hay's opinion crisis represents a moment of decisive state intervention (Hay, 1999, p. 323). With the emphasis accorded to '*decisive* intervention', he is therefore able make an important distinction between 'failure' (an accumulation or condensation of contradictions) and crisis (a moment of decisive intervention during which those contradictions are identified). The latter scenario clearly invokes a sense in which there is a wider public perception of crisis. In this view crisis refers to a set of conditions in which systemic failure has been recognised, or rather it has become politically and ideationally mediated. Crisis is understood as a 'moment of institutional change', a 'moment of rupture' (Hay, 1999, pp. 320–324).

There is much in this portrayal of crisis that is illuminating and it is hardly surprising that in many ways I should find this persuasive. However, there are number of important themes which we need to address before we can attempt to periodise the crisis of the mid- to late 1980s in Ireland. The first two themes refer to what I see as a rather odd turn of phrase: crisis as 'decisive state intervention'. Here the aim is not to reduce Hay's invaluable ideas to a discussion of semantics, because in many ways I agree wholeheartedly with much of his position. Rather, it is to suggest that in posing a crisis in terms of decisive state intervention there is a tendency to attribute far too much independence, autonomy and coherence to state action in a period that should be conceived as more chaotic and incoherent. If state action is designed to manage and achieve political stability, this assumes that even as a crisis emerges (and they rarely fall out of a clear blue sky) the state's initial terms of reference will be a defence of the status quo. A crisis defines the need for (new) and decisive state action and thus occurs prior to 'decisive state action'. The preference therefore should be to view crisis as a moment of realisation in which competing political discourse(s) fail to resonate among a wider audience. Within the ensuing political vacuum a new, emerging set of political arguments may claim ascendancy. It is at this moment, when a political and ideological vacuum emerges, that the struggle takes place between competing discourses, and this more accurately corresponds to the point of crisis.

In other words, the principal difference between Hay's view and mine lies in my preference for viewing a crisis as a moment of realisation (a moment in which the ideational and the material become interwoven) which takes place *before* decisive state intervention. This is a period of chaos, which by definition implies that decisive state action (at least analytically) must take place after a crisis. There is one significant advantage in this move. While it may seem a moot point, even close to splitting hairs, it does allow us to problematise any future trajectory of a state project prior to 'decisive state action' rather than in the aftermath of a decisive form of intervention. In the work of those such as Jessop or even Hay there is always a latent tendency to problematise after the event. Put simply, the adoption of terms such as 'strategy' necessarily infers a level of coherence. However, these authors often need to query that coherence by suggesting that success is not inevitable, that it is always open to question. To the more sceptical audience, such clauses stand ill at ease with phrases such as '*decisive* state intervention'.

On the other hand, if we suggest that decisive state action should occur at the *beginning of the end* of crisis this allows us to problematise the character of the political project at its moment of inception, rather than after the event. A crisis occurs only at the moment in which the challenge begins to take shape, a period of instability, political contestation and struggle. It is during this period, and prior to the decisive state action, that competing discourses begin to present alternative visions of state action. If we wish to retain Hay's view of decisive state action (and I see no reason not to), then we must maintain its positive, possessive sense. In analytical terms (although this may well remain fuzzy in empirical terms) it represents the beginning of the end of crisis, for it assumes that a new and perhaps radically different trajectory for state action will be implemented. That is what makes it *decisive*, for it signals a new departure. It suggests that something has been agreed upon, that action has been taken and that a response to crisis has been made. As a crisis emerges or unfolds, competing discourses will begin to engineer a new vision that will be successful (tendentially)

only if it resonates with the wider, lived experience of a succession of contradictions and policy failures.[6]

This new political and ideological discourse and its accompanying policies are not plucked out of thin air, or pulled like rabbits from a hat. The
choice of policy (or what is acceptable) is influenced, shaped and constrained by the particular economic, political and ideological terrain. As
the burgeoning literature on policy transfer indicates, governments, ministers and think tanks seem increasingly predisposed to search for policy
instruments and policies from other countries.[7] While this provides a
source of potential policy responses to crisis, they are filtered through the
political process, encountering either resistance or sponsorship from
vested interests, influential lobby groups or those with privileged access to
policy networks.

Neither is policy devised by civil servants acting simply at the behest of
ministers. I have no difficulty in accepting the argument that on occasion
policies may carry the imprint of a particular minister or that they bear the
scars of a political crisis; but what I want to suggest is that the overall trajectory of a political project is shaped and constrained by the structural
conditions of capitalism that pervade both national and international levels. It need not, and should not, be interpreted as some form of inevitable,
often linear development (a problem usually exacerbated by phrases such
as 'a political project').

This is not to ignore the characteristics of party politics peculiar to Ireland. On the contrary, it is important to acknowledge how the structural
exigencies of global capitalism are refracted through Irish political structures. Here the role of the electoral system, the nature of party competition
and the nature of competition between political representatives at the local
level are all important features of the Irish polity.

Unlike many of its west European counterparts that opted for propor-
tional representation (PR) with a list system, Ireland opted for PR with a
single transferable vote (PR-STV). In instances where PR is linked to a list
system, the voter's choice is along party lines (Sinnott, 1999). However,
under PR-STV, political representation also includes an important connec-
tion between parliamentary candidates and their constituency. In both
instances it is commonly argued that PR leads to the proliferation of parties, coalition governments and/or political instability (Sinnott, 1999,
p115). However, as the Constitution Reform Group observed, this is by no
means inevitable, since the presence of smaller parties has been contained
by party discipline.[8] It is an issue upon which Sinnott remains more circumspect, noting that the review group's conclusion may be 'too sanguine', largely because it ignored the potential for PR-STV to increase the
likelihood of independent candidates gaining election. In such circum-

stance two important themes emerge. First, there may be an increased propensity for minority governments, with independent TDs, to be constructed. Secondly, it places a greater emphasis upon the role of constituency work and intra-party competition.

Minority government sustained by independent TDs has occurred three times since the 1980s. Thus, while political instability may not necessarily be a feature of PR-STV, it 'does increase the probability of government reliance on independent deputies whose support may be delivered only at a disproportionate price and even then may not be durable' (Sinnott, 1999, p. 117). This may be compounded if PR-STV accentuates the possibility that 'competition between parties tends to be delivered on the basis of services rendered, rather than policy differences' (Sinnott, 1999, p. 118).

There can be little doubt that brokerage continues to have an important influence on Irish politics, or that it has an important bearing on much of the implementation of policy. As Sinnott notes, it often involves individual TDs conducting lengthy clinics to deal with welfare benefits and the complaints of resident associations and local pressure groups, as well as the perceived need to be present at political demonstrations, sporting events or funerals (Sinnott, 1999, p. 119). As public figures, TDs are increasingly expected to perform the onerous task of traversing the corridors of the civil service or local government on behalf of their clients. In addition, TDs' portfolio subsumes the role of 'local promoter', advancing the interest of local business, preventing or mediating in factory closures and securing public investment (Gallagher and Komito, 1999, pp. 206–207).[9]

Amid increasing concern over the state of public finances during the post-election year of 2003, the issue of brokerage and incoherence in the Irish political system has been increasingly to the fore. The former Taoiseach Garrett Fitzgerald has argued that the Irish political system has failed to cope with the 'competitive stresses of a multi-seat electoral system' that has generated tensions between candidates of the same political persuasion (Fitzgerald, *Irish Times*, 6 December 2003). In part, he attributes this development to the fact that whereas previously a party had financed constituency campaigns, individual candidates now raise funds for political campaigns. More disconcertingly, it seems that the practice of ministers using their position to divert public resources to their own constituencies has been allowed to flourish. In turn, Fitzgerald laments that what 'had previously been a natural source of local pride, in seeing one of their constituency TDs in government, has gradually turned into a justified belief . . . that only by having a minister of their own could local interests be effectively promoted'. In addition, he argues that searching for a cabinet with 'geographical balance', rather than the most effective team, has simply exacerbated the problem. Such issues present a serious difficulty to a government faced with decisions that may be locally unpopular.[10] They also provide an important influence upon the nature of policy construction, delivery and regulation.

Party competition

The origins of the Ireland's party system lie in the split within the original Sinn Fein party, whose success in the 1918 Westminster election led to Irish independence in 1922. Despite its electoral success the nationalist issue remained unresolved, with partition and the British-imposed oath of allegiance the most contentious elements in the Treaty settlement (Mair, 1999). Indeed, division between pro- and anti-agreement supporters in Sinn Fein was intense in the first decade of independence (Mair, 1999, p. 131). In 1926 a minority of the party led by Eamon de Valera broke away and, after electoral victory in 1932, remained in office until 1948. It was to mark the second of 'three watersheds in the development of the Irish party system' (Mair, 1999, p. 133).[11]

During the 1920s and 1930s the Labour Party had struggled to provide a radical political alternative. Limited industrialisation and the prominence of nationalist issues on the political agenda had been significant contributory factors. After 1948, and as a result of the strategies pursued by the minor parties and Labour, the political lines were drawn between Fianna Fáil and the rest (Mair, 1999).[12] It was a political divide that was sustained until 1989, when Fianna Fáil opted for the first time to enter into coalition.

By the early 1970s Labour had shifted to the Left of the political spectrum and, rather surprisingly, was accompanied by Fine Gael. Fine Gael's rejection of its free market ethos ensured that a social democratic vision was firmly on the Irish political agenda. Meanwhile Fianna Fáil's agenda remained fairly similar: single-party strong government allied to an economic policy which endorsed the view that increased economic growth would benefit all (Mair, 1999, p.140). The economic recession of the 1980s persuaded Fine Gael to change tack. A commitment to redistribution was replaced by an enthusiasm for curbing public expenditure. In turn, Labour lost crucial political ground to the newly formed Workers Party and many Labour supporters shifted to Fianna Fáil and Fine Gael. Moreover, as Mair observes, the Irish political landscape became increasingly populated and fragmented, with the arrival of the Workers Party on the left and the Progressive Democrats (PDs) on the right (Mair, 1999; Collins and Cradden, 2001, p.25).

In Mair's opinion, the 1989 election marked the final watershed, as the pattern of party competition opened up and Fianna Fáil chose to enter into coalition with the PDs. Political competition would no longer be based on Fianna Fáil and the rest, and from here on in Fianna Fáil would constitute simply another big party. (Mair, 1999). And yet, almost perversely, this may have strengthened Fianna Fáil's hand. While its electoral success may have subsided it now offers the potential for coalition on both a centre right and a centre left position (Laver and Shepsle, 1992).

There can be little doubt that globalisation and the increasing influence of supranational institutions on the Irish polity continue to stimulate moves towards further deregulation and privatisation, curtailing a range of mechanisms for governance. However, this does not necessarily mean an end to national politics or the assertion of the national interest in the international arena. New relationships of governance will emerge and be contested. This is a position that contrasts with those that assume that nation states will have little autonomy in the global order. As the discussion below on welfare and civil service reform indicates, policy learning has clearly been influential in shaping the thrust, content and pace of change. However, we should not read this as a process in which the Irish state simply ambles along, pilfering policy from an international menu of reform. In the field of environmental policy reform, for example, there have been clear instances in which the policy learning has been undertaken from within, suggesting an historical element to the learning process, one which presents problems for those who see globalisation as an all-encompassing linear process. Moreover, it is also clear that even in areas such as rural governance, where reform has been particularly pronounced and the role of global markets has been influential in framing change, there is still an important national dimension to our explanation. In this sense, policy developments that emanate from the international arena, and which are shaped by its attenuated processes, are refracted in politics at the national level.

The crisis of 1987 in Ireland

Throughout the 1980s the Irish economy found itself mired in a succession of financial and economic difficulties. Inflation for the period 1982–87, for example, averaged 20.5 per cent and unemployment levels were at record highs. Indeed, during the early years of the 1980s Ireland actually recorded falls in GNP while pressure mounted on the government's ability to cope with the problem of escalating public sector debt. The national debt had risen from IR£1,009 million (65 per cent of GNP) in March 1970 to IR£21,611 (129 per cent of GNP) by 1986 (MacSharry et al., 2000).

As early as 1982 there had been a widespread disenchantment with Ireland's economic performance, and yet there existed little in the way of a consensus on a vision for the future. However, by 1987 the nature of the crisis had altered. While similarities in the problems encountered between 1982 and 1987 undoubtedly exist – most notably the return of a minority Fianna Fáil government and the parlous state of public finances – there were also important differences.

Debates about the prescriptions for change in 1987 were largely dominated by cuts in public expenditure and the imperative of reducing the national debt. These were issues addressed by the National Economic and Social Council (NESC) in its report of 1986, *A Strategy for Development*, and provided an important stimulus to the debate that ensued. Events were also influenced by the nature of the ignominious collapse of the Fine Gael/Labour coalition in January of 1987. The Labour Party had opted out of the coalition, largely on the grounds that the spending cuts (particularly on health) were unpalatable. This was to signal a period of political vacuum from which a 'political consensus on fiscal policy' would emerge (MacSharry et al., 2000, p.62).

This tentative consensus would bear fruit only in the aftermath of an influential speech delivered in early 1987 by the leader of the opposition, Alan Dukes, in Tallaght (later dubbed 'the Tallaght strategy'). Dukes declared support for the government's position, arguing that the 'resolution of our public finance problems is the essential key to everything'. More startling perhaps was his admission that 'when the government is moving in the right overall direction, I will not oppose the central thrust of policy' (Dukes, cited in MacSharry et al., 2000, p.77). As MacSharry notes in his recollections of this period: 'quite remarkably, the economic consensus extended from a shared analysis of the problem to a common prescription of the solution – with spending cuts accepted as a necessary part of the remedy' (MacSharry et al., 2000, p.46).[13]

It is plausible to suggest that that this period constitutes a moment of crisis. However, while I would concede that the declaration put forward in the Tallaght speech, and the government's determination to cut spending and reduce the national debt, arguably form part of a new vision for change, it does not form the moment of decisive state intervention. That moment came later that year, signalling the *beginning of the end of crisis*. At this point the government embarked upon an attempt to establish an agreement with business and the trade unions over a package of public policy commitments, welfare benefits and tax cuts which would take effect in the Programme for National Economic Recovery (PNER) (1987–90). It is this that represents more accurately the moment of decisive state intervention, when a discursive project becomes embedded in a political programme.

It is important to recognise that the ideological and political character of this project does not remain ossified, that the material and discursive are always challenged and therefore need to be reconstituted. The failure to appreciate this has been the source of the confusion that surrounds discussion of the national agreements in Ireland. Thus, for those of a social democratic persuasion the initial enthusiasm for these agreements has given way to disenchantment, as critics contend that they are little more than 'Thatcherism in sheep's clothing'. On the other hand, those of a more conservative political orientation have argued that such agreements are no longer necessary as the economy moves towards full employment, and that they place business in a political straitjacket, denying it the opportunity to improve Ireland's competitiveness.

At the heart of this debate lies a political conundrum. There can be little doubt that in contrast to many other European countries Ireland has persisted with a political project formed around a succession of macro-political bargaining agreements. And yet, almost perversely, these institutionalised forms of intermediation appear to have become a vehicle for imposing a neo-liberal political agenda. The problem stems from the fact that social democrats have assumed that national-level agreements should necessarily be concerned with a political project that includes demand management strategies, a passive welfare state and/or a social democratic project to reduce unemployment and poverty through state intervention. Such a narrow focus restricts our capacity to explain elements of this project which do not appear to lie within the 'traditional ambit' of a free market response to many of Ireland's difficulties.[14] Alternatively, among the legion of free market 'revisionists' which now appear before us the preoccupation is to expunge the role of government and the unions in this economic revival, arguing that it has been grossly overstated. In other words, one of the more distinctive (and perhaps appealing) features of bargaining Irish style has been its attempt to construct a form of governance capable of delivering a 'world-class economy' while retaining a *modicum* of commitment to avoid social dislocation.

It was by no means clear that the unions or business would agree to this strategy. However, the unions were only too well aware of what had been taking place in the UK, where the union movement had been increasingly ostracised from the corridors of political power. Business was also anxious about the level of industrial unrest, high levels of taxation and the state of public finances. For its part, the government's position was precarious, demanding that it juggle the terms of the agreement without destabilising its own minority voting position in the Dáil (MacSharry et al., 2000). Having won support from the social partners for the PNER the government advanced with some caution.

The structure of this book

The rest of this book is divided into five chapters. The first examines the attempt by the Irish State to construct a new form of governance. In contrast to many other European states, Ireland has persisted with a succession of macro-political bargaining agreements that have extended beyond the simple issue of pay to embrace wider concerns of public policy. Moreover, as this chapter argues, such political intermediation has been central to the creation of a set of conditions in which national and international capital has prospered.[15] It is an interpretation that differs significantly from the contention of some that such agreements act as a constraint upon the restructuring of the supply side of the economy. Thus, Lash, Urry and Streeck, for example, have argued that macro forms of political bargaining are inappropriate and counterproductive in an era of flexible specialisation, when 'standard solutions for regulating employment are of decreasing relevance' (Streeck, 1992, p.213; see also Lash and Urry, 1987). In contrast, the arguments presented here suggest that such mediation has contributed positively to the creation of a set of political and economic conditions in which management has been able to secure changes in working practices and introduce new technology. In other words, this neo-corporatist strategy has *allowed* a restructuring of the supply side of the economy.

It seems clear that as the new millennium opened the final death knell of the KWS sounded. In an ever more competitive global market the critics of the KWS contend that it is an increasingly anachronistic structure. Moreover, as the experience of the 1980s and 1990s has shown, the search for alternatives to the KWS has been stimulated by the emergence of a new underclass, a socially excluded layer which has been progressively ostracised from labour, housing and educational markets. Whereas the themes of the 1960s and 1970s were predominantly about inclusion, public policy now seems dominated by measures designed to justify exclusion (Hoggett, 1994). The debate is concerned no longer with equity and redistribution but with the complicated process of organising consent around new definitions of poverty and justifiable entitlement. It is worth noting at this juncture that the search for a 'third way', a politics which straddles if you like 'inefficient and rigid corporatism' and 'divisive Thatcherism', also presents a new dichotomy between passive and active policy paradigms. The policy recommendations of this new, active paradigm are condensed into a persistent call for an overhaul of an archaic, passive, universal welfare regime.

In a subtle, but none the less crucial fashion, the view of this reconstructed social democracy distinguishes itself from the neo-liberal critique of welfare by the fact that we are no longer exclusively concerned with the role of individual self-responsibility. A policy paradigm that attributes the *cause* of unemployment to the failings of individuals (and subsequently constructs a neo-liberal safety net) has been supplanted by one which creates 'opportunities' and generates 'incentives' for those individuals who 'possess' the capacity to respond actively to their predicament. It is a policy paradigm populated not by individuals per se, but by 'categories of individuals' whose membership is defined by their 'particular circumstance' and experience of unemployment (lone parents, the young unemployed, or absent fathers). We no longer have a 'catch-all' experience of unemployment (or receipt of welfare) and consequently the policy response can no longer be universal. Rather, we have a series of 'unemployment experiences' in which policy is tailored to 'categories of individuals'. Unemployment is no longer ascribed to the failure of individuals, and responsibility does not lie at the door of the state. The active dimension to this welfare regime resides in the tensions that exist between state support and individual responsibility. The state functions to create opportunities from which to assist those individuals who 'wish' to respond to their predicament (this is its possessive dimension) (Taylor, 2002b).

In this context it is important to recognise that while a new regime of accumulation may prove successful it will not necessarily be predicated on the redistribution of wealth between active and inactive members of the labour market. The ill-fated budget presented by Charlie McCreevy, minister for finance, towards the end of 1999 encapsulates the problems that reside within this political and economic project. As the Fianna Fáil/PD coalition has accelerated the shift towards a more conservative/neo-liberal economic strategy it has renewed tensions within the partnership framework. This was most emphatically expressed in the fallout from a budget that generated improved tax benefits three times greater for those on higher incomes. Ultimately, the success of this strategy will rest on its ability to reconcile the tensions that exist between the need to regulate social division and the drive towards a flexible economy.

The search for alternative approaches to welfare provision has also been marked by the emergence of a plethora of diverse relations between the state and civil society, as moves to restructure the nature of service delivery take place. In essence, it represents a shift away from the rigid bureaucratic structures of the welfare state, where the emphasis is placed upon rules and regulations, to new forms of service delivery. As such, the provision of welfare has been progressively undertaken by a combination of state, para-state, voluntary and private organisations that have reduced any clear distinction between the state and civil society. For many, these new institutional arrangements form the basis of a response to the globalised economy and the changing nature of the labour market and of household structures. In part, it has involved the adoption of performance criteria and private sector management techniques by the public sector in order to encourage competition in public service delivery (see Rhodes, 1996).[16]

The lexicon of this 'new managerialism' is replete with concepts that signify a shift from a preoccupation with inputs (bureaucratic regulation) to a concern with outputs; quasi-markets, consumer choice and empowerment. Indeed, it may well be the case, as Rhodes observes, that it is about 'less government' and more 'governance', but its pervasive influence rests surely on the fact that it is not about 'less politics', since at its very heart lies a move to politicise public service delivery (Rhodes, 1996).[17] Citizens, or 'clients' as they are more commonly referred to, are endowed with the capacity to seek redress from faceless bureaucrats through rights which are enshrined in mission statements. It is a debate infused with ideas not simply about 'modernisation' or the need to create new participative structures, but rather about how to establish a consensus around the virtues of restructuring public service delivery. More often than not the debate is motivated by an attempt to confront the political imbalance purported to exist in the public sector, seen as a cosy idyll isolated from the insecurity and more onerous inequities which pervade the private sector. If these are issues that form part of the political discourse in which changes to the supply side of the welfare state are debated, there have also been a number of measures designed to alter the demand side. Here a succession of moves has been made to introduce more stringent forms of welfare entitlement.

Within European public policy circles, changes to public service delivery are deemed to signal part of a process of 'hollowing out' the state. For those of such disparate political persuasions as Jessop (1994) and Rhodes (1996) it seems that we are now witnessing the emergence of polycentric states involved in a subtle but none the less formidable task of *enabling*, rather than organising, political activity.[18] Policy outcomes are no longer perceived as the simple result of central government directives. Rather, government is now engaged in a succession of new relations with local government, para-state and private sector organisations, all of which have an important bearing upon the nature, direction and implementation of policy (see Taylor, 2003; Taylor and Millar, forthcoming)

The kernel of this debate has been exemplified in the striking influence of international changes upon the Irish civil service, a process that forms the concern of the third chapter of this book. The overhaul of the Irish civil service has been crystallised in an attempt to create an effective, efficient and more democratically responsive set of political institutions. For those in the civil service it has involved the adoption of flexible working practices, new forms of accounting, greater transparency, reductions in cost and the introduction of measures designed to enhance 'client services' (Boyle, 1997a,b,c).

In essence, this restructuring of the Irish civil service has sought to challenge systematically the presence of bureaucratic and managerial rigidities. If efficiency provides the very crux of improvement, flexibility has been the basis of reform. Conversely, while such reforms are often presented as a panacea for all our ills, more often than not they neglect to consider that when the legitimacy of state actors is questioned, new forms of control undermine the safeguards usually assigned to public servants. What remains quite clear, however, is that Ireland has followed a succession of states that have embarked upon a reorganisation of civil service structures. On the one hand, governments have increasingly demanded greater control of civil servants, reducing the level of discretion available to them. On the other hand, the importation of 'new managerialist' techniques to the public sector has witnessed an increasing emphasis upon the citizen as consumer, creating a climate in which civil servants are expected to respond in a 'market-oriented' fashion (Rhodes, 1996; Boston, 1999).

Debates about the 'hollowing out' of the state have also figured prominently in the area of rural and urban development. In this area of public policy, which is examined in chapter 4, the Irish state has been at the forefront of moves to develop innovative responses to the social dislocation associated with the drive towards a modern flexible economy. It is not that the social dislocation associated with uneven economic development is a particularly recent phenomenon; rather, the problem (in its new guise), and by definition the character of the political response, have been shaped by debates that surround public policy in both a national and an international setting. Here, one of the more novel features of this programme has been the extension of a remit which embraces themes such as empowerment and political participation. This chapter seeks to assess critically whether such programmes form the bedrock of moves designed to create a new set of relations between the state and its citizenry through the creation of genuine participative structures.

The final chapter examines the changes that have occurred in environmental regulation. To environmental activists and political commentators alike, the construction of the Environmental Protection Agency (EPA) in 1992 appeared to confirm that Ireland had finally embraced the modernising imperative at the heart of the EU, and that its environment would not be sacrificed at the altar of the Celtic Tiger's economic performance. It was envisaged that the EPA would replace the rigid demarcation of bureaucratic responsibilities between different public bodies with a flexible, integrated and administratively transparent institution. It was to be a significant portent of change that ecological modernisation was finally emerging within the Irish polity.

This chapter offers an alternative interpretation, one in which the EPA represents an institutional response to a series of environmental conflicts which had begun to undermine the traditional influence of the agricultural and business lobbies. It challenges the view that at the heart of the EPA's conception was the simple realisation on the part of the Irish state that its environmental regulatory regime was inadequate. Indeed, while many within the higher political echelons of the Irish state recognised the need to revamp its environmental policy, the government's principal, overarching objective was to ensure that further regulation would not be detrimental to the performance of the Celtic Tiger. At the forefront of this process was a struggle to construct a new political discourse on the environment that would accommodate the environmentalist critique of the 1980s without threatening the free market ethos which underpinned the politics of the Celtic Tiger. Put simply, environmental policy debate in Ireland is concerned no longer with the extent of ecological degradation, environmental democracy, the quality of the environment or encouraging environmental sensitivity, but with the complicated process of organising consent around new definitions of acceptable pollution.

Notes

1 Examples abound but perhaps the most prominent was the decision by Telecom Éireann, formerly the state-owned telecommunications provider (see n.14 below), to organise a competition in which the winner, Ennis, would be converted into the first 'information-age town', a move which captured the feeling that Ireland was at the cutting edge of the .com economy.

2 This is a line of thought promulgated by those such as Fintan O'Toole, who has argued that the source of change lies in the declining influence of the Catholic church and the emergence of a new 'pluralist orthodoxy' in Ireland.

3 The move by union members outside of Ryanair to support the action of Ryanair baggage handlers in 1999 can be understood in the context of an ongoing struggle to achieve trade union recognition, an issue that was not resolved successfully under the terms of Partnership 2000. The dispute was not simply about Ryanair, or its outspoken management, but it did make political sense to stand against a high-profile comany such as Ryanair rather than a multinational company located at a greenfield site. For more detail on these arguments as they relate to the taxi drivers' dispute in 2000, see Taylor (2002b).

4 Ironically, it may well be that at the very moment of crisis a greater level of cohesion and unity within the state is achieved as it attempts to alter or transform its constituent elements (Hay, 1999, p. 321).

5 The latter may subsequently prove decisive in terms of the transformation of the system (either because it maintains the stability or exacerbates its latent contradictions) (Hay, 1999, p. 325).

6 This is not that far removed from Hay's position, since he succinctly observes that: 'the process of narration operates through the discursive "recruiting" of policy failures, and the lived experience to which they give rise, as symptoms of a crisis of the state. The discursive construction of crisis can thus be seen as a process of abstraction and narration in which the disparate effects of a great variety of independent policy failures and contradictions are brought together in a unified, and deeply political, crisis discourse' (Hay, 1999, p. 333).

7 For an overview of this literature, and the development of a framework, see Dolowitz and Marsh (1996). For a discussion of a particular example of policy transfer in Ireland see Taylor and Horan (2001).

8 For an excellent summary of the way in which PR-STV operates, and the debates that have ensued, see Sinnott (1999).

9 Thus, for example, Maire Geoghegan-Quinn TD was moved to remark that 'once you get elected you become public property. You are on call 24 hours a day, 365 days a year . . . they will raise these issues with you when you are shopping, relaxing in a pub on Sunday night or at any other time they happen to run into you. Alternatively, they might decide to, and indeed often do, call to your home to discuss their problems . . . working in the Dáil doesn't get you re-elected', Geoghegan-Quinn, cited in Gallagher and Komito, 1999, p.207).

10 The political demonstrations over the proposed Hanly Reform in healthcare (2003) are a case in point. A Cabinet minister was forced to make a public apology to the Taoiseach after becoming involved in a conflict between his 'loyalty to the local constituency' and cabinet responsibility. The minister 'perceived' a need to place his head above the parapet at the proposed closure of facilities at two local hospitals (Nenagh and Ennis), a move that conflicted with his duty to adhere to Cabinet responsibility. For an interesting account of debates on clientelism and brokerage see Collins and O'Shea (2003).

11 The first had come in 1927 when Fianna Fáil emerged from the wilderness and decided to take its seats in the Dáil. In so doing it ensured that the intense conflict which had once been fought out as a civil war would become largely the focus for electoral competition (Mair, 1999).

12 For more detail on these issues see Mair (1999).

13 Given MacSharry's conservative political persuasion, it is hardly surprising that he should locate the origins of the Celtic Tiger in a combination of the robust political leadership of C. J. Haughey and an economic policy that rejected the country's 'growing addiction to debt'. The phenomenon of the Celtic Tiger was therefore born from the 'radical and painful correction in the national finances that got underway in 1987 and pavedthe way for the benign economc conditions of high growth and low inflation that followed' (MacSharry et al., 2000, p.47).

14 The recent initiative to construct a public pension fund from the proceeds of past and future privatisations and an annual contribution of 1 per cent of GDP

from the Exchequer for the foreseeable future spring to mind, as do the moves made to encourage people into low-paid work through the retention of welfare benefits and medical cards. And yet the picture is clouded further by the fact that, while there is undoubtedly considerable sympathy for free market solutions to Ireland's difficulties, there are areas such as industrial policy where there is a view that there should be 'continued provision of some direct state supports'. In 1998 the government initiated the full deregulation of the telecommunications sector with the privatisation of Telecom Eireann. Regulation now resides in the Office of the Director of Telecommunications Regulation, which was charged with ensuring fair competition. Its remit extends to 'unbundling the local loop' (allowing competing telecom firms to gain access to land lines owned by a monopoly provider), issuing Global System for Mobile communications (Ireland's third GSM) licence, and disclosing the conditions for awarding third-generation mobile phone services. Reform of public sector transport will prove a thornier branch to grasp. While there have been moves to address the regulation of Irish airports with a view to changes in airport charges, handling services and the licensing of Irish airlines, the proposed privatisation of the state-owned airline, Aer Lingus, has been delayed. Proposals to introduce competition for franchises for public bus services and the restructuring of railways have all been mooted, but government will face strong and determined opposition from the public sector unions. See Green (2001, p. 13).

15 While the build-up to the latest national agreement revealed a number of tensions between the social partners, interpretations of the source of Ireland's economic success have usually emphasised the importance of Partnership agreements. Indeed, in a spirit Marcuse would have appreciated, there appears at times to be almost a 'paralysis of criticism'. See the comments of the Taoiseach, Bertie Ahern, in his article 'Social Partnership Formula has made us the Envy of Europe' (*Irish Times*, 10 March 2000). Garrett Fitzgerald has been one of the more prominent critics, suggesting that such agreements have undermined the role of the Irish parliament in the formation of public policy.

16 Take, for example, the changing nature of funding in higher education. Traditionally the universities had been funded by a combination of central government grants and student fees. Under current structures the universities are now funded centrally – the removal of fees, which have been reintroduced recently, was motivated not so much by any democratic will to improve the intake of students from underprivileged backgrounds as by an intent to establish efficiency in the higher education system. The government now holds the capacity to define (and redefine as the political and economic climate changes) the relationship between research grants, capital grants and subject areas. Witness, for example, the recent competition between universities for state funding for research grants and capital spending projects.

17 Rhodes adheres largely to the position offered by Kooiman (1993), who argues that there is a need to distinguish between the process of government (goal-directed interventions) and governance (the result or total effects of socio-political administration) (Rhodes, 1996, p.657).

18 'Enabling' refers to the process in which government encourages a variety of delivery responses to problems that emerge. In the Irish case we have seen the emergence of public–private partnerships, co-operatives and joint entrepreneurial ventures. Recently, sources within the Department of Education (DoE) have suggested that it should explore the possibility of creating a new agency to operate exams in secondary schools, a move motivated by the 2002 dispute with the teaching profession over pay and conditions.

1

Negotiated governance in the era of the Celtic Tiger

Within European political science it has been fashionable to question the efficacy of macro-political forms of bargaining. Goldthorpe (1984), Lash and Urry (1987), Streeck (1992) and Gobeyn (1993), to name but a few, have expressed reservations about the compatibility of these political arrangements with the prevailing global structures of capitalism. Such scepticism has not been confined to those of a social democratic political persuasion. Throughout the 1980s and 1990s conservative political commentators argued vehemently that such interest intermediation was anathema to an entrepreneurially driven economy, generating as it did rigidities in the labour market and excessive political influence for trade unions.

The problem with such approaches is not just that they tend to overemphasise the level of rigidity within macro-political bargaining arrangements, but that in doing so they ignore the extent to which such agreements develop as a response to economic and political crises. It is not simply a question of being misled by the rhetorical assurances of either Thatcherism, Reaganism or Kohlism. Rather, contemporary political commentators have been seduced by neo-conservative interpretations of alleged administrative failure: that the real problem facing west European capitalism has been an explosion in the institutional impediments to economic growth. This neo-conservative critique rests on a series of critical postures informed by a succession of disappointments with the political and economic developments of the 1970s that failed to conform to what were essentially affirmative images of western industrial societies. The argument runs that a surge in popular aspirations provided the spur for a dramatic increase in state intervention and exposed the limitations of the KWS (Habermas, 1989).

Not surprisingly, the central feature of this neo-conservative critique has been a call for a reduction in state intervention and a corresponding increase in the role of the free market (Habermas, 1989). It is not just that this form of bargaining has fallen out of fashion; rather, it is deemed no longer compatible with the prevailing structures of global capitalism. It is a situation reflected in the current lexicon of political science and public administration, replete as it is with concepts apparently antithetical to the machinations of macro-political bargaining: flexible labour markets, polyvalent work structures and competitive international markets. Add to this the mobility of transnational capital and a purported 'hollowing out of the state' and it is hardly surprising that pessimism should envelop any role for macro-political bargaining in the new global economic order. And yet, in Ireland macro-political bargaining has formed the cornerstone of government strategy since the beginning of the 1990s. Indeed, while many Irish politicians may have been initially sceptical, few are now willing to decry publicly the role performed by national-level agreements in revitalising the Irish economy.

This chapter seeks to challenge, therefore, a political orthodoxy that rejects a role for national-level agreements in the new global economic order. In particular, it cautions against the inclination to portray sectoral or decentralised forms of negotiation in a more favourable light, as if there is a natural complementarity between such forms of negotiation and the new, emerging structures of capitalism. It is an approach that assumes *a priori* that such forms of negotiation are somehow better suited to the current 'needs' of capital. This problem is compounded by the failure to consider fully the complexity of the managerial function, where the tendency is to conflate the interests of individual businesses with business in general or, alternatively, to restrict the parameters of the managerial function to the issue of pay.

Within this literature there has been a discernible tendency to associate national-level agreements with demand management strategies, a passive welfare state and/or a social democratic project to reduce unemployment and poverty through state intervention. To those of a social democratic disposition the national agreements are viewed as little more than a 'sheep in wolf's clothing', Thatcherism without the accompanying rhetoric of 'trickle-down economics'. To others, they appear quite the opposite: excessive state intervention rescued only by the fortuitous influx of American multinational capital. It is this paradox, the restructuring of the supply side of the Irish economy undertaken within an ambit largely framed by macro-political bargaining, which has so perplexed Irish political scientists and which forms the basis for this chapter.

Here, this chapter argues that the rhetoric that has accompanied reform has emphasised commitment to avoid the social dislocation often associated with that of the UK. Thus, while the type of calculated assault upon the welfare state that took place in the UK during the 1980s has been largely absent, welfare payments have increased only in line with inflation. A succession of governments has presided over a period of unprecedented economic growth and yet poverty persists. Debate is concerned no longer with equity, redistribution or efficiency but with organising consent around new definitions of 'acceptable poverty'. In an attempt to confront these disparate issues the chapter is divided into three sections. The first explores the arguments surrounding the role of macro-forms of political bargaining in the new global era. The second examines a series of critical postures on the role of such agreements. The final section details the contours of the principal agreements that have been negotiated over the last decade.

National-level bargaining in the global economy

Appraisals from a wide variety of political commentators have argued that capitalism has moved into a new, dynamic phase in which the flexibility of productive systems, personnel and organisational strategy is paramount. Business, it is argued, can no longer sustain the level of economic growth upon which both the welfare state and trade union influence upon public policy were predicated (Goldthorpe, 1984; Lash and Urry, 1987; Streeck, 1992; Gobeyn, 1993). The contention is that the explosion in social and political rights that accompanied such bargaining increased rigidities in the labour market and created institutional impediments to economic growth. Put simply, macro-political bargaining procedures are viewed as increasingly anachronistic structures within an era of flexible specialisation (Taylor, 1996a).[1]

It is an argument that has figured prominently in the work of Streeck (1992), who has questioned the viability of macro-political bargaining in the new, emerging global economic order. Streeck maintains that the decay in national corporatisms can be attributed to a qualitative change in an economic and social structure that has undermined the structural and cultural foundations of corporatism (Streeck, 1992, p. 212). The simple dichotomy between capital and labour, the central pivot on which neo-corporatist negotiations were secured, has been usurped as volatile international markets, advances in technology and new political cleavages challenge the alliance forged between social democracy and the trade unions (Streeck, 1992, p. 213).

In a similar vein, Lash and Urry contend that corporatism was largely 'a matter for compromise between social classes in very much a national context of resource distribution' (Lash and Urry, 1987, p. 233). The fact that the penetration of global capital has dislocated national economies has made an assessment of what is an 'appropriate sacrifice' in the national interest a precarious exercise (Lash and Urry, 1987, pp. 233–34). The capacity to engage in national-level negotiations has been compromised further by the internationalisation of capital markets and a corresponding shift towards 'disorganised capitalism', manifest in an increase in company- and plant-level bargaining (Lash and Urry, 1987, p. 5). Thus, Lash and Urry conclude that a transformation in production techniques, a growth in the service sector and the internationalisation of production have all impacted detrimentally upon those areas of the economy that formed the basis for the centralised bargain of neo-corporatism (Lash and Urry, 1987, p. 234)

Pessimism about such negotiated forms of governance has also found sympathy in the work of Gobeyn, who has sought to identify a 'capitalist oriented' explanation for the decline of macro-political bargaining. For Gobeyn, the persistent levels of entrenched structural unemployment in those sectors of the economy that enjoyed high levels of trade union density were compounded by the increased mobility of capital and a reduction in international barriers, which have 'rendered obsolete' the 'extensive, nationally based concertative linkages' (Gobeyn, 1993, p. 4).

There are clearly discernible similarities between the respective positions of Streeck, Lash and Urry, and Gobeyn. All emphasise the importance to management of being released from the constraints imposed by macro-political bargaining, the deregulation of national and international labour markets, the internationalisation of capital and the corresponding shift in the composition of workforces. The tone of this chapter remains more cautious, particularly with regard to the premise that decentralised forms of bargaining offer a more flexible response to the 'rigidities' imposed by corporatist tendencies. In particular, this chapter identifies concern over the manner in which 'rigidity' is used as a concept. More often than not it is applied only to corporatist tendencies and presumably, therefore, denotes problems not experienced in a market-based response to crisis. As such, the term becomes laden with negative connotations. A more useful distinction, and one that does not carry the assumptions of efficiency implicit within the metaphors of rigidity/flexibility, would be to argue that both corporatist *and* market-based responses to crisis offer *opportunities* and *constraints.* Formulated in such a manner, the framework does not assume *a priori* that a market response is more flexible than a corporatist response to crisis.

It may well be the case that a reduction in the size of the public sector offers the state an opportunity to depoliticise any programme of restructuring and avoid undue conflict in vulnerable areas. However, we need to acknowledge that, in the process of relinquishing responsibility, the state may also lose strategic control in key sectors. This may be compounded by a reduction in the state's capacity to provide collective goods that are in the long-term interest of the economy, but which may not emerge from the rational decisions of individual firms in a free market. In this vein it is preferable to see market-based approaches as offering both opportunities and constraints.

A further problem implicit in the work of Streeck, Gobeyn, and Lash and Urry is the tendency to assume that decentralised forms of wage bargaining are necessarily more efficient in responding to the needs of business. This is compounded by the inclination to perceive this form of bargaining to be inherently more beneficial and recognised uniformly as such by management. There is, needless to say, little evidence in countries such as the UK to support such a sweeping conclusion (see Brown and Walsh, 1991; Black, 1993; Black 1994).

Arguments that defend a move towards decentralised bargaining tend to emphasise the gains to be made from the flexible deployment of employees, enabling management to establish a closer link between pay, performance and the local labour market (Purcell, 1991). However, as Walsh's research shows, decentralised forms of bargaining present management with alternative problems, and any tendency to see these forms as inherently more 'efficient' should be resisted. In particular, she argues that decentralised wage bargaining procedures may actually generate intra-firm bargaining pressures, thereby reducing the possibility of securing productivity gains. Moreover, where productivity is determined by interdependent technologies, as opposed to employee performance, management may encounter obstacles to the introduction of individual incentive schemes (Walsh, 1993, p. 416).

Debates about macro-political bargaining almost invariably coalesce around the alleged propensity of such agreements to promote rigidities in the economy. Neo-liberal economists have argued that there are obligations that accompany such negotiations, effectively placing governments in a political straitjacket. In such circumstances efficiency is undermined as governments attempt to balance the conflicting demands of unions to defend jobs and management to make the 'tough decisions' on restructuring.

In a subtle and far more persuasive fashion, neo-liberal economists have argued that it is not just that public sector industries suffer from poor management–union relations, but that the state imposes a series of institutional rigidities that are a burden upon *any* industry operating within an internationally competitive environment. Decisions to downsize, or confront unions about restrictive working practices, almost always involve political clearance. This becomes an increasingly precarious exercise in a global economic order where management is required to enact decisions in a shorter time. A further theme, one mentioned only occasionally in the accompanying political rhetoric, is that involvement in macro-level negotiations allows unions to secure wage increases above the market level, a situation that reinforces a 'rates for the job' consciousness and prevents management from reducing job demarcations (Dore, 1988, p. 400).

If such arguments remain largely within the realm of the economic, the neo-liberal critique also extends to the political. State intervention, or more accurately the changing nature of citizenship that allegedly results from state intervention, is identified as a source of difficulty. The objection centres on the impact and burden imposed by improved citizenship rights as the level of security assumed under the auspices of a welfare state increases (Hayek, 1960). It is not simply a question of the level of entitlements, although this in itself tends to raise the hackles of any committed neo-liberal economist; rather, the problem is the very structure of those entitlements. The expansion in social citizenship rights envisaged in a social democratic project increases welfare benefits, which, in turn, foster a culture of dependency that serves to increase rigidities in the labour market.[2] It is an argument that critics of the New Right have found difficult to resolve.

Dore's response has been to concede that the presence of such rights has an inevitable impact on the take-up of low-paid jobs (Dore, 1988). In his opinion there is a complex relationship between equity (the redistribution of productive resources) and efficiency in periods of high unemployment. This, he believes, can be resolved only through some form of macro-political bargaining which ensures specific levels of employment, thereby reducing the impact of 'unproductive rigidities' (income maintenance schemes) (Dore, 1988).

It is an issue upon which Streeck remains more circumspect. He has argued that in the absence of any internationally agreed form of self-restraint and/or Keynesian employment-creation scheme, the institutions that once served the weak have become defences for the employed. Indeed, there can be little doubt that governments throughout western Europe have made little in the way of a sustained attempt to reduce the division between the employed and the unemployed. As Streeck succinctly observes, it seems almost perverse that:

> the real champions of equality now seem to be those who have always fought on the side of inequality: the proponents of 'market clearing', wages and flexible employment devices which, while they would increase the wage spread between skill groups, firms, industries and regions, at least promise to close the gap between employed and the unemployed by allowing the latter to compete. (Streeck, 1988, p. 415)

In contrast to Dore, however, Streeck is willing to concede that the existence of some forms of rigidity need not present an insurmountable problem, providing there is a reduction in productive rigidities. In countries like the United States and Britain, for example, there has been a trade-off between flexible access to the external labour market (hiring and firing workers to change the size and composition of their workforce) and strong 'rigidities' with respect to internal deployment, redeployment and retraining (Streeck, 1988, p. 417). This contrasts sharply with the case of Germany or Sweden, where unions have managed to secure rigid entitlements to long-term employment in exchange for high levels of internal shop-floor flexibility (Streeck, 1988, p. 419). The advantage in the latter cases, as Dore is only too well aware, is that measures which seek to improve employment security (a significant source of labour market rigidity) may actually motivate firms to adapt to market change through intra-company diversification. In addition, they may also serve to stimulate employers to pursue retraining programmes. Within such working environs Dore believes that employees may be more receptive to the introduction of new technology and changing work practices (see Dore, 1988, p. 401).[3]

The debate that surrounds labour market regulation has also attracted the attention of Rhodes, who has argued that although the UK has been successful in its move away from a 'cluster of southern European states with rigid labour markets', this has not transformed the productive fortunes of the British economy (Rhodes, 1998). For Rhodes, it is plausible to suggest that greater external flexibility (the hiring and firing of workers) has been achieved. Moreover, there may well be a case for arguing that the breakdown of union control over the workplace has induced more internal flexibility. However, he warns that such gains have been achieved without a corresponding increase in the 'levels of trust (except in inward investing Japanese firms which, in some sectors, have revolutionised work organisation)' (Rhodes, 1998, p. 8). Neither has the associated fragmentation of employers and trade unions assisted in the 'provision of collective goods such as an effective training system', hampering any concerted move away from a 'low skill equilibrium'. Consequently, while the relationship between external flexibility and internal flexibility has altered, the UK's regime is still a 'price based' rather than 'quality based' productive structure (Rhodes, 1998, p. 8).

It seems clear that a pattern of high wages and rigid job entitlements is unlikely to result from the enlightening forces of the free market. In such circumstances, social peace, worker commitment and high and flexible qualifications tend to be undersupplied if left to the rational decisions of individual firms. In other words, certain rigidities (collective goods which are in the long-term interest of the economy) are important prerequisites to the development of an arena in which enterprising firms respond and diversify in quality competitive markets. Streeck suggests that a system of wage determination that keeps wages higher than the market would otherwise dictate may actually encourage firms to diversify and invest in training and retraining. Similarly, employment protection appears to enhance individual firms' awareness of the need to invest in training programmes to retain expensive skills (Streeck, 1988, 1992).

This is an argument that contains two themes of relevance to this chapter. First, it presents a challenge to the dominant neo-liberal interpretation of what constitutes an *enterprising* firm. Second, it raises the crucial question of why certain rigidities imposed upon management 'force' innovation and others do not. Why, for example, do the (alleged) rigidities imposed by macro-political bargaining arrangements not provide a stimulus towards innovation? On this matter it seems that Streeck is willing to accept that *certain* forms of political regulation are beneficial, when he states that 'political regulation not only need not be detrimental to economic success, but may constitute a central precondition for it' (Streeck, 1988, p. 419). This is reiterated in his opposition to the neo-liberal perspective, when he suggests that rigidities may well stimulate managerial innovation:

> A polyvalent organisation whose sub units are capable of flexibly crossing the boundaries of their assigned functions is expensive, and the return on investment in polyvalence is difficult to establish. This is why the de-Taylorisation of work organisation, profitable as it undoubtedly is for firms pressed for higher product quality and diversity, seems to proceed faster where there is additional and independent pressure for reorganisation of work, for other than economic reasons. In the same way in which institutionally imposed obligations to train improve firms' skill base, legislation or industrial agreements mandating employers to enlarge and enrich job definition may contribute to operational flexibility. *In both cases competitiveness increases as a result of adjustments individual firms would or could not voluntarily have made.* (Streeck and Schmitter, 1991, p. 19, my emphasis)

In Streeck's view, then, rigidity and flexibility are not mutually exclusive. However, he appears unwilling to concede that 'beneficial political regulation' extends to macro-political bargaining. This discrepancy is intelligible only when we realise that for Streeck, political regulation is beneficial *only* if it is directed towards the *supply* side of the economy, a role unsuitable for macro-political bargaining because in his opinion it remains circumscribed by its function as a tool for demand-side change. Streeck's argument (and for many it is a persuasive one) is that:

> some sort of effective Keynesian expansionist capacity seems indispensable for the kind of corporatist concertation and social contract bargaining that

> was to stabilise non-American capitalisms of the 1970s. As much as these systems may otherwise have differed, under the rules of corporatist bargaining a state that cannot with any reasonable prospect of success promise to apply its fiscal and monetary tools to alleviate unemployment cannot possibly hope to gain concessions from unions or to influence settlements between unions and employers by, for example, offering to improve the terms of the bargain through corresponding economic policy. (Streeck, 1992, p. 211)

Within reconstructed social democratic thinking (the third way if you prefer) there has been a temptation to reject macro-political forms of bargaining and accept, albeit reluctantly, the neo-liberal charge that there is a need to overhaul the archaic, passive, universal welfare regime to which macropolitical bargaining is often assimilated.

Within reconstructed social democracy we are no longer concerned with the role of individual self-responsibility. The difficulty that reconstructed social democrats have with neo-liberalism is that it attributes unemployment to the failing of the individual. In contrast, reconstructed social democracy seeks to create 'incentives' for individuals who 'possess' the capacity to respond actively to the predicament of welfare dependency. That Streeck's work sits comfortably within reconstructed social democracy can be deduced from his use of the term 'beneficial political regulation'. Where political regulation is beneficial (employment protection and training) his vocabulary is infused with terms such as 'stimulate', 'encourage' or 'innovate'. These are positive, 'possessive' categories and, as such, are suited to an active policy paradigm. Where political regulation is not beneficial it is usually associated with income maintenance schemes or welfare benefits (demand management). The assumption behind Streeck's position is that macro-political bargaining is synonymous with a *passive* welfare state.

The intention here is not to reduce many of Streeck's succinct observations to a discussion of semantics; rather it is to highlight the fact that macro-political bargaining tends to be (mistakenly) equated with economic demand management strategies and/or a passive welfare state. Neither would I wish to downplay the importance of pressures emanating from the global economy which clearly pose significant problems to Ireland's form of negotiated governance. The increasing penetration of multinational companies in the Irish economy, and their capacity to relocate production rapidly in periods of volatile market conditions, raise difficulties for successful macro-level concertation (that is, governments, business and trade unions acting in concert to agree on policy) and any coordinated policy response. It would also be naive to assume that in such circumstances international capital will not seek more flexibility in the search for an optimal balance in labour market regulation. However, we should caution against a vogue in which a neo-liberal approach to labour market regulation is perceived to be 'better suited' to the prevailing conditions of global capitalism. In the short term it may well deliver greater external flexibility, but this may fall short of providing the collective goods (training and education) or the political and economic stability from which to pursue that most elusive prize: a high-tech, high-wage economy.

This is a view with which Rhodes would appear to concur. Thus, he suggests that 'successful economic adjustment, including greater flexibility in labour markets and the organisation of welfare states, may require, in turn, a flexible form of "market" or "competitive" corporatism rather than attempted moves in a neo-liberal direction' (Rhodes, 1998, p. 1). However, there are important differences in our respective positions. Rhodes, for example, places considerable emphasis upon the role of pay flexibility at the local level, suggesting that: 'in sum there are pressures for both a decentralisation and a centralisation (or in some cases a recentralisation) of industrial relations systems. An "optimal" solution would combine some form of incomes policy or national wage co-ordination with *pay flexibility within certain margins at the level of the firm*' (Rhodes, 1998, p. 3, my emphasis).[4]

As the discussion of local pay bargaining below indicates, flexibility in pay negotiations has been an important contributory factor in the success of macro-political bargaining in Ireland. Indeed, I am more than willing to concede that the existence of local clauses in macro-level negotiations allows consideration for the plight of individual companies during periods of volatile market conditions. However, I also want to suggest that the success of macro-political bargaining should not be attributed solely to the issue of pay flexibility. While local clauses may establish a closer tie between pay, performance and the local labour market, they also provide a focal point for both management and unions to negotiate changes in *work practices* and the *introduction of new technology*.

In other words, the type of issues involved in national-level agreements (and that includes local pay clauses) extends beyond the parameters of pay (increases) to embrace a discussion about changes in the supply side of the economy. If these agreements were simply about adding an element of flexibility to pay negotiations (without removing productive rigidities, as Streeck so usefully points out) then presumably they would increase wage rigidity over time, given the constant desire to seek competitive international advantage. Above all, we need to recognise that the success of national-level agreements is not simply due to the introduction of pay flexibility (Rhodes), and they are not exclusively concerned with economic demand management and/or a passive welfare state (Streeck). Neither should we assume that macro-political bargaining constrains the capacity of management to engineer changes in production methods, the introduction of new technology or work practices, as is so often portrayed in the literature of neo-liberal economists.

The remaining sections of this chapter return to these themes at an empirical level and address at least three key arguments. First, the rigidities normally attributed to macro-political bargaining agreements are not necessarily inherent and, far from being a constraint, may assist management in the restructuring of the supply side of the economy. Second, to date analyses have focused predominantly upon the role of macro-political bargaining in setting wage rates in both the public and private sectors. There is a tendency therefore to ignore the fact that in Ireland there have been moves to introduce flexibility into public sector service provision.[5] The final section examines recent attempts to expand the experience of partnership and the role this performs in the construction of a new form of governance in Ireland.

From the Programme for National Economic Recovery to the Programme for Prosperity and Fairness

The origins of Ireland's experience with macro-political bargaining can be located in the negotiated institutional arrangements first mooted in response to industrial conflict during 1960s. To those inside government, the debilitating experiences of such industrial strife could be attributed to the particularities of Irish trade union organisation, multi-union representation and a relatively weak level of centralisation. In a concerted attempt to restore stability to wage negotiations, and subsequently reduce the incidence of strikes, the government prompted a series of national wage agreements (NWA) and national understandings (NU) with employers and trade unions. These agreements, which lasted between 1970 and 1980, involved negotiations over pay between employers and unions and a series of non-pay negotiations between unions and government (Hardiman, 1988, p. 53).

During the 1970s the NWAs assumed an increasingly structured format. Largely at the behest of the Services, Industrial, Professional and Technical Union (SIPTU), the largest trade union, attempts were made to ensure that future negotiations would pursue social and economic policies in a more integrated fashion. The unions were cognisant that any wage increases secured in a national agreement could be lost in budgetary policies that placed an unfair burden upon employees. Although greater success on this issue was achieved in later agreements, the strategy was severely hampered in the early 1980s as the combination of political instability and economic crisis led governments to abandon negotiations with the trade union movement.

Management had become disenchanted with national-level agreements, as was apparent in its concerted campaign to decentralise wage negotiations and tie pay increases to either local labour market conditions or the profitability of individual firms. However, the emergence of the PNER in 1987 and the Programme for Economic and Social Progress (PESP) in 1990 signalled a renewed enthusiasm for national-level negotiations.

The PNER had been negotiated amid a crisis in public finances, with government debt peaking at 117 per cent of GDP. A large part of the programme's remit was thus directed towards reducing the debt/GDP ratio to 96.5 per cent by 1990 (O'Riordan, 1996). However, the programme also delivered higher living standards for employees as modest wage increases were coupled with tax reforms. Not surprisingly, its success led to negotiations for a successor, the PESP. By 1992 the success of these programmes had ensured that national-level wage negotiations, particularly in the manual and clerical sectors, were the norm.

If the PESP were to prove successful then it was imperative that it would perform a pivotal role in restructuring the supply side of the economy. Here, the introduction of clause 3 (a pay clause that allowed companies to negotiate pay increases to a maximum of 3 per cent outside of those negotiated at national level) was an important first step, allowing management to tie negotiations to local labour market conditions, achieve changes in productive rigidities and yet retain moderation in wage demands at a macro-level. As Table 1.1 shows, under the arrangements set out in clause 3 of PESP, managers were able to secure concessions in a wide range of operating areas. This was confirmed in research undertaken by the *Industrial Relations News* (IRN) which showed that in almost half (48 per cent) of the 96 local bargaining deals recorded at the beginning of 1991, 'significant concessions' were made (IRN, 1992, Vol. 37).[6] The IRN study also made an important distinction between items such as 'agreements to co-operate with on-going change or the tightening up on tea breaks' and agreements on cashless pay, increased productivity, or major reorganisation or rationalisation. When both of these broad categories (significant and minor trade-offs) are put together, the overall figure for companies where concessions were agreed in return for clause 3 came to a total of just over 79 per cent (IRN, 1992, Vol. 37).

The type of change agreed by unions in a trade-off for payment of clause 3 included productivity improvements, rationalisation or reorganisation, regrading, co-operation with new technology or new machinery, the introduction of 'just in time' working practices and, of course, the all-encompassing 'co-operation with on-going change' (IRN, 1992, Vol. 36). Clause 3 was not simply a local pay-bargaining clause. Although it introduced an element of flexibility into macro-level negotiations (allowing management some latitude on pay), it also realigned discussions towards the issues of new technology, changing work practices and job demarcations. In other words, it engineered a situation that demanded consultation, negotiation and compromise.

Table 1.1 Breakdown of clause 3 agreements, 1992

Terms of agreement	%
3% with 'significant' trade-offs	48.0
3 per cent with 'minor' trade-offs	25.0
3% *without* trade-offs	14.6
Over 3% radical change	6.2
Less than 3 per cent	4.1
Other	2.0
Total	*100.0*

Source: IRN, 1992, Vol. 37.

A further appealing feature of clause 3 was the fact that payments could be made in phases, ensuring that delays could be sought in 'periods of financial stricture'. This latter element to the agreement, subject to approval from both the Labour Court and the Labour Relations Commission (LRC) of the financial state of an individual firm, was particularly interesting since it allowed a 'breathing space' to emerge during volatile market conditions or a currency crisis. Although the data is more limited, Table 1.2 indicates that while the majority of companies (55.5 per cent) paid clause 3 in a single phase, a phased payment was made in 27 per cent of cases, a process that became more prevalent as 1992 progressed. It is a feature of the agreements that has persistently found favour among employers and was retained in the Programme for Prosperity and Fairness (2001–3).

Table 1.2 How the 3 per cent was applied, 1992

Full 3% (starting date, phase II of PESP)	53	(55.5%)
Full 3% on a phased basis (starting date, phase II of PESP)	26	(27.0%)
Full 3% (starting date before phase II of PESP)	5	(5.2%)
Full 3% (starting date after phase II of PESP)	3	(3.0%)
Deals in excess of 3%	6	(6.2%)
Interim deals	3	(3.0%)
Total	96	(100.0%)

The data presented in Table 1.3 provides a breakdown of the changes that were secured during this period. There are two important themes that emerge. First, despite the predominance of macro-political bargaining structures, Irish management was extremely successful in altering working practices among core employees. Second, many of the changes that took place relate specifically to the status of employees. As the first column of Table 1.4 shows, the type of responses associated with flexible strategies designed to increase an organisation's ability to adapt to volatile market conditions altered radically, as companies increased the use of part-time employees, temporary or casual workers, fixed-term contracts and subcontractors.[7] The incidence of such change clearly reveals a significant disparity between the rhetoric of national-level employer organisations, which often allude to the restrictive nature of macro-political bargaining agreements, and the experience of such negotiations.

Table 1.3 Has there been a change in the use of the following working arrangements over the last three years? (1992: percentages)

Arrangement	More	Same	Less	Not used	Don't know
Weekend work	14.5	50.7	14.5	14.5	5.8
Shift work	15.2	54.3	8.0	15.9	6.5
Overtime	23.2	34.1	34.1	2.9	5.8
Annual hours contract	4.3	17.4	9.4	50.0	1.4
Part-time work	31.2	26.8	4.3	26.1	11.6
Temporary	37.7	36.2	8.7	6.5	0.7
Fixed-term contract	37.7	29.0	4.3	19.6	0.7
Home-based work	1.4	4.3	–	70.3	0.7
Government training scheme	13.0	29.0	–	36.2	2.2
Subcontracting	36.2	29.7	3.6	20.3	0.7

Source: IRN, 1992, Vol. 38.

An additional but nevertheless crucial component of the success of macro-political bargaining in Ireland has been the institutional apparatus designed to resolve disputes between management and unions. As Tables 1.4, 1.5 and 1.6 show, there has been a substantial reduction in the incidence of strikes, the level of unofficial strike activity and the number of days lost in disputes. Indeed, a comparison between the periods 1982–87 and 1988–93 provides clear evidence of the success of the PNER and PESP in reducing the level of strike activity in the economy.

While the data confirms the success of macro-political bargaining in reducing industrial conflict, it is worth noting that industrial strife has not simply disappeared. Any success in macro-level concertation also demands a conciliation service (accepted as legitimate by all parties) that provides an institutional setting in which antagonism may be resolved. As Table 1.7

indicates, the combination of the Labour Court and the LRC proved remarkably successful in resolving disputes between management and unions. Clearly, while national-level agreements contributed significantly to a period of sustained political consensus, we have witnessed an impressively high ratio of settlements through the institutional mechanisms designed to alleviate antagonism.

Table 1.4 Number of strikes and of work days lost under decentralised wage bargaining, 1982–87, and under PNER/PESP, 1988–93

Decentralised wage bargaining			PNER/PESP		
Year	Strikes	Days lost	Year	Strikes	Days lost
1982	131	434,000	1988	65	143,000
1983	154	319,000	1989	38	50,000
1984	192	386,000	1990	49	223,000
1985	116	418,000	1991	54	86,000
1986	100	309,000	1992	38	191,000
1987	80	264,000	1993*	48	65,000
Total	*773*	*2,130,000*	*Total*	*292*	*758,000*
Average number of days lost per annum: 355,000			Average number of days lost per annum: 126,000		

Source: Central Statistics Office/*Department of Enterprise and Employment.

Table 1.5 Number of strikes commenced, 1987–91

Year	Total	Official	Unofficial
1987	76	54 (71%)	22 (29%)
1988	72	46 (64%)	26 (36%)
1989	41	28 (68%)	13 (32%)
1990	51	35 (69%)	16 (31%)
1991	52	39 (75%)	13 (25%)

Source: Department of Labour, 1991.

Table 1.6 Days lost, 1987–91

Year	Total	Official	Unofficial
1987	260,000	235,000 (90%)	25,000 (10%)
1988	130,000	123,500 (95%)	6,500 (5%)
1989	41,400	29,800 (72%)	11,600 (28%)
1990	203,700	196,000 (97%)	6,800 (3%)
1991	82,900	73,600 (89%)	9,300 (11%)

Source: Department of Labour, 1991.

Table 1.7 Settlement of industrial disputes in the public and private sectors, 1990–96

Year	Referrals (number)	Meetings (number)	Settled (%)
1990	1,474	2,074	73
1991	1,880	2,385	85
1992	1,935	2,450	75
1993	1,844	2,379	71
1994	1,551	2,055	66
1995	1,692	2,072	70
1996	1,487	1,999	81

Few would take issue with the view that the PESP was an outstanding success. However, the latter stages of this agreement coincided with a particularly unstable European economic climate and a national interest rate crisis during 1992–93. While growth rates in the economy were significantly less than those achieved during the late 1980s and early 1990s the picture was far from disastrous, since the levels attained were still above the European average and, in contrast with other EU states, Ireland achieved modest growth in employment. However, the legacy of high rates of long-term unemployment coupled with an above average rate of expansion in the labour force meant that Ireland continued to struggle with the seemingly interminable problem of long-term structural unemployment. It was against this backdrop of uncertainty that the social partners embarked upon negotiations for a third agreement: the Programme for Competitiveness and Work (PCW) (1994–96).

The debilitating experience of currency instability in 1992/93 had a profound influence on the parameters struck for the PCW. As a result of the slow-down in economic growth, employers were reluctant to concede wage negotiation at a local level over and above that agreed for the national level (O'Riordan, 1996). Thus, in terms of the basic pay negotiations, the PCW involved a series of staged payments to be made over a three-year period from 1994 to 1996. Basic pay increases of 2 per cent in 1994, 2.5 per cent in 1995 and 2.5 per cent in the first six months of 1996 were agreed. An additional 1 per cent would be made in the remaining six months of 1996.

The objective of the PCW was to alleviate the burden of taxation on workers with low incomes and raise the threshold at which higher rates of taxation come into play. With regard to the first priority, the increase in the level of income exempt from tax as a result of the government's 1996 budget did give a real relative improvement to the very low paid. However, it did so only after an inadequate increase in the exemption limit in the previous budget. Not surprisingly, from the trade unions' perspective the over-all experience of the PCW was disappointing, as little in the way of real progress was achieved in reducing the burden of taxation on the low paid (O'Riordan, 1996, p. 6).

The principal reason for the government's failure to meet its tax reform commitments was connected to its decision to over-fulfil the PCW's agreed fiscal policy objective. All parties to the PCW supported a policy of main-taining the government deficit within the Maastricht ceiling of 3 per cent of GDP, and by staying at 2.2 per cent the Irish deficit met that condition by a wide margin. In addition, all parties to the PCW were in agreement with meeting the other Maastricht guideline in respect of fiscal policy, namely that of making satisfactory progress towards a debt/GDP ratio of 60 per cent (O'Riordan, 1996). And yet, during the period of the PCW the Irish economy experienced (at that time) an unprecedented level of economic growth, averaging 6.5 per cent between 1994 and 1996. The period of the PCW also witnessed a particularly low level of industrial strife and a record low of industrial disputes in 1994, with just 25,550 working days lost (see Table 1.8).

Table 1.8 Industrial disputes, 1993–98

Year	Disputes	Firms Involved	Workers involved	Total days lost
1993	48	48	12,789	61,312
1994	29	238	5,007	25,550
1995	34	34	31,653	130,300
1996	32	30	13,339	114,584
1997	28	28	5,364	74,508*
1998	34	62	8,060	37,374

* This period falls under Partnership 2000. A significant element of this figure is attributed to the Irish Life insurance company dispute, which accounted for 10,080 days.
Source: Central Statistics Office.

If the data reveals a substantial decline in political conflict, the evidence from the LRC confirms that pay and conditions were no longer the primary source of industrial strife in Ireland (LRC, 1997). Issues such as poor human relations between shop floor and line managers, the absence of communications or consultation, and the introduction of major change were now the most significant issues of contention. It was a situation in which the Commission was moved to remark that 'significant and constant change is the order of the day', as the impact of new technology, deregula-tion in state industries, international competition and the changing nature of the workplace took effect. Reflecting this change, its conciliation service was now increasingly concerned with disputes about new management or production techniques and changes in work practices, particularly in the public sector (LRC, 1994). What is more, the Commission noted that while a relatively low level of disputes had been recorded on the issues of disclosure of information and union recognition, there had been a 'notable increase' (LRC, 1997, p. 18). It was, for the unions, an important issue, and assumed greater political visibility.

There can be little doubt that under the terms of the PCW (which had been narrower than the PESP) management had been able to pursue with continued vigour the restructuring of the supply side of the economy. This was confirmed in a study which showed that during the 1990s, 75 per cent of firms introduced new plant and technology and over 60 per cent secured changes to working time arrangements, working practices and new employee involvement initiatives. In addition, payment systems and promotional criteria were revised or altered in nearly half of all workplaces. As the authors of one study note, 'while it is difficult to estimate the depth of such change from these data, the level of workplace change and the range of issues addressed appear very significant. Evidently workplaces in the Celtic Tiger are indeed highly dynamic' (Roche and Geary, 1998, p. 3).

Keen to avoid the experience of unions in the UK, which had found themselves isolated from the wider decision-making agenda of public policy, trade unions in Ireland were willing partners in the search for new investment and the introduction of new technology. This was confirmed in research undertaken by D'Art and Turner (1999) which showed that while a 'them and us' attitude to management–union relations may not have disappeared altogether, there were important developments in the 1990s. For D'Art and Turner, the intensity of a 'them and us' attitude in management–union relations is significantly related to 'employee awareness of the need for firm survival, greater discretion in work, satisfaction with industrial relations procedures and a cohesive union organisation' (D'Art and Turner, 1999, p. 112). Their research suggests that the presence of a strong and functioning union at firm level had the potential to address problems such as 'lack of trust' between workers and management or the lack of institutional support from upper management. In addition, these researchers argue that collective bargaining allows workers to participate and negotiate for a share in the surplus of the firm and increases worker confidence in dealing with management (D'Art and Turner, 1999, p. 113). These are certainly themes that attracted the attention of Irish Congress of Trade Unions (ICTU) in the early 1990s as it sought to encourage firm-level participation. There can be little doubt that the conditions of political and economic stability fostered under the PESP continued throughout the duration of the PCW.

Almost all parties to the macro-level negotiations concur that in the area of employment expansion the PCW was a qualified success. What remains in doubt is the adequacy of this achievement, given the inherited unemployment problem and the level of resources used to tackle long-term unemployment (O'Riordan, 1996, p. 7). Under the terms of the PCW the government was committed to introducing a new Community Employment (CE) venture that would enable the unemployed to undertake work of public or social value while it provided work experience and development training. In order to reduce any 'disincentive' to take up such opportunities the government agreed that secondary welfare benefits would be retained. The government was thus committed to providing 40,000 places on a voluntary basis by 1994.

The PCW also required the government to consider the findings of the National Economic and Social Forum (NESF), a consultative body that embraced diverse interests such as the unemployed and women's groups. In June 1994, the NESF issued a report on Ireland's long-term unemployed and called for the development of an employment service targeted at those registered as unemployed for more than six months. In January 1996, the government responded with four initiatives. First, 30,000 or 75 per cent of CE places would be allocated to those over 21 and unemployed for at least 12 months. A further 10,000 CE places (25 per cent) would be reserved for those over 35 and unemployed for three years or more, and places would be provided on a pilot basis for those over 35 who had been unemployed for more than five years. Finally, a new scheme would be introduced and aimed at those who had been unemployed for six months and were likely to become long-term unemployed.

The attractiveness and subsequent success of this initiative resulted in a conflict between the government and unions. Although participation averaged 31,800 the figure of 40,000 had been passed by the end of the year, encouraging calls in some quarters for cutbacks. As far as the unions were concerned, the programmes had been jeopardised by an over-zealous pursuit of fiscal rectitude (O'Riordan, 1996).[8]

As with many such agreements, the PCW involved a political balancing act. On the one hand, government acknowledged the demands of the trade union movement to improve the living standards of its members, while, on the other hand, government's objective was to sustain an environment in which global capital would seek to reside. As such, the main tenets of the programme (as its title so eloquently reveals) were designed to engineer a consensus around the need to embrace more fully the 'realistic economic strictures of the global market'. In this sense, it represented a subtle, but none the less crucial, shift towards a more conservative economic outlook, one that effectively abandoned any serious pretension to the social democratic ethos that may have permeated elements of earlier agreements.

If we avoid being seduced by the political rhetoric that surrounded the PCW, it remains patently clear that while it may have embraced the language of inclusion it did little to alleviate the vast inequalities that persist in Ireland. Neither did it address fundamental questions about industrial democracy. This latter issue, which attracted the sobriquet of 'plant-level partnership', altered little during the tenure of the PCW and changed only marginally during Partnership 2000.

The backdrop to Partnership 2000 was very different to that for the PCW. The unions sought radical tax reform to provide tax relief for public sector workers, a flexible pay agreement that would benefit the low paid, and new initiatives designed to include profit sharing in companies. Local pay clauses were reintroduced and linked to productivity gains in the private sector and modernisation programmes in the public sector. It is not that the agreement sought to appease the more conservative elements of the Irish media or its academe, who have voiced continued opposition to the 'spiralling' public sector wage bill. Rather, the agreement acknowledged the 'imperative' to build upon measures that had induced change in the public sector (*Partnership 2000*, 1997, p. 68). With regard to this, Chapter 10 of the agreement represents the culmination of almost a decade of concern at reorganising public service provision. A succession of policy developments sought to engineer reform: Delivering Better Government, Shaping a Healthier Future: A Strategy for Effective Healthcare in the 1990s, Charting our Educational Future, and the Strategic Management Initiative.

Reflecting the international trend towards the restructuring of civil services, emphasis was accorded to improving the quality of service provision, flexibility in the deployment of resources and the use of performance measurement. Here, Partnership 2000 contained a local bargaining element that linked ongoing discussions about new and flexible working arrangements in public sector service provision. Indeed, the agreement explicitly stipulated that adjustments in pay (at the local level) would 'be conditional upon there having been verified progress to a satisfactory level on implementation of the modernisation programme set out in chapter ten of the agreement' (*Partnership 2000*, 1997, p. 80).

Few would doubt that the overhaul of the Irish civil service was long overdue or that reform achieved thus far was significantly assisted by national-level negotiations. However, while many of these reforms are well under way, and a trajectory is well established, there remain important questions over the detail and extent of change. The Department of

Finance, for example, remains sceptical, convinced that the reform programme is infused with aspirations but has delivered rather less in terms of tangible change.

Nevertheless, the Department of the Taoiseach's office remains confident that significant steps forward have been made, providing the basis for future change. Negotiations with unions through national-level agreements institutionalise the accepted need for change, allowing future revision of public sector working practices. However tentative these developments may have been, they nevertheless confirm the ability of national-level bargaining to provide a framework from which to establish change in the supply side of the economy. Moreover, they are important in persuading business that gains in efficiency made in the private sector will not be sacrificed at the altar of public sector inefficiency.

One of the features that distinguished Partnership 2000 from previous agreements was the emphasis accorded to increasing the role of plant-level partnership in Ireland. In particular, the agreement implemented a new body, the National Centre for Partnership, designed to promote workplace partnership in both the public and private sectors. However, as O'Dowd, joint director of the Centre acknowledged, while there was 'growing interest' in these ventures, partnership was practised only in a minority of cases (IRN, 1998, Vol. 31).

It is a finding confirmed in the University College Dublin study on workplace change, which argued that the incidence of partnership at the firm level was only 'very modest' in unionised companies. At most, 20 per cent have established partnerships, and fewer used this as a means for organising change. The study also revealed that partnership was generally limited to 'operational issues' and rarely formed part of the strategic decision-making of a business (Roche and Geary, 1998, p. 17). Indeed, Roche and Geary's work confirms that moves to sustain the managerial prerogative remain the most common form of 'handling change'. Here, Ireland 'has much in common with other western economies' where the 'pattern of change tends to be piecemeal and fragmented, with strong areas of continuity and inertia even in workplaces experimenting with new modes of collaborative production' (Roche and Geary, 2000, p. 29). Moreover, this work suggests that 'the uneven and far from widespread diffusion of new practices, and the uncertain prospects of innovation based on partnership' met with 'substantial barriers and not uncommonly deep resistance from employers' (Roche and Geary, 2000, p. 4).

The reluctance on the part of management to embrace partnership may be attributed in part to risks commonly perceived to be carried in such forms of negotiation. Management expressed the fear that decisions might be delayed, or that the managerial prerogative would be diluted (Roche and

Geary, 1998, p. 18). Even where partnership arrangements at the firm level have taken place, an element encouraged in Chapter 9 of *Partnership 2000*, they were agreed only in conjunction with significant changes to work practices. The research by IRN clearly show that of 48 such agreements made since mid-1996, as many as 16 involved major changes in work practice such as teamworking, world-class manufacturing or some other form of new work organisation (IRN, 16 1999). A further twelve 'Chapter 9' deals involved setting up some form of partnership forum that was less controversial because it involved no financial commitment by the company.

There can be little doubt that the issue of firm-level participation is a crucial one. As Regini has succinctly observed, concertative efforts during the 1970s were characterised by political exchange and a compensatory role for the state. Whereas for the state these relationships offered immediate and tangible rewards (stability, legitimation and self-restraint), the 'reverse was almost never the case' (Regini, 1996, p. 17). In other words, a tension emerges between, on the one hand, the insulation from rank-and-file pressures offered by monopoly representation and, on the other hand, a risk of a crisis of union representation as the leadership becomes distanced from its membership. As Regini points out, the recent Italian situation shows that 'concertation without explicit political exchange may succeed precisely when interest organisations become less centralised and insulated from rank and file pressures; and especially, when workplace representation acquires a greater role vis a vis the union bureaucracy' (Regini, 1996, p. 19).

Representation which is rooted in the workplace and which enhances participation may overcome a crisis of representation because it reaffirms the relevance of trade union activity to the rank and file. In this context it seems plausible to suggest that local-level bargaining clauses, such as clause 3, or any serious move to endorse plant-level partnership may have unintentionally resurrected the role of plant-level union activity. In so doing it provides a focal point for management-union discussions, thereby reaffirming the relevance, value and (partial) success of a trade union presence.

Such developments provide tangible reasons for caution against those who see macro-political bargaining in terms of rigid, static structures, populated by actors implacable to the changing circumstances of the global economy. Negotiated forms of governance should therefore be seen in a more dynamic light, recognising its capacity to change over time and in response to influences emanating from outside national borders.

There has also been considerable debate about whether changes to workplace industrial relations have been instrumental in driving forward the Celtic Tiger. McCartney and Teague, for example, have argued that workplace reorganisation incorporating change such as job rotation, quality circles, total quality management and teamworking have been a familiar theme in Ireland. In their view, we have witnessed a move away from low-value-added commodity production, which tends to be cost sensitive, to quality-sensitive markets (McCartney and Teague, 1997, p. 384). It is an issue upon which Roche and Geary (2000) do not concur. Citing evidence generated both in the survey they undertook for University College Dublin and the wider international literature, they suggest that workplace innovation and change in industrial relations has been rather more 'partial, piecemeal and fragile in character' than presented by McCartney and Teague (Roche and Geary, 2000, p. 4).

In the survey, teamwork was found in 59 per cent of workplaces, whereas the McCartney and Teague study suggests only 27 per cent of establishments have moved in this direction. The difference in the distribution of quality circles was in the opposite direction, with a far greater incidence in the McCartney and Teague survey. Both studies found the diffusion of total quality management high (see Roche and Geary, 2000, pp. 9-11). However, Roche and Geary's work also adopts two indicators that provide further evidence for the level of employee involvement: periodic or ad hoc task forces and joint consultative committees and works councils.

While Roche and Geary acknowledge that the incidence of new forms of work organisation in Irish workplaces has indeed 'been impressive', they emphasise the fact that a closer examination of the research data shows that changes which have taken place 'permit employees limited discretion and narrowly circumscribed decision-making authority'. Certainly these researchers reject the idea that new forms of partnership have been at the forefront of any form of change which has been undertaken (Roche and Geary, 2000, pp28–9).

The issue of trade union recognition developed in Partnership 2000 was also a source of consternation to many trade unionists. Throughout the 1990s trade unions were alarmed at the tendency (particularly among multinational companies) to establish non-union organisations. While the negotiations for Partnership 2000 embraced the idea of union recognition it became clear that it was not resolved to the satisfaction of the unions. The Irish Business and Employers' Confederation (IBEC), which has a significant proportion of members for which non-union human resources (HR) policies are a core value, could not agree to a legally binding mechanism for union recognition disputes. As a result, a series of proposals was drafted that involved voluntary negotiations taken in conjunction with the LRC, which would be concluded in a non-binding recommendation (see IRN, 1998, Vol. 3).

Partnership 2000 also sought to widen the nature of partnership by introducing voluntary organisations to explore new policy approaches to social exclusion and inequality (O'Donnell, 1998, p. 87). It was a response to growing concern that macro-level agreements between the social partners had failed to deliver to the marginalised sections of Irish society. However, this attempt at expanding the number of participants in negotiations to include elements of the voluntary and community sectors (the fourth pillar) has not been without its problems. These groups tend to bring normative arguments to the negotiating table. While this may expand the range of issues, include alternative visions of economic development and therefore alter the nature of debate, it also introduces strains between the old and new social partners.

On this matter, O'Donnell has noted that while bargaining as a concept distinguishes social partnership from more liberal and pluralist approaches, in which consultation is more prominent, it 'does not entirely capture the partnership process' (O'Donnell, 1998, p. 102). For O'Donnell, partnership entails the 'players in a process of deliberation that has the potential to shape and reshape their understanding, identity and preferences'. This is an important theme, since it recognises that identity (and presumably interests and strategy) 'can be shaped through interaction'. As such, he suggests that one of the more notable features of the partnership experiments has been the reluctance to engage on 'ultimate social visions'. Under such circumstances the social partners are more concerned with a problem-solving approach where consensus is no longer a 'pre-condition' as much as an ' outcome' (O'Donnell, 1998, p. 102). A further element of innovation, as far as O'Donnell is concerned, has been the shift away from partnership being the exclusive preserve of the peak organisations. Social partners are no longer concerned purely with their role as representatives of given occupational groups but are now actively engaged in 'mobilising citizens who have problems that need to be dealt with'. Fixed functional roles have been supplanted by the need to co-ordinate between groups and extend the functions of public advocacy (O'Donnell, 1998, p. 103).

These new forms of social partnership have induced changes in the relationship between policy making, implementation and monitoring, in ways which place monitoring at the centre of policy (O'Donnell, 1998, p. 104). It is a set of arguments with which I have a good deal of sympathy, not least because it reinforces the view that macro-political bargaining structures are not necessarily rigid and static structures, but involve the dynamic (re)construction of relationships aimed at forging political and economic stability.

The Programme for Prosperity and Fairness

With economic growth approaching stratospheric levels during late 1998 and early 1999, the political terrain upon which negotiations took place for a successor agreement to Partnership 2000 presented a new set of challenges. In particular, two prominent issues emerged in the ensuing debate. The first was the widespread view among union members that any new agreement would have to address the fact that the budgets of 1998/99 had disproportionately favoured those on higher incomes. The second issue, one that was to emerge forcefully in the latter part of 2000 and which threatened to unravel the agreement, was that of inflation. Negotiations throughout 2000 proved protracted and tortuous and were made all the more difficult because the government opted for budgets that appeared to ignore an inflation rate so significantly above those of its European counterparts that it earned a rebuke from other European finance ministers.

The deal, which aimed to alleviate the distortions introduced by earlier budgets, was to provide tax cuts of around IR£1.5 billion over three years and a series of social exclusion measures that would run to a further IR£1.5 billion. Over the course of the agreement it was estimated that the low paid would receive 20.5 per cent cumulative pay increases and those on less than IR£200 a week would no longer contribute to Pay Related Social Insurance (PRSI).

In order to prevent a repetition of the public sector pay disputes that had beset the early and middle stages of Partnership 2000, two proposals were included in the Programme for Prosperity and Fairness (PPF): an 'early settlers' clause of 3 per cent for those working in the public sector, and the promise of a 'benchmarking' review body that would address changes in work practices and pay relative to the private sector. Irrespective of any gains to be made from the benchmarking review process, those in the public sector could expect to receive around 15.75 per cent pay increases over the full term of the agreement. Those that settled early were likely to experience an increase of 19 per cent. Such increases in public sector pay would see the exchequer pay bill rise by IR£1.2 billion or 17 per cent by 2003.

The PPF was to run for 33 months and involved an agreement on pay, employment, tax reform, lifelong learning and childcare. The projection on pay was that it would rise by 5.5 per cent in each of the first two 12-month periods (or by a minimum of IR£12 per week) and by 4 per cent in the final nine months. The minimum wage was negotiated upwards to IR£4.40. In addition, there were commitments to improve spending on childcare payments and the removal of those on the minimum wage from the tax net, although both of these were subject to economic growth remaining above a ceiling of 5.6 per cent.

Initially, sentiment among the social partners appeared up-beat. Thus, for example, the General Secretary of ICTU was moved to remark that it was the 'best deal that can be got out of this process for workers and people on low paid incomes' (*Irish Times*, 9 February 2000). It was an argument that found favour in the higher echelons of IMPACT, the largest public service union, whose general secretary, Peter McLoone, suggested that 'when IMPACT members are filling in their ballot papers they must ask themselves is there any other process that would guarantee increases of at least 25 per cent over the next thirty three months. The answer has to be no' (*Irish Times*, 9 February 2000). However, it was not a view shared by all within the trade union movement.

In its special conference in February of 2000 the country's second-largest trade union, MANDATE, unanimously rejected the deal. Its principal objection was that, as the voice of low paid workers, it found it unacceptable that they would receive increases of only IR£32 a week when those on average incomes could expect to earn double that amount. The union was appalled at the failure to implement a minimum wage of IR£5 per hour or secure the right of shop stewards to represent members or attend training courses in working hours. MANDATE's members voted overwhelmingly to reject the dea, by 89.7 per cent to 10.3 per cent (*Irish Times*, 24 February 2000, and 23 March 2000).

MANDATE was not alone in its objection to the PPF, with discontent also being voiced widely among the teaching profession. Although the Irish National Teachers' Organisation (INTO) had endorsed the agreement, albeit by a slender majority of 51 per cent to 49 per cent, the teaching profession more generally felt aggrieved that pay levels had fallen behind those in professions such as nursing and the gardai. Within INTO the most marked opposition emerged from the Dublin area, concerned with the failure of pay to keep up with escalating living costs in the capital. The Teachers' Union of Ireland (TUI) also voted against the PPF, by a margin of 55 per cent to 45 per cent. However, the most concerted and vociferous critic of the PPF was the Association of Secondary Teachers in Ireland (ASTI), a union involved in a prolonged industrial dispute over its pay claim of 30 per cent.

The government hoped that opposition from the public sector to the deal would be assuaged by its promise for a benchmarking review body that would attempt to break with the old system of pay relativities. The body was charged with examining pay and working practices across a wide spectrum of the civil and public service. Benchmarking has been a controversial process, one not alleviated by the rise in unemployment and reduced government finances that accompanied the budget of December 2003. Its critics have argued that the process remains flawed, that the criteria for adjudicating on pay increases are overly complex and lack transparency. More importantly perhaps, and even at this early date, there appears little in the way of a systematic appraisal of the changes set to arise in public sector work practices.

If low pay and public sector relativities were prominent issues that hampered negotiations prior to the signing of the PPF, the rise in inflation threatened to unravel the agreement altogether. As early as March 2000 the SIPTU president, Des Geraghty, had warned against complacency and that the issue of partnership at the local level and rising inflation would have to be addressed. While SIPTU had strongly endorsed the PPF, by a margin of 69 per cent to 31 per cent, its leadership was concerned that rising inflation and a further escalation in house prices would rapidly undermine any gains achieved by the unions. It was an argument echoed by Peter Cassells, general secretary of ICTU, who stated that the PPF was an 'interdependent package and, if one element is not delivered, then other elements are in immediate danger'. Indeed, he went on to caution that if the 'government allows markets forces to push inflation to a level that impacts upon living standards, this will force workers to seek compensation through higher wages' (*Irish Times*, 24 March 2000).

The government's initial reaction was to dampen the hysteria. As far as the minister for finance was concerned, the headline inflation figure, which stood at 4.6 per cent in April of 2000, would peak during the summer and fall back by the end of the year. However, as SIPTU pointed out, 'when workers were balloting on the PPF it was on the basis that inflation would rise to four per cent' (*Irish Times*, 19 April 2000). By the summer of 2000 rising inflation had become a serious political issue, with many in the union movement calling for negotiations to be reopened. By September of 2000 the situation had deteriorated seriously. The tension surrounding the future of the deal was clearly evident in an internal memorandum leaked to the *Irish Times* which revealed that Jack O'Connor, SIPTU's vice-president, had argued that the PPF was predicated upon strong non-inflationary economic growth and that while this was outstripping the anticipated 5.6 per cent target, inflation was at 6.2 per cent and showing all the signs of increasing further. In O'Connor's opinion, the position had become 'untenable' (*Irish Times*, 13 September 2000).

In a succession of hastily arranged meetings, and with one eye on the forthcoming December budget, a renewed package was agreed that would offset the impact of rising inflation on the original deal. As a consequence the government and IBEC acceded to a further 2 per cent pay rise from April 2001, which meant the pay increase would move from 5.5 per cent to 7.5

per cent, and a one-off payment of 1 per cent in April 2002 to offset the impact of inflation (*Irish Times*, 5 December, 2000).

Some concluding remarks

There can be little doubt that Partnership 2000 and the PPF succeeded in firmly embedding national agreements and 'partnership' within the Irish political psyche. Indeed, they have confidently proclaimed the basis for a new political architecture in Irish politics. No longer are such agreements simply about compensatory state action or crisis management; they now involve more crucially the construction of a new form of social and political regulation. They do not remain circumscribed as incomes policies or pay agreements, integral though these remain, but are about providing the basis for new forms of policy making. They show shift from a concern with the exchange of resources in order to secure political acquiescence (redistribution) to an allocation of economic policy authority (regulation) (Regini, 1996, p. 17).

The arguments presented here suggest that despite the presence of macro-political bargaining arrangements in Ireland, management has been proactive (and at least partially successful) in pursuing a programme of productive restructuring. In stark contrast to neo-liberal criticisms of interest intermediation, this chapter has argued that the very presence of such arrangements may have assisted in engineering an environment more conducive to constructive negotiations on flexible work practices, employee status and social organisation. This would appear to suggest that the optimism embedded in Streeck's view, that flexibility and rigidity are not mutually exclusive, is not misplaced. The problem for Streeck (and he is not alone on this matter) lies in the failure to appreciate the role macro-political bargaining can play in restructuring the productive (supply side) of the economy. It is not simply that management in Ireland has been able to trade off a particular clause of the wage agreement in exchange for the introduction of new working practices and technology (although this has clearly been an important element). Rather, such agreements contribute positively to the creation of a stable environment in which management may be encouraged to innovate and reduce productive rigidities. Social peace, worker commitment, and the recognition of the need to encourage long-term investment in new plant and technology are all a part of the political dimension to managerial strategies shaped by macro-political bargaining agreements.

The political furore that accompanied a severe currency crisis in the early 1990s was weathered, political and economic stability was maintained, and the problem of long-term unemployment eased through the late 1990s. This is not to suggest that all will be plain sailing. In the aftermath of an unprecedented economic boom the trade unions remain perturbed at escalating house prices and the failure to redistribute more evenly the economic gains of the 'Celtic Tiger'. There are also difficulties surrounding the extent of plant-level partnership, the persistence (indeed expansion) of marginalised groups in Irish society and the thorny issue of trade union recognition. However, there are few politicians not willing to subscribe to the view that national-level agreements have contributed significantly to Ireland's economic regeneration. It seems, therefore, that considerable though these hurdles may be, the continued appeal of macro-political bargaining is unlikely to be diminished.

Notes

1   The term 'flexible specialisation' has emerged as an umbrella concept encompassing a wide range of processes within contemporary capitalism. For those such as Piore and Sabel (1984) the mass production techniques of the long post-war boom have been replaced by a new paradigm in which flexibility in production and consumption becomes axiomatic. It is an extremely contentious concept. In general terms the components of this new paradigm include changes in both product and labour markets, new forms of flexibility in the workforce (both numerical and functional), product diversification and the emergence of smaller production units operating for niche markets. For alternative views on the main features of this new, emerging era see Jessop (1990) and Hirst and Zeitlin (1991). For a critical discussion of this concept see Clarke (1988, Hyman (1988), Pollert (1988) and Warde (1994).
2   An interesting comparative analysis of some of the complex themes associated with this type of argument can be found in Pfaller and Gough (1991). They suggest that their findings *do not* prove that welfare statism is linked to diminishing economic performance.
3   Rowthorn (1992) argues that such wage-efficiency considerations have an important bearing upon the issue of centralisation and decentralisation of bargaining. Moreover, the issue is perhaps a little more complex than either Dore or Streeck acknowledges. For example, Calmfors notes that there are least two types of firm that would prefer centralised forms of negotiation to decentralised forms of negotiation (Calmfors, 1993).
4   The first sentence of this echoes the position held by Calmfors and Driffil (1994), who accord a priority to either a centralised or decentralised approach.
5   It is plausible to suggest that Ireland is simply an exceptional case. However, there are a number of features of the Irish polity that make it a good example in which to analyse the allegedly inherent rigidities of macro-political bargaining structures. As a small, open economy located on the periphery of western Europe, its need to respond quickly to changes in international markets is particularly pressing. Rigidities that emerge as a result of such bargaining would

   presumably compound the perceived economic costs of peripheral location and
   relative underdevelopment.
6 The SIPTU report was based on 187 cases covering 749 companies. See IRN,
   1992, Vol. 37.
7 It is important to add a note of caution here. While these figures suggest that
   part-time work is common, this applies only to the relatively small proportion
   of organisations that responded to the Price Waterhouse Cranfield Project, a
   survey of changing employment patterns (Morley *et al.* 1994). However, as an
   emerging feature the survey found it was common across organisational ownership (Irish, UK and US).
8 It is an issue that continues to raise controversy, as when the government
   announced that it would cut these programmes as part of budget proposals for
   2003–4.

2

'All boats rise on a new tide': reconstructing welfare in the era of the Celtic Tiger

Any discussion of the manner in which the Irish state has forged political and economic stability demands an examination of its welfare state. Crucial though this is, it is important to recognise that it is an area of debate where confusion persists. To those of a social democratic persuasion there appears to have been a discernible (and uncomfortable) reorientation in priorities: a drift away from a concern with the redistribution of wealth, as a succession of governments embrace more forcibly the strictures of neo-liberal economics. For some this is reflected in the changing lexicon of Irish politics, which appears increasingly redolent of the Conservative administrations of Ronald Reagan and Margaret Thatcher: the handbag may be missing but it has been supplanted by the metaphor of 'all boats rising on the new tide'. It is a statement that sits comfortably within the rhetoric espoused by those who support trickle-down economics.[1]

To others, it appears quite the opposite: obtrusive state intervention and excessive welfare benefits are proving an increasingly onerous burden upon the Celtic Tiger.[2] It is an argument which, more often than not, revels in a 'straw man' account of the welfare state: that its labyrinthine bureaucratic structure has crowded out investment, serving to sustain a culture of dependency and undermining the emergence of an entrepreneurial spirit. Towards the end of the 1990s such political arguments assumed greater prominence, as government confronted the novel (and almost incomprehensible) prospect of a tightening labour market while many remained in the category of the long-term unemployed. There was little mention of the nature of the 'available' work, its rates of pay or working conditions. Needless to say it was also an arena in which the clichés of tabloid journalism prospered, an environment where incessant calls for more stringent eligibility to welfare entitlements were made.

In such circumstances, it is often difficult to avoid the feeling that an attempt to ward off the neo-liberal 'bogeyman' may have excessively eulogised the KWS in its period of ascendancy. Convinced that within global capitalism there is no alternative to neo-liberalism, it has been all too easy for critics of this new order to lapse into a tendency to portray the welfare state in a positively reverential light. Here, the dark forces of neo-liberalism are contrasted with the autumnal glow of a bastardised form of Keynesian welfarism.

I have no difficulty in accepting the view that what sustained the appeal of Keynes's vision of managed capitalism was its ability to reconcile the conflicting interests of both capital and labour through a political promise to deliver full employment. One of the more prominent themes to emerge in this social democratic project was that it was predicated not upon establishing a minimum level of welfare, but rather upon an extension of social as well as civil and political rights. As a consequence, the welfare state extended beyond the realm of education, health and income maintenance to encompass full employment policies, environmental regulation, work safety, low wage councils and retraining programmes (Pfaller *et al.*, 1991, p. 2). However, as a conception of citizenship, it fell short of endorsing the need to establish formal equality. It may well have been anticipated that an expansion in social rights would lead to a 'general enrichment of the concrete substance of civilised life', a reduction in risk and insecurity, and an 'equalisation between the more or less fortunate at all levels' (Marshall, cited in Bottomore, 1992, p. 20). Although the alleviation of poverty was certainly a crucial consideration for any progressive democratic polity, formal equality remained an aspiration, not an explicit policy objective. As Marshall has noted:

> The more you look on wealth as conclusive proof of merit, the more you incline to regard poverty as evidence of failure – but the penalty of failure may seem to be greater than the offence warrants . . . as the social conscience stirs to life, class abatement . . . becomes a desirable aim to be pursued *as far as is compatible with the continued efficiency of the social machine.* (cited in Bottomore, 1992, p. 20, my emphasis)

Popular support for the welfare vision provided by those such as Beveridge may have rested on the ability of those on the left to 'read into it' a collectivist vision, while the concerns of those on the right could be assuaged by an interpretation that stressed the importance of individual responsibility. Such ambiguity was compounded by later interpretations of the interventionist thrust of Beveridge or Keynes, which remain tarnished by the ideological hostility of the New Right to state intervention. Certainly, the early years of conservative government under Thatcher in the UK, and the Republican administrations of Reagan in the USA, were marked by a determination to distance themselves from the root evil of modern capitalism:

the claustrophobic embrace of the state. And yet, while Hayek's work was often hauled forward as an exemplar of anti-statism, it is often forgotten that the real difference between Keynes and Hayek concerned the issue of where to draw the line between intervention and non-intervention. Keynes thought this a pragmatic issue, whereas Hayek thought it a matter of principle (Gamble, 1996, p. 159).

By qualifying the free market, Keynes's vision found a ringing endorsement in the work of Titmuss, who had rejected the narrow interpretation of 'choice in welfare' to be found in the liberal economic thinking of those such as Milton Friedman. In areas such as medical care Titmuss derided the work of liberal economists who failed to realise that 'consumers' did not know in advance their needs, how much meeting them would cost, or what categories of medical care they would be purchasing. Indeed, for Titmuss the inappropriateness of market provision in healthcare was revealed in the fact that as a commodity it could not be returned to the seller. Moreover, he queried whether consumers could ever exchange comparable information about 'good or bad' medical advice (Titmuss, 1967, pp. 37–8).

The fervent opposition of Titmuss to the unfettered forces of the free market was to find its most cogent expression in his advocacy of a blood-supply system that did not use 'professional donors from skid row denizens'. He believed that the system should involve free donations *by* the community *for* the community (Titmuss, 1967). In advocating this he felt that it would improve the 'choice of all' in welfare and confirm that altruism and solidarity could form the basis for *efficient* state intervention. Socialism was about community as well as equality, and it was therefore important to recognise and value our contribution to that community (Titmuss, 1967).

The defence of state intervention offered by Titmuss carries force not only because it argued the case for efficiency, but also because it identified legitimate state intervention, or *responsible* government, in terms of its capacity to reduce the unpredictability and uncertainty of risk to unemployment, poverty, ill-health, homelessness or ignorance. It is this which gives the interventionist state of the post-war period the imprimatur of the public. It was not about providing the 'institutionalised pledges of safety and welfare' often referred to by those such as Beck (1995); rather it was about regulating (and thereby alleviating) the worst excesses of the free market. As Titmuss was only too well aware, consumers could not estimate in advance the nature or extent of hazards and a free market would simply neglect and 'punish the indigent, the coloured, the dispossessed and the deviant' (Titmuss, 1967, p. 38).

From the mid-1970s onward political debate throughout the Anglo-saxon public policy world was dominated by the issues of public sector debt, inflation, unemployment and excessive levels of taxation. Under the leadership of Thatcher the Conservative Party in the UK extolled the virtues of competition, arguing that consumers would benefit from greater choice and that business would respond positively to the invigorating forces of the free market. Indeed, much of Thatcher's vitriol was directed towards a public sector dominated allegedly by the last vestiges of socialism. For those such as Thatcher, Hayek's work provided a thorough-going critique of socialism (Gamble, 1996, p. 151).

Hayek's damning critique of socialism was based upon a view that it destroys the basis of morals, freedom, responsibility and wealth produc-tion, so that, sooner or later, it leads to totalitarian forms of government (Gamble, 1996). His antipathy to socialism rests on the fact that two of its core principles, altruism and solidarity, provide the two greatest obstacles to sustained economic growth. Perturbed by the fact that even anti-social-ists regard such concepts as virtuous, Hayek asserts that altruism can extend only to the needs of known other people and that in an extended order, its practice is impossible (Gamble, 1996, p. 28). In stark contrast to the vision of state intervention in post-war Britain, Hayek proposed that the morality of the Great Society was one constructed upon individual free-dom and responsibility. Its foundations could be found in the free 'exchange of equivalents' or, as Smith argued, 'a society in which you give me that which I want, and you shall have this which you want' (Adam Smith, cited in Gamble, p. 28).

In Hayek's opinion, few people understood, or were prepared to accept, that an extended order was not an expression of our fundamental moral instincts, but a denial of them (Gamble, 1996, p. 29). In contrast to an extended order based upon state intervention, one defended on the grounds of altruism and solidarity, Hayek proposed an alternative, sponta-neous order in which there is no single directing centre and which is dom-inated only by the unintended consequences of all agents. It is a societal order that explicitly rejects constructivist rationalism – the view that insti-tutions and action can be based upon reason. Indeed, Hayek explicitly argued that 'before we can remould society intelligently . . . we must realise that, even when we believe that we understand it, we may be mistaken. What we must learn to understand is that human civilisation has a life of its own, that all our efforts to improve things must operate within a work-ing whole which we cannot entirely control' (Hayek, 1960, p. 70).

Not surprisingly, the notion of social justice that pervades the KWS was viewed as pernicious, for not only does it deny the freedom of individuals (the state 'decides' what is fair and defines 'just'), but it undermines indi-vidual responsibility. In Hayek's view, liberty and responsibility were insep-arable and a free society would not function or 'maintain itself unless its members regard it as right that each individual occupy the position that results from his action and accept it as due to his own action'. It was, he conceded, a position 'which evokes the outright hostility of men who have been taught that it is nothing but circumstances over which they have no control that has determined their position in life' (Hayek, 1960, p. 70).

Entrenched firmly within an anti-rationalist perspective, Hayek believes that knowledge is imperfect and that the cost of any economic activity is subjective. Knowledge in a market economy is dispersed, fragmented and decentralised, and any attempt at central planning or state control is flawed because it assumes that knowledge could somehow be collected by a central authority and employed to construct a more perfect market (Gamble, 1996, p. 68). For the intellectuals of the New Right, Hayek's work provided a political and economic blueprint, calling for a reduction in state intervention, a retrenchment in the welfare state and a corresponding shift in power away from the trade unions.

A concern with excessive public expenditure, the role of the state, the burden of high taxes and the reordering of the relationship between the public and the private were all essential components of the New Right critique of the KWS. However, it is important to recognise that it is erroneous to regard social citizenship as the equivalent of civil and political rights; instead it is important to distinguish between rights and redistribution. While civil and political rights are indivisible and non-transferable rights belonging to the individual, social rights are redistributive and are premised upon the fiscal capacities of the state (Klausen, 1995, p. 245). Certainly, a closer scrutiny of welfare programmes throughout western Europe questions the veracity of the assertion that social citizenship involved granting social rights with no strings attached. Ideas such as universalism, citizenship and solidarity may have pervaded the rhetorical themes of social democracy, but few programmes ever lived up to their expectations. Entitlement policing, based on the willingness to work or market availability, was an integral feature of most welfare programmes throughout the post-war period.

If the sterility of debate has been framed partially by the tendency to see the welfare state through rose-tinted glasses, it has also been characterised by discussions which extend little beyond the benefits (or not) of reductions in taxation or increases in welfare provision. This is compounded by a confusion which surrounds the fact that, if there has been a social democratic element to certain policies designed to ease the passage into the labour market, there has also been a distinct neo-liberal tinge to the preference for more stringent criteria for eligibility to welfare entitlements, a marked increase in the use of fraud squads, and a determination to resist increases in welfare payments above the rate of inflation.

The origins of this confusion can be located primarily in the (mis)conception that negotiated forms of governance are always linked to demand-side macro-economic policies, a social democratic political project and/or an interventionist state. This fails to recognise that these new policies involve an attempt to construct a political discourse that abandons the core principles of the New Right.

A considerable amount of the appeal of the policy recommendations of this new, active paradigm lies in the persistent call for an overhaul of an archaic, passive, universal welfare regime. In contrast to that of neo-liberalism, the focus is no longer upon individual self-responsibility. It is a policy paradigm inhabited not by individuals, but by categories of individuals with diverse experiences of unemployment. The policy response can therefore no longer be universal as it was under the KWS. Rather, the welfare regime under reconstructed social democracy must balance state support and individual responsibility. Not surprisingly, the political discourse accompanying this reform has also been transformed.

Performing a function akin to pit props in a mineshaft, a new welfare vocabulary has been constructed that seeks to assuage the concerns of those who remain sceptical of this new regime. Gone are the days when welfare recipients were cosseted though benefits or assistance, for now the welfare environment operates under a new maxim: 'supportive conditionality'. If the nature of welfare demand has changed, supply needs to be altered accordingly. While controversy over the 1999 budget that generated improved tax benefits three times greater for those on higher incomes may have been anticipated, few would have predicted the scale of the furore. It was largely due to the government's attempt to 'individualise' the tax system in an effort to provide incentives for married (non-working) mothers to return to the workforce.[3]

And yet, one of the more distinctive features of bargaining 'Celtic style' has been the attempt to secure a seat at the table of the global economic leaders without enduring the social division that has been observed in countries such as the UK. Ultimately, the success of the approach will rest on the ability to drive towards a flexible economy while managing to respond to demands for a more equitable distribution of economic resources.

Constructing an active welfare state: tax, welfare and labour market policy

To a large extent, and with only some minor variations (most notably Sweden), states throughout western Europe and the wider Anglo-saxon public policy environment had, prior to the mid-1970s, performed a largely passive role vis-a-vis labour markets. In a period of long-term economic growth, unemployment was viewed predominantly as a cyclical aberration, with the state's function being simply to provide financial protection and alleviate the more onerous excesses of unemployment. After two oil shocks in the 1970s, and with inflation rampant, there were many of a social democratic persuasion presented with the stark proposition that unemployment was becoming a semi-permanent feature of the political landscape. Whereas the concerns of the 1960s were about inclusion, generating policies to do with housing and poverty among the elderly, the focus of the 1980s shifted towards the problems of the long-term unemployed. In line with other major European states, Ireland experienced not only an increase in unemployment but also an extension in the average duration. There were important sectoral differences to consider as well, where employment in areas such as agriculture, forestry and fishing haemorrhaged between 1979 and 1986 by 54,000 (NESC, 1988a).

By the late 1980s, and influenced increasingly by a neo-liberal economic agenda, the search for policy alternatives throughout western Europe shifted towards a concern with supply-side issues. Training programmes designed to enhance the skills of the unemployed were married to 'support measures' aimed at improving the search for work and more stringent eligibility entitlement for welfare benefits. Thus, while the economies of western Europe had undergone a significant structural change, a renewed emphasis upon the individual's experience of unemployment came to the fore. Integral to these arguments was the belief that the longer people remain unemployed the less likely they were to leave unemployment, either because they had become disillusioned or because employers interpret such periods of unemployment in a negative light (NESC, 1988a, p. 37).

While an active labour market policy was deemed essential, it was by no means novel. As far back as the 1950s Sweden had been using such polices as part of a macro-economic management tool to offset inflationary pressures arising from full employment. By the 1980s they were firmly on the agenda of almost every government in the Anglo-saxon public policy world. The search for alternatives was accompanied by criticism of the existing skills competencies of the workforce and the failure of education to meet the needs of business (see Finn, 1989). These were moves defended largely on the grounds that active programmes would (re)train workers with new skills, allowing those unemployed to adjust more easily and efficiently to changes in the labour market.

It was also anticipated that there would be a positive 'knock-on' effect as the economy benefited from increased productivity, sustaining further improvements in employment. The argument ran that an increase in the number of skilled workers would reduce the pressure to increase wages, given that competition for jobs would be greater. The aim was to construct a set of polices designed not only to address the level of skills (and adjust the balance of those skills to a changing economy) but to provide a set of services to the disadvantaged that might encourage 'active job searching'.

In line with developments taking place in other Organisation for Economic Co-operation and Development (OECD) countries during the 1970s and 1980s Ireland shifted progressively towards a more active-oriented set of labour market policies. As O'Connell and McGinnity observe, in 1975 the government initiated the formation of AnCO, a state training body that provided basic training with work experience for young unskilled workers (O'Connell and McGinnity, 1997, p. 25). It was the precursor to a succession of schemes introduced during the late 1970s which included temporary wage subsidies, later replaced by the employment incentive scheme, community training workshops and work experience programmes (1978). Introduced on an ad hoc basis with responsibility assigned across a range of government departments, these were largely short-term measures to alleviate temporary unemployment. However, as the economy lurched into a prolonged period of stagnation, and unemployment became a more stubborn feature of the Irish economy, many of these schemes (or their variants) became a permanent feature of employment policy (O'Connell and McGinnity, 1997, p. 25; see Table 2.1).

Table 2.1 Labour market trends, selected years, 1981–96

Year	At work (000)	Unemployed (000)	Labour force (000)	Net migration (000)	Unemployment rate (%)
1981	1,146	126	1,272	2	9.9
1986	1,081	228	1,308	−28	17.4
1991	1,134	208	1,342	−2	15.5
1993	1,146	230	1,376	−6	16.7
1996	1,285	190	1,475	6	12.9

Source: O'Connell and McGinnity 1997.

In its review of these developments the NESC (1988A) remarked that an expansion and, by implication, fragmentation of schemes ranging across different departments had led to problems in co-ordination. In such circumstances it was difficult to establish objectives. Indeed, it was clear that in many instances places were being offered to candidates whose motivation and qualification ensured high placement rates, marginalising further the disadvantaged (NESC, 1988A). Given the economy's poor performance during the 1980s, it was hardly surprising that the number of schemes should expand or that the number of participants should double between 1983 and 1994. While employment subsidy schemes fluctuated in terms of numbers, direct employment schemes increased strongly, particularly in the early 1990s with the introduction of the Social Employment Scheme (SES) and its successor CE. Participation in employment subsidies also increased rapidly between 1992 and 1994 from under 4,000 to over 21,000. This included the Back to Work Allowance Scheme and the PRSI Exemption Scheme

With long-term unemployment remaining a stubborn issue in the early 1990s, a succession of reports emerged from national bodies such as the NESF and the Task Force on Long-Term Unemployment, and influential international bodies such as the EU and the OECD. As policies throughout the OECD testify, by the 1990s active labour market policies were widespread and constructed with the intention of avoiding the likelihood that income maintenance schemes would institutionalise unemployment. The focus of policy thus fell on the relationship between moves to enhance employment prospects (training and subsidies) and welfare entitlements and policing.

The pessimism which had engulfed Irish politics in the mid- to late 1980s had largely dissipated during the 1990s as the economy effected a turnaround remarkable not only in its scale but also in its duration. And yet, considerable debate persists about whether active labour market schemes are as effective as their proponents suggest, or whether they have contributed as significantly to the resurgence in the economy as their supporters would have us believe. Calmfors, for example, has argued that if compensation levels are high then they may have the effect of increasing wage levels (Calmfors, 1994). In addition, there is considerable scepticism about whether such schemes contain high levels of dead weight – that is, where reductions in unemployment would otherwise have been achieved without the existence (and therefore attenuated cost) of such schemes. As O'Connell and McGinnity observe, while some material would suggest that active labour market policies (ALMPs) do have an impact upon wage moderation and improve job creation, the OECD's research would appear to be more circumspect. A cross-national survey conducted by the OECD found that in 21 countries studied, active labour market expenditure was negatively associated with economic growth. It is a view with which Calmfors confers, suggesting that such programmes should be one among a number of policies designed to alleviate the problems of unemployment (Calmfors, 1994).

With the introduction of the SES and the CE, the number of participants in ALMPs experienced a dramatic expansion between 1992 and 1995, from 17,600 to 55,000 (O'Connell and McGinnity, 1997, p. 27). However, the rate of placement appears to have been low, and the impact upon the long-term unemployed (at least during the early 1990s) appeared to be marginal. In O'Connell and McGinnity's opinion it was a situation unlikely to improve, given the fact that the training component extended to no more than 20 days. In their opinion such a low level of training was unlikely to 'counteract the accumulated educational and labour market disadvantages of the majority of long-term unemployed' (O'Connell and McGinnity, 1997, p. 142). Indeed, according to these authors the expansion of such schemes represented a 'policy choice which favours high volume programmes at the expense of quality and effectiveness' (O'Connell and McGinnity, 1997, p. 142).

In a similar vein, the NESC noted that training was 'expensive with potentially low or negative returns unless carefully targeted so as to provide relevant skills for potential niches'. It also cautioned against taking 'too sanguine' a view of the potential of training as a remedy for unemployment, since its success rests on a mismatch between labour demand and skills (NESC, 1996, p. 192). The Council was of the opinion that training schemes might well prove successful at preventing unemployment but were inappropriate in areas such as Ireland where unemployment had become entrenched. The Council believed that training, if targeted astutely, might be most effective among the recently unemployed or for those who had qualifications and who wished to re-enter the labour force (NESC, 1996, p. 192).

The NESC was keen to extol the view that such schemes should operate in tandem with counselling and information packages with a strong view to placement. Moreover, the Council was circumspect with regard to direct job creation or social employment because it felt that the long-term benefits remained limited. It was willing to concede, however, that such schemes had the potential to provide ongoing employment for the disadvantaged and were therefore likely to assist 'employment readiness' (NESC, 1996, p. 192). The preference of the NESC was for subsidies to employment in existing or new enterprises that offered the most potential for the long-term unemployed, particularly if targeted at those who found it hardest to find employment. Such schemes reproduce the routines of work and are more likely to address the problems of 'stickiness', such as employers finding difficulty with the length of time for which applicants have been unemployed. The argument runs that recent work, however limited in its duration, tends to be valued by employers.

In the Irish context, the research undertaken by O'Connell and McGinnity offers a more up-beat assessment. In their opinion, and providing that a distinction is made between active labour market policies which are market oriented (skills training and employment subsidies) and those which are not, such schemes have the potential to improve the employment prospects of participants (O'Connell and McGinnity, 1997, p. 121). However, even in this more optimistic assessment they concede that there are groups within the unemployed (women and the long-term) who face particular difficulties associated with uneven representation and access to schemes. The problem appears to reside not in the criteria for eligibility, but in the procedure by which candidates are selected. It seems that a process of 'creaming off' takes place, in which administrators, faced with the unenviable task of managing the limited places available for the number of unemployed, opt for those candidates more likely to succeed. As a consequence, the long-term unemployed and other disadvantaged groups are not only 'marginalised in the labour market, they are also disadvantaged in selection for reintegration programmes.' (O'Connell and McGinnity, 1997, p. 122).

In recent years counselling, mentoring and the use of employment placement services have moved increasingly to the fore. In Ireland, the NESF successfully proposed that a local employment service (LES) be introduced to offset the prevailing tendency towards over-centralisation in training and employment services. The focus of the LES was upon local co-operation and service delivery, with priority for the categories that were more difficult to place (NESC, 1996, p. 195). Such moves indicate a concern with events which take place at the fringes of the labour market where stickiness or rigidity persist, and which could be alleviated through better co-ordination between tax and welfare policies.

The problem is that the combination of high tax levels on the low paid and increasing welfare benefits may reduce the incentive to re-enter employment. It raises the prospect of either unemployment or poverty traps emerging. The former arises when low levels of pay compare unfavourably with benefit levels, whereas the latter relates to problems that occur as net income rises but is met with a higher tax burden. A succession of policies throughout the 1990s attempted to address these quandaries. In general terms, it is a debate that involves a set of scenarios in which welfare benefits impact at the lower levels of pay. This is often termed the income replacement ratio (IRR), or the proportion of after-tax income that is replaced by welfare benefits (which may include non-cash payments).

Between 1987 and 1991 the IRR rose by 10 percentage points as unemployment assistance increased. However, after 1991 the IRR fell as unemployment assistance increased at a lower level in absolute terms and direct taxation on the low paid was reduced (Tansey, 1998, p. 231). As Tansey observes, it is possible to draw two conclusions on these matters. First, for single people earning around IR£7,100 in 1996 cash unemployment benefits did not constitute a significant deterrent to work. Second, once pay below this level is included the picture becomes rather more blurred, as welfare benefits replace between three-fifths and four-fifths of net income from employment (Tansey, 1998, p. 234).

Working with a different set of assumptions (the inclusion of private sector rent, for example), the Irish National Organisation for the Unemployed (INOU) was able to show further the dilemmas faced by people in low paid work or receiving unemployment benefit who might wish to return to the labour market. In the INOU's model, where private sector rent was pitched at around IR£40 a week, state benefits would replace all net income up to a range of IR£6,000 a year. In other words, as Tansey notes, there is little incentive to return to work when annual pay levels are at or below IR£6,000 (see Table 2.2).

Table 2.2 Single people: adjusted IRRs, 1997–98.

Gross pay (IR£)	Direct taxes (IR£)	Rent (IR£)	Net income from work after rent (IR£)	Social income after rent (IR£)	IRR (adjusted) (%)
6,000	551	2,080	3,369	3,342	99.2
7,000	856	2,080	4,064	3,342	82.2
8,000	1,161	2,080	4,759	3,342	70.2
9,000	1,466	2,080	5,454	3,342	61.3
10,000	1,771	2,080	6,149	3,342	54.4

Source: Tansey (1998, p. 238).

Where high IRRs tend to discourage the unemployed from seeking employment, poverty traps penalise those at work when incomes rise but the tax take increases. The effect of this can clearly be seen in Table 2.3, which shows that for a single-income married couple with two children, net income falls despite the fact that gross annual income rises from IR£7000 to IR£11,000.

In an attempt to remove or, at the very least, reduce the incidence of such anomalies, the government introduced employment subsidies and reduced the tax burden on low paid work. As Tansey succinctly observes, policy shifted from one that subsidises unemployment to one that subsidises low paid employment. Family Income Support (FIS) was pivotal in this because it topped up net incomes among the low paid. However, as the Department of Finance acknowledged, there was a disappointingly low level of take-up of FIS, with 60 per cent of those eligible failing to make claims (Tansey, 1998, p. 242). And yet, without such supports poverty traps remain. Indeed, in many instances, without FIS there was little incentive to take up low paid positions. Even in jobs where annual pay was around IR£9,000, for example, net income would have been only marginally above that of the social wage (by IR£700 a year) (Tansey, 1998, p. 242). What is more, even when FIS was claimed, a household's income was lower if it earned IR£12,000 than if pre-tax earnings from employment amounted to IR£8,000 (see Table 2.4).

Table 2.3 The poverty trap: less income for more pay, 1995–96 (married couple, two children, one earner)

Annual earnings (IR£)	Net Weekly (IR£)
5,000	142
6,000	147
7,000	153
8,000	152
9,000	151
10,000	147
11,000	149
12,000	158
13,000	166
14,000	176
15,000	187

Source: Tansey (1998).

Table 2.4 The impact of FIS, 1997–98 (married couple, two children, one earner)

Gross pay (IR£)	Direct taxes (IR£)	Rent (local authority) (IR£)	Net pay from work (after rent) (IR£)	FIS (IR£)	Total income (IR£)	Social wage (IR£)
8,000	173	1.083	6,744	2,340	9,364	6,990
9,000	258	1,135	7,607	1,768	9,375	6,990
10,000	703	1,129	8,168	1,177	9,345	6,990
11,000	1,395	1,112	8,493	753	9,246	6,990
12,000	1,862	1,117	9,021	260	9,280	6,990

Source: Tansey (1998, p. 242).

The budgets of the late 1990s responded to this by strengthening the Back to Work Allowance (BTWA) scheme for the long-term unemployed over the age of 23. This scheme allowed those returning to work to retain 75 per cent of their existing benefits for the first year, 50 per cent for the second and 25 per cent for the third and final year. Attracting no income tax or PRSI deductions it was a scheme that proved attractive, with numbers rising from 10,000 in 1996 to 27,000 in 1998 (see Table 2.5).

Table 2.5 The impact of the BTWA scheme, 1997–98 (long-term unemployed single people returning to work)

Gross pay (IR£)	After tax income (IR£)	Rent (IR£)	Net pay after rent	BTWA benefits	Net income from work (IR£)
6,000	5,449	2,080	3,369	4,544	7,913
7,000	6,144	2,080	4,064	4,544	8,608
8,000	6,839	2,080	4,759	4,544	9,303
9,000	7,534	2,080	5,454	4,544	9,998
10,000	8,229	2,080	6,149	4,544	10,693
14,000	11,009	2,080	8,929	2,072	11,631

Source: Tansey (1998, p. 242).

As Tansey has pointed out, participation in the scheme made virtually any low paid job more attractive than unemployment assistance, particularly during the first two years. These were initiatives that represented part of a range of active policies introduced in the 1990s, which also included changes to the eligibility for medical cards and the introduction of area-based employment schemes.

In Ireland, access to free medical care is available only to those whose income is below a specific threshold, and it is a means tested non-cash benefit. It has long been argued that the cost of medical care was an important consideration to those unemployed presented with an opportunity to return to the labour market. Defending the interests of your family can be an uncomfortable and complex juggling act, where the decision to enter low paid (and often insecure) work is countered by the potential threat of high medical costs. It was certainly a view recognised by the Expert Working Group on Integrating Tax and Social Welfare, which observed that:

> The effect of the medical card on the incentive to work is generally accepted to be significant. This is particularly marked where recipients percieve that there is a high risk of illness for themselves or their families . . . recipients can understandably put a contingent value on the card much in excess of the value imputed from estimates and . . . in these circumstances an unemployed person might be unwilling to take up a relatively well paid job. (cited in Callan and Nolan, 1999, p. 67)

In its interim report the group recommended that irrespective of future income, those registered as long-term unemployed should retain a medical card on re-entering the labour market. It was a measure implemented in the 1996 budget, with the period of retention being three years as opposed to the two years recommended by the expert working group. While the impact of such measures is often difficult to assess, Callan and Nolan have suggested that the survey data would appear to indicate that it is a policy measure 'likely to be important for only a small minority of the unemployed, but for that minority the impact could be quite substantial' (Callan and Nolan, 1999, p. 2).

It is important to recognise that it is not simply a matter of improved public finances allowing an increase in the threshold for eligibility (a passive policy reaction). Rather, a relaxation in the rules governing eligibility has introduced a more dynamic element to policy so that those unemployed can retain their medical card for a period of three years as they re-enter employment. It is a policy that clearly attempts both to overcome the vagaries of employment insecurity associated with low paid work and to increase flexibility at the fringes of the labour market. It has also been one of the clearest indicators of a shift towards a concern with the relationship between welfare policies and their impact upon the supply side of the economy.

Since 1991 Ireland has also been engaged in an attempt to produce a series of innovative programmes aimed at alleviating long-term unemployment. As part of the PESP, the government initiated the development of 12 area-based partnerships in urban and rural communities. One of the more important features of these new schemes was the manner in which a relaxation of rules governing eligibility for social welfare payments was made. For those such as Sabel, such adjustments made 'participation in these programmes broadly affordable and attractive', removing disincentives which might 'deter the most needy from exploring these possibilities' (Sabel, 1995, p. 10; see also Craig and McKeown, 1994). These developments were also mirrored in the Area Allowance (Enterprise) scheme, in which long-term unemployed people who established their own business could retain their welfare benefits for one year. At the end of 1992, 223 had availed themselves of this benefit. By 1993 the number had risen to over 740 (Craig and McKeown, 1994).

The Area Allowance (Enterprise) scheme was but one of a series of welfare policies designed to introduce flexibility into the labour market, the origins of which can be located in developments emanating from the EU. Following the extraordinary meeting of the European Council in November 1997, member states were obliged to introduce National Action Plans (NAPs) in response to unemployment. In Ireland, the NAP contained a succession of active welfare policies targeted at the long-term unemployed. The back to work allowance scheme (27,000 places) allowed for 100 per cent retention of welfare entitlements for those taking up self-employment. In a similar vein, the Job Assist scheme offered those long-term unemployed returning to work a tax allowance of £3,000 (plus £1,000 per child) tapered over three years, with a double deduction for employers who employ them. Similarly, the introduction of the one-parent family payment in 1997, which enabled lone parents to earn up to £6,000 per annum without affecting their entitlement to payment, formed part of an incentive structure built into welfare entitlements.[4]

A further set of policy ideas that surfaced in discussions on long-term unemployment during the 1990s was the potential role for the social economy. It was an issue which the NESC had endorsed in *A Strategy for Competitiveness, Growth and Employment*(1994a) and was aimed at encouraging new forms of social service provision and useful social employment along a continuum from commercial service provision to pure statutory provision. Such policy initiatives had their origins in debates that surfaced in the late 1980s and early 1990s about the role of basic incomes.

Disillusioned with a welfare paradigm organised around the right to work, one that had palpably failed, Healy and Reynolds argued that we need to reconstruct our view of citizenship and reject the traditional dichotomies of modern society: feminism and patriarchy; capital and labour; economic growth and ecological degradation. These authors argued that one of the essential changes required was that the promise of 'wealth, power, control and economic growth' associated with full-time employment needed to be complemented with the 'dynamics of belonging, nurturing, caring, receptivity and self-giving' (Healy and Reynolds, 1993, p. 69; for criticisms see Taylor, 1996b).

In the light of the difficulties experienced by the KWS, those such as Healy and Reynolds argued that a radical departure was required, one that recognised meaningful work as dependent upon: 'the introduction of some system of income distribution which provides a guaranteed basic income to every person in society . . . an income paid unconditionally to all on an individual basis without means test or any requirement to work' (Healy and Reynolds, 1993, p. 73). As the Irish economy continued to struggle with long-term unemployment during the early 1990s, these were arguments that temporarily gained credence. However, interest waned as the economy surged ahead from 1994 onwards and the government's taste for such a radical overhaul of tax and welfare subsided. Indeed, the preferred option was to examine the benefits of the social economy, a move that fitted more comfortably with events taking place in Europe, where there was an emphasis on a role for the market.

It was anticipated that the social economy could replace certain market failures or play a role where people in need could only afford part of the cost of a useful social service (NESC, 1996, p. 204). It would therefore entail limited forms of subsidised provision through a quasi-market arrangement. This offered the prospect of going beyond existing forms of community employment, where little in the way of saleable commodities was produced, and link with both CE and local area-based initiatives (see below).

As the Irish economy moved towards full employment in the latter part of the 1990s there could be little doubt that such moves found favour within influential political circles. The Tánaiste, Mary Harney, for example, announced that an increase in funding of IR£41m would be made available for initiatives falling within the ambit of the social economy, providing some 2,500 jobs (although many of these would be displaced from the CE schemes) (*Irish Times*, 19 September 2000). In the view of the Tánaiste it was a shift that signalled the changing character of unemployment. When the CE programme had been initiated, unemployment stood at 17 per cent, with seven unemployed people to every CE position. By September of 2000 it was a one-to-one relationship. The CE programme had been devised during a period of high unemployment, where the spin-offs were to the community. The social economy would involve programmes that would concentrate upon creating benefits to the community, with the spin-off being employment.

Nevertheless, concerns were raised. John Butler of the Dundalk Employment Initiative, for one, expressed reservations about the fact that while some secondary benefits would be retained, rent allowances could fall to as low as 25 per cent (*Irish Times*, 19 September 2000). Moreover, it was by no means clear whether, under the new funding arrangements, these schemes would have to be self-financing community business initiatives or should include deficient demand social economy enterprises.

While many of these new measures could be interpreted as positive, active, even inclusive policies, they were accompanied by more stringent criteria for eligibility to welfare entitlements and a marked predisposition to increase the use of fraud squads. The line drawn between a policy aimed at constructing a more inclusive society (and one that is optional) and a policy that attaches punitive conditions can often be very thin. In the Irish case, for example, there has been evident and persistent discord between the ministers for social welfare and for enterprise and employment over whether social welfare payments should be discontinued if a person fails to take up the offer of a training scheme.

Following the publication of the Central Statistics Office investigation into differences between the Live Register and the Labour Force Survey measures of unemployment in the 1990s, the issue of fraud emerged as a significant political issue. While many of the arguments were shrouded in complex statistical differences between the two surveys, they nevertheless generated intense political debate about the extent of welfare fraud. In its summation of this controversy, the NESC (1996) argued that it was difficult to draw any substantial conclusions because there was a good deal of 'room for speculation' (NESC, 1996, p. 200). The only previous research of substance on this matter had been undertaken in 1987 by the Department of Social Welfare, which found that 2 per cent of claims in Dublin had a clear element of fraud. While suspicion hung over a larger number of claims, the department's conclusion was that fraud probably accounted for around 5 per cent of claims.

As the focus of policy shifts away from passive measures, and debate is generated about fraud, the issue of conditionality is inevitably raised; that is, whether particular (often more stringent) conditions should be attached to the receipt of welfare benefits or more punitive measures should be taken in the event of a refusal to take up placement on a scheme. To some, this signifies a shift towards a neo-liberal preoccupation with a more penal attitude to the unemployed, further seeking to reduce welfare entitlements. To others, it represents a logical, reasoned and politically justifiable attempt to prevent the possibility of unemployment becoming institutionalised.

In the heat generated in debate on such matters, it is all too easily forgotten that conditions have always been attached to the receipt of unemployment benefit, where eligibility depends on being 'available for work' or 'actively seeking' employment. Following the Task Force on Long Term Unemployment's report, a new phrase has gained ascendancy in this field of public policy: supportive conditionality. As the NESC report observes, targeting is an application of qualifying conditions to aggregates, whereas supportive conditionality involves some form of corresponding action by individuals: an individual has a duty to be available for consideration for appropriately targeted measures. The NESC was of the opinion that supportive conditionality, once allied to targeted measures and tax or benefit changes to remove traps and disincentives, was altogether different to standard measures designed to counter fraud.

It was a welfare philosophy that underscored the Youth Progression Programme (YPP) in 1996: after six months, continued eligibility for unemployment assistance (UA) benefits depended on registration for the YPP. The NESC was of the opinion that given the huge waste in human potential there could be little justification for not applying supportive conditionality to other categories of the unemployed. Indeed, it suggested that the targeting of schemes should be closely allied to this form of conditionality in order to offset the potential for dead weight (NESC, 1996).

Within policy-making circles it seems ever more clear that the idea of a 'catch-all' experience of unemployment has been effectively consigned to the distant past. The type of changes to labour markets and household structures synonymous with the new global economic order has meant that unemployment is seen neither as the result of an individual's particular failing nor as an outcome of the inadequacy of state policy.

Ideas such as 'supportive conditionality' are rarely if ever politically uncontested. To the unreconstructed social democrat who believes firmly in the KWS, there is the real fear that the 'supportive element' will somehow lapse in periods of renewed hostility to the unemployed. In other words, such ventures may represent little more than a wolf in sheep's clothing. More disconcerting perhaps is the fact that supportive conditionality is a beguiling, almost evasive phrase, successful because it distracts our attention from the tension which lies at the heart of this principle. On paper, or perhaps more accurately in meetings between civil servants and ministers, it may appear a straightforward task to assure the 'public' that this will not form the basis of a new, draconian welfare order. In practice, however, and certainly in times less conducive to outlays in public expenditure, an important distinction may be drawn between what is supportive and what is conditional.

From the outset we need to ask ourselves what constitutes success in these areas. Are we engaged in a serious process of providing opportunities to those who avail themselves of such schemes, and of making a social democratic commitment to circumvent the social dislocation that occurs as a result of accumulated structural inequalities? Or are we in the business of people moving in and out of temporary forms of employment or training schemes, reproducing a tranche of low skilled/low paid workers (at times probably operating in the black economy) who benefit only when the labour market tightens?

The NESC has acknowledged that 'supportive conditionality' can be adequately fostered only where sufficient jobs or placements are available and where there is the capacity to offer a package of proper quality options to all comers (NESC, 1996, p. 202). What constitutes a set of 'proper quality options' is clearly open to considerable debate. It is certainly a phrase that could fall prey to the unintelligible semantics of free market economics, where these programmes can quickly become 'fiscally irresponsible', a phrase in vogue, and one often favoured by the current Fianna Fáil/PD coalition government.

Prior to 1994, and despite positive economic growth, the Irish economy was unable to generate a substantial shift in unemployment levels, particularly among the long-term unemployed. However, from 1994 onwards there has been both a discernible increase in job creation figures and a corresponding decrease in unemployment figures. It is a transformation in the economic fortunes of the Irish polity that has impacted significantly on the trajectory of policy. It is important to recognise, however, that this new direction in policy (embracing a more active-oriented set of welfare initiatives) should be understood not simply as the outcome of healthier public finances. Certainly, it would be difficult to take issue with the view that the economy's continued vibrancy has generated increasing tax revenues, allowing for policy experimentation in areas previously prone to stasis. There are, however, other features of this period that have had an important bearing upon policy, or perhaps more accurately upon the choice of policy alternatives.

The transformation of labour market policy in Ireland since 1994 should be understood against the backdrop of reform in the Anglo-saxon public policy world, where there has been an ongoing search for more active-oriented policy interventions. There has also been a marked predisposition for coalition governments in Ireland increasingly to endorse a political discourse that favours restraint in public expenditure. It was a shift influenced by the political opportunism afforded by an extended period of economic prosperity. The impact of this latter point should not be underestimated. As late as 1993 the NESC report *A Strategy for Competitiveness, Growth and Employment* was arguing that the long-term unemployed were unlikely 'to gain significantly from any general improvements in labour market conditions resulting from structural reforms or the emergence of a more positive external environment' (cited in NESC, 1996, p. 190).

The desire to applaud many of these new initiatives is often informed by the view that they present the tantalising prospect of redefining relations between citizens and state bureaucracies, stimulating enterprise. For some, however, such optimism needs to be tempered by the fact that any short-term success of these policies may simply be the natural by-product of an economy in a period of boom.

Housing

If the introduction of area-based unemployment schemes and changes to the eligibility criteria for medical cards are examples of intervention which display at least some form of concern with inclusivity, housing is one which clearly does not. This should surprise few, for while housing in both the public and private sector receives state support, it is on private ownership that government policy has always been predominantly focused. It is a policy predisposition strikingly reflected in the fact that since 1987 public housing has remained stubbornly below 10 per cent of all new houses constructed, despite an increase in waiting lists and a startling escalation in the cost of private sector houses. It is also a feature of public policy which contrasts sharply with the norm for the decades prior to 1980, where public housing occupied a range between 10 and 20 per cent (see Table 2.6).

Table 2.6 Dwellings by type of tenure in Ireland, 1946–91 (%)

Type	1946	1961	1971	1981	1991
Owner occupied	52.6	59.8	68.8	74.4	79.3
Social housing	N/A	18.4	15.5	12.5	9.7
Private rented	N/A	17.2	13.3	10.1	8.0

Source: Fahey (1998).

As the role of public housing diminished during the 1990s, the gap between public authority housing and private sector housing provision widened considerably. This occurred largely as a result of a deliberate government policy to encourage (and maintain) private ownership as the mainstay of housing policy. Throughout the 1990s we witnessed the retention of tax reliefs on mortgage interest, grants for first time buyers of £3,000, and a succession of tax schemes designed to encourage further expansion in private sector provision of rented accommodation.[5] Although the latter schemes operated under the auspices of government attempts to stimulate urban renewal or target seaside resorts (tourism), the effect was, nevertheless, to encourage private speculation through government subsidies to promote private sector rented accommodation. In addition, there have also been changes to stamp duty (tax) designed to offset 'temporary aberrations' in the market and alleviate the 'plight' of first time buyers. There can be little doubt that while tax relief on mortgage interest relief was gradually eroded during the 1990s, state support for the private sector persists. Against a backdrop of state subsidies, and despite a massive escalation in house prices, owner occupation was maintained at around 80 per cent throughout the 1990s (Fahey, 1998).

The failure on the part of successive governments to restore the cutbacks in the construction of social housing in the 1980s, and policies designed to encourage the privatisation of public housing stock through tenant purchases, ensured that 200,000 of 320,000 local authority houses are now in the private sector. That this process of privatisation has continued unabated is evidenced in the fact that in 1996 local authorities assisted 3,450 households into owner occupation (2,284 tenant purchases and 1,166 shared ownership ventures), while only 3,593 units were added to their portfolios. It is only when we include the contribution (917 units) of the voluntary sector expansion in the social housing element to local authority activity that the total increases above that for owner occupation (Fahey, 1998, p. 290) (see Tables 2.7 and 2.8).

As data from the *Housing Statistics Bulletin* (1999) demonstrates, during the late 1990s the sale of housing authority houses showed no signs of decline. In 1999, 3,234 sales were approved and a further 4,846 applications were received. As Table 2.9 shows, the number of new houses built remained static at around 2,800 houses while acquisitions declined from over 800 to around 500. During 1999 the figures for completion remained similar, although there were signs of a marginal improvement with new projects in progress reaching 4,099.

Table 2.7 Sale of local authority houses, 1995–99

Year	Sales completed
1995	950
1996	2,284
1997	2,139
1998	2,006
1999	2,256

Source: Housing Statistics Bulletin, 1999.

Table 2. 8 House completions, 1995–99

Year	Local authority	Voluntary or non-profit	Private sector	Total
1995	2,960	1,011	26,604	30,575
1996	2,676	917	30,132	33,725
1997	2,632	756	35,454	38,842
1999	2,771	485	39,093	42,349
1998	2,909	579	43,024	46,512

Source: Housing Statistics Bulletin, 1999.

Table 2.9 Local authority housing: new building and acquisitions, 1995–98

Year	Completions	Acquisitions
1995	2,960	882
1996	2,676	897
1997	2,632	658
1998	2,771	511

Source: Housing Statistics Bulletin, 1999.

As Fahey succinctly observes, the cumulative effect of these policies meant that for the majority of tenants, renting accommodation from the local authority had become a 'staging post' on the route to the heavily subsidised owner occupied sector (Fahey, 1998, p. 290). While this was a policy framework beneficial to some, it presented an altogether different set of problems to others. For those on low to middle incomes the increase in private sector house prices placed this avenue largely out of reach. It was a problem compounded by the fact that social housing produces little in the way of a viable alternative. Social housing in Ireland now accounts for only 10 per cent of the total housing stock and has remained around 100,000 units, the lowest share of any country in Europe (Fahey, 1998, p. 4). There can be little doubt that while the overall quality of housing in both the private and public sectors has improved, there is considerable concern that local authority housing has become the preserve of the marginalised in society. It is a feature of policy which raises important political questions about segregation and social exclusion (Fahey, 1998).

Although the surrender grant scheme operated for only a short period of time during the 1980s it was, for many people, a significant contributory factor in the acceleration of a process of residualisation in local authority housing. The scheme provided a group of incentives including a £5,000 grant to encourage local authority tenants (and purchasers) to cede occupation and move into the private sector. It was a policy riven with conflicts. On the one hand, it seemed an eminently reasonable method of releasing social housing at a time when construction was being cut back. On the other hand, it also sat comfortably with a government policy that emphasised private ownership and wished to stimulate construction in the private sector. As the NESC reported, 7,700 people availed themselves of the scheme (NESC, 1988b). The major difficulty was that they were from households located predominantly in the worst-off estates and represented the best-off households there. A temporary but nevertheless significant shift in the social profile of the estates occurred, with the mix moving predominantly towards welfare dependants (Fahey, 1998, p. 40).

Given that the size of the social housing sector has diminished, and that the social profile of that sector has been distorted, it is hardly surprising that the residual nature of social housing has become accentuated. This was confirmed by Nolan, who has argued that the risk of poverty among local authority tenants increased sharply between 1987 and 1994 (Nolan *et al.*, 1998). The data generated in the Labour Force Survey also reveals that only 24 per cent of households in social housing had one or two members at work (Fahey, 1998, p. 41). The low levels of educational achievement often compound such problems. Thus, as Fahey points out, over 60 per cent of household heads in social housing attained primary education and less than 1 per cent of such households attended third-level education. With regard to household structure, the most significant divergence from other forms of tenure is in the numbers of lone parents with children under 15 (Fahey, 1998, pp. 42-3).

There can be little doubt that shortcomings in this area of policy are inextricably linked to the limited political and financial powers of local authorities. There are few policy avenues available that may counteract the preoccupation with owner occupation. What is more, there is little that local authorities can do to respond to issues associated with residualisation which lie in other areas of government policy: low incomes, long-term unemployment or low levels of educational attainment (see Fahey, 1998).

With the shift towards the privatisation of social housing there has also been a corresponding increase in the role of the private sector in the provision of rental accommodation. To some extent, this can be attributed not so much to housing policy as to eligibility for discretionary welfare entitlements that contribute towards the costs of rent. As Fahey points out, this was a minor area of government expenditure between 1988 and 1998 (IR£6.1 million) but has exploded in the interim period (IR£115 million). Indeed, the figures contained in a consultants' report for the Department of the Environment (Bacon and Associates, 2000) suggest that there are now 42,000 people availing themselves of rent supplements under the supplementary welfare allowances, or 40 per cent of the total private rented stock.

Despite fears of the type of house-price 'bubble' which blew up in the British economy in the late 1980s, government policy has steadfastly refused to consider public housing as a potential way out of the impasse of escalating house prices. Indeed, the government's neo-liberal instincts have been all too clearly displayed in its preference for a private sector solution to the 'housing crisis'. In an attempt to create 'affordable housing', regulations are to be introduced which stipulate that any new private sector developments will have to have at least 20 per cent of housing in the 'affordable category'.

Education

If the maxim of the estate agent is location, location, location then it is tempting, if more than a little exaggerated, to suggest that what is positive, even dynamic about the Celtic Tiger ultimately has its origins in education, education, education. As Boylan among others has observed, between 1960 and 1985 Ireland had one of the highest rates of investment in human capital of any OECD country, and this was one of the more influential factors in spawning the Celtic Tiger (Boylan, 2002). Even for those a little more sceptical, such as Leddin, the fact that participation in the third-level sector in the past was below the OECD average may well form part of an explanation for the slow economic growth and its acceleration in recent years (Leddin, 1997, p. 8).

Irrespective of whether investment in education was the primary factor in generating the conditions for the emergence of the Celtic Tiger, there can be little doubt that governments from the 1960s onwards have continued to affirm their support for the expansion of education. However, if the debates about access and equity were to the fore during the 1970s, the prominent issue of the 1980s and 1990s was the relevance of education to the economy. By the late 1980s it was a debate that had begun to coalesce around the urgent need for reform, as the relationship between the minister, the DoE and schools became the focal point of scrutiny. Policy in the form of a white paper was slow to materialise, as control passed through the hands of a succession of ministers (in different governments), all keen to put their own imprint on policy. If the passage of policy was convoluted, this was due to the fact that Mary O'Rourke's successor at the DoE, Niamh Breathnach, opted to hold a National Convention on Education in 1992 to ascertain views and establish the basis for a consensus on reform. It was hardly surprising, therefore, that the final draft of the white paper did not materialise until 1995, or that certain features of policy should emerge and then fall by the wayside.

From the outset, the prevailing view had been that administrative procedures in education were in need of urgent reform. For far too long, important policy directives had been made with only a tenuous link to legislation, a situation compounded by a significant growth in the use of circulars to set objectives (Walshe, 1999). Concerned at the inordinately centralised nature of administration, the reorganisation of school governance emerged as the key point around which reform would be organised. It was argued that devolved responsibility would allow schools greater autonomy over budgeting, establish a clearer separation between church and school, and ensure a closer link between state funding and an admissions policy that did not discriminate on the grounds of means, educational level or social background (Walshe, 1999, pp. 15–16). It was also envisaged that restructuring would entail new roles for the DoE and school boards and the establishment of local educational authorities (Coolahan, 1993, p. 12).

These were certainly educational objectives that sat comfortably with a managerialist ethos that government wished to instil, emphasising the need to establish closer links between educational curricula and the needs of business (see Culliton, 1992). Some of the proposals had an extremely limited shelf life, most notably the intention of introducing an obligatory 'enterprise and technology studies' subject and representation from the business community on each board of school management. Nevertheless, the green paper (DoE, 1992) displayed the government's determination to acknowledge the importance of the business ethic within educational policy.

A concern with the relationship between education and business was by no means new. In the wake of two oil crises, economic stagnation and rising public sector debt, governments throughout western Europe had been preoccupied with the phenomenon of structural unemployment. Prior to the 1970s and with the economies of western Europe basking in the golden age of capitalism, unemployment had been perceived largely as a temporary phenomenon. However, with high unemployment proving a stubbornly persistent feature on the political agenda, attention turned to the manner in which education had failed the 'needs of business'. It was a theme that resonated through the 1980 white paper on education, which argued that there was a need to revise a curriculum that could be described as 'excessively academic in content' and which contained a 'pronounced bias' in college courses towards the professions. It was an argument contained in the document *The Programme for Action in Education 1984–87* which suggested that the major challenge to education lay in relating the 'relevance of the educational process to the world of work and to the need to adapt the system to meet changes in employment patterns' (DoE, 1984, p. 3).

If an attempt to establish a closer link between business and education was by no means new, under the stewardship of Seamus Brennan, minister for education, policy took on a distinctly 'managerialist' outlook. Brennan recommended a shift away from county educational committees to executive agencies, responsible for payrolls, educational property management, curriculum and assessment (Walshe, 1999, p. 26). Displaying a willingness to endorse many of the themes commonly associated with the New Public Management, Brennan observed that 'in Education I found a department that was the biggest property holder in the country. Too much time was spent on decisions about fixing slate roofs. I felt all that should be contracted out and that the department should concentrate on deciding policy' (Brennan, cited in Walshe, 1999, p. 26).

Reform of the administrative structure surrounding education had been an issue addressed at an earlier stage by the OECD in its report on education policies in Ireland. The report noted that, 'although a small system, it has the same administrative apparatus and faces the same problem of control, management and monitoring as large systems . . . the schools are locally managed . . . but in so far as the exercise of its specific powers are concerned, the Department of Education functions like a highly centralised bureaucracy' (cited in the green paper, 1992, p. 139). On whether regionalisation would be suitable, the report remarked that 'the department is concerned with such minor matters because there is no administrative layer interposed between it and individual institutions. The question arises, therefore, whether it would not be desirable to devolve some of the department's routine functions to regionally based administrative units' (cited in Walshe, 1999, p. 64; see also Coolahan, 1993, p. 15).

In its response the DoE acknowledged that the devolution of responsibilities would be a 'painful process for some' and that, while there might be benefits, these might be outweighed by the difficulties encountered. However, the department went on to conclude that 'the tendency to refer demands for additional resources, funding and difficult decisions and choices to central government is deeply ingrained in Irish public life . . . the challenge is exceptionally difficult, but the potential benefits could be worth the effort, (Coolahan, 1993, p. 12).

While the idea of introducing executive agencies was later dropped, it nevertheless revealed the government's preference for redefining the role of education. It was a shift in policy not welcomed by all. As the Association of Management of Catholic Secondary Schools (AMCSS) caustically pointed out, the 1992 green paper was driven by 'economic pragmatism, acquisitive individualism and functional efficiency' (Walshe, 1999, p. 33). It was a view with which the Catholic Primary School Managers' Association (CPSMA) was in accord, suggesting that there had been a 'disproportionate emphasis' on promoting an enterprise culture and preparing young people for work. As far as INTO was concerned, if the green paper appeared 'superficially attractive' in that it seemed to provide a 'proximate response to a pressing demand', there was the distinct possibility that it could lead to 'bad practice' (Walshe, 1999, p. 33).

The green paper's remit was far-reaching, embracing as it did reform of school governance, internal management, promotion and performance. As far as school governance was concerned it endorsed the view that greater responsibility should be devolved from the DoE to individual schools. Citing the arguments of the Primary Education Review Body (1990), the green paper recommended that boards should be given greater autonomy and play a more 'meaningful role in the operation of the school'. Indeed, while the review body acknowledged the positive contribution of local clergy on school boards, it noted that not all 'clergy are suited to this role' and envisaged strengthening the position of school boards (1992, p. 140). In addition, the board would be responsible for appointing staff, ensuring that the quality of teaching was maintained and, where necessary, addressing any weaknesses identified.

The 1992 green paper also recommended greater representation for parents on management boards, although both O'Rourke and later Brennan were keen to ensure that this did not exceed the representation of teachers and school owners on management boards (see Coolahan, 1993). Indeed, government was of the view that, given the fact that 80 per cent of capital spending and 90 per cent of current spending were provided for by the state, there should be a requirement to establish a board with the necessary authority to manage. It was an issue around which a complicated

set of discussions ensued. At the hub of this dispute was the issue of representation, or perhaps more accurately the level of representation the
teaching profession would secure, on the boards of management. Certainly, the government's proposal that business representation on school
boards would be mandatory was to many people disconcerting (Walshe,
1997, p. 98).

A further issue that raised eyebrows in the green paper was the move to
reform internal management procedures. In an attempt to introduce a
more flexible framework the green paper recommended changes to the role
of principals, the composition of selection boards for appointments and
positions of responsibility (Coolahan, 1993, pp. 48–49). Here, the role of
the principal was deemed pivotal, responsible as it was for determining the
educational aims of the school, developing the school's curriculum and
outlining the methods by which the aims would be achieved. The evaluation of staff and relations between staff and parents would also fall within
the principal's remit.

If the concentration of functions in the principal's remit was to attract
criticisms, the persistence of promotion based on seniority, which had long
been felt responsible for undermining the efficiency of middle management, was to prove a particularly thorny issue. Not surprisingly, changes to
the nature of school governance met with considerable adverse reaction.
INTO was opposed to the idea of a 'chief executive'-style leadership of the
management boards, favouring a more organic scheme in which school
heads would share responsibility with senior teaching staff. The Church of
Ireland also rejected the thrust of the change contained in the green paper
and in particular the vision of one model of school board for every school
irrespective of size, origin or ethos (Walshe, 1999, p. 101).

The attempt to alter the nature of school governance was linked to the
perceived strength of the teaching unions. Unlike their counterparts in
both the USA and the UK, the teaching unions in Ireland have traditionally
held considerable bargaining strength. Any attempt to alter the balance
between parent and teacher representation on management boards could
thus be seen as a measure designed to undermine the political power of the
trade unions.

Any discussion of the reform of school governance that involved the
introduction of school boards and changes to internal management also
inevitably impinged upon the controversial issue of 'unsatisfactory teaching'. During the draft stage of the 1995 white paper, it was argued that if
in-service training for the teacher did not result in an improvement then
the department would assist the board of management. As the paper suggested: 'in the event that remediation is not successful, it may be necessary
to pursue withdrawal of recognition. This may involve recourse to special

severance conditions that would be worked out in Conciliation' (white paper, DoE, 1995, p. 12). It was to prove an extremely contentious issue, one not resolved until the productivity talks of the PCW. Another feature of the white paper, which raised important issues, included a stricter adherence to the school year. Concern had been expressed that the length of the school year in Ireland was significantly shorter than that of other European countries and that even this had been subject to erosion (Walshe, 1999, p. 14).

There could be little doubt that any move towards greater forms of devolved responsibility would impact significantly upon the regulative role of the state. The green paper proposed that the inspectorate withdrew from direct involvement in schools to concentrate on observing, monitoring and evaluating policy. It was anticipated that it be linked more closely with the administrative section of the DoE. Whole school inspections would evaluate and monitor the school plan and individual teacher planning, student achievement, pupil–teacher interaction and the deployment of staff. In addition they would focus on the extent to which education guidelines were met, the provision for meeting individual needs in students, the quality of buildings, and the manner in which all resources in the school were being used (Coolahan, 1993, p. 61).

Neither the teaching profession nor the management of parent associations was in favour, treating the proposals with scepticism. In particular, there was concern at the frequency of inspections, the responsibilities and authority invested in the inspection team, and the nature of any 'appropriate action' to address deficiencies. Moreover, there was concern over whether the team making the inspection should also be involved in the implementation of the proposals. It raised the issue of whether there should be a two-tier system, a national inspectorate for conducting whole school inspections and a local school inspectorate providing advisory support (Coolahan, 1993, p. 63).

The issue of school performance, or perhaps more accurately variable school performance, attracted the attention of the ombudsman, Kevin Murphy, who was responsible for implementing the freedom of information bill. His intervention was necessary because of the requests from two national newspapers, the *Sunday Times* and the *Sunday Tribune*, and a regional paper, the *Kerryman*, for information on exam performance on a school-by-school basis that would allow 'league tables' to be constructed (*Irish Times*, 12 October 1999). The teacher unions, the parents' body and the DoE were all opposed to the dissemination of this information on a number of grounds. The DoE cited section 53 of the Education Act, which authorises the minister to refuse access to information in 'a particular set of circumstances'.

Following extensive consultation with a wide range of interested parties, the ombudsman argued that Section 53 did not apply retrospectively and that a public body could not object to the publication of information on the grounds that some bodies were 'more worthy than others' (*Irish Times*, 12 October 1999). The DoE objected (successfully), arguing that such a request would place an undue burden upon its staff in the compilation of data, that it might lead to a withdrawal by teachers in the conduct of the exam, and might place a strain on industrial relations between teachers and the department.

After a period of consultation and negotiation stretching through the best part of a decade, there can be little doubt that education at both primary and secondary level has undergone substantial change. However, while there appeared to be consensus at the consultative stage, there were still difficult hurdles before legislation could be enacted. In particular, attempts to 'tighten' agreement upon the length of the school year, an issue addressed in both the green paper and the white paper, led to 'difficulties' in relations between the DoE and the teaching unions. It was resolved only after a complex package had been agreed with the unions that entailed concessions on increased allowances, a shortening of the incremental pay scale and an early retirement scheme. As part of that agreement additional promotion posts were also offered with defined tasks, and teachers were asked to accept non-teaching duties as part of their posts. The offer signalled the end of seniority as the main determining factor in deciding who attained middle management, in a system that was moving from one dominated by religious owners of schools to one dominated by teachers (Walshe, 1999, p. 183).

There was also considerable resistance to the introduction of whole school inspections, which had been put forward as early as 1996. The intention was that these would be piloted in a small number of schools and thereafter further consultation would take place. Not surprisingly, the unions were not enamoured of the prospect. ASTI was concerned that professionals 'aware' of the difficulties schools encountered should be involved in the process. ASTI thus hoped to identify resources and facilities as important indices in the assessment of school performance. Little progress was made for a further two years, although ASTI and INTO agreed to a pilot project. The TUI resisted such moves.

The main elements that surfaced in the legislation included the provision for establishment of boards in all schools in receipt of public funding and for parents, teachers and patrons to have rights under law to be involved in the management of schools. The legislation also gave statutory recognition to the National Parents' Council and stipulated that parents have a right to receive any reports on the operation and performance of schools. It defined more closely the function and roles of teachers and principals, setting out the responsibilities of the various stakeholders in education. It also made provision for appeals and grievances and allowed, for example, students over the age of 18 to have access to their own school records. There was also the right of appeal to the board of management on a decision taken by a member of staff, or to the DoE on any decision by the board of management (Walshe, 1999, pp. 205–207).

After a prolonged and often tortuous process of negotiation, the legislation enacted in the 1990s attempted to engineer a reform of school governance as part of a wider political project designed to deliver an educational system attuned to the demands of the new global economy. It has been a far from straightforward task. Education remains a policy environment populated by well-organised vested interests that have successfully resisted some of the more contentious, neo-liberally inspired efforts to effect a change in the relationship between education and work.

Higher education

In Ireland, the number of students in full-time third-level education increased dramatically from the 1960s onwards and, despite the severe constraints on public expenditure during much of the 1980s, third-level education continued to expand and diversify. What is more, despite a falling birth rate that had generated decreasing cohorts in the elementary and post-primary schools, demand for places in higher education continued to grow throughout the 1980s (O'Buachalla, 1992, p. 69). While the rate of increase was most pronounced in the technological sector, increased enrolment throughout higher education was facilitated by government policies to augment the capacity of the system: the upgrade of existing institutions, the utilisation of spare capacity in colleges and the funding of special schemes. The former national institutes for higher education at Limerick and Dublin, for example, were established as universities in 1990 and a former college of education was annexed by University College Dublin as a business school (O'Buachalla, 1992, p. 70). In 1990, following the work of a special government–university working party, the universities undertook to provide 3,600 new places over three years, with government providing the funds to cover related capital, equipment and recurrent costs.

Policy in the 1990s was concerned with a perceived discrepancy between the emphasis accorded to reflection and scholarly work in the higher education system and the demands of a flexible economy. Government sought to align more closely the provision of third-level education with the 'demands' of students and business, a policy driven essentially by an attempt 'to evaluate academic life as an economic commodity with market value, rather than as an intellectual pursuit for its own sake' (Farnham, 1999, p. 11).

The motivation and desire on the part of government to initiate reform of higher education was revealed in the green paper (1992), which argued that there should be rationalisation in provision and more attention to costs, efficiency and quality. The minister of education, Niamh Breathnach, was concerned about the drop-out rates of some institutions, cost effectiveness and the need to instil better quality assurance. The last of three issues was to be a theme that figured prominently in higher educational discourse throughout the 1990s (Walshe, 1999, p. 123).

Rather unexpectedly, however, the issue that dominated debate was the alleged intrusion on academic freedom. Indeed, a political furore broke out over the intention to amend university governing structures, the appointment procedures for presidents, provost or masters, and the balance of the membership of governing bodies (Walshe, 1999, p. 135; Coolahan, 1993, pp95-105). The first of the problems to surface was the possible dissolution of the National University of Ireland structure. It had been mooted that legislation would be made that sought to amend the 1908 Irish Universities Act and give independence to University College Cork, University College Dublin, University College Galway and the University of Maynooth. As Walshe observes, this had been an issue initially raised during the late 1980s. On that occasion, however, the views of the constituent colleges had been influenced by new developments in funding, which were to be a threat to the traditional institutions, but also by the government's perceived desire to intervene in university autonomy. Caution, it was argued, should be exercised in giving any opportunity to the state through a major new Universities Bill (Osborn and Fisher, cited in Walshe, 1999, p. 133).

The second serious difficulty arose over the provision for new governing structures. The government wanted to expand representation to include junior and senior academic staff, non-academic staff, students and business interests. Such difficulties were compounded by the fact that the Bill also received stern criticism for the eight sections it contained that sought to hand over control of key elements of university operations to the Higher Education Authority (HEA). Issuing strategic development plans, annual reports and evaluative material on the performance of universities would all come under its remit (Walshe, 1999, p. 143).

Amid a concerted campaign from the universities and influential Senators, the final Bill witnessed a number of proposals designed to reduce tension. Amid an acrimonious debate a plethora of amendments was secured, as government struggled to come to terms with the well-organised and vociferous lobby. Indeed, significant concessions were made on all the major issues (Walshe, 1999, p. 142).

While the issue of academic freedom made 'good copy' for the broadsheets, the more profound sources of change in higher education came in areas that received rather less attention: the change in fees, the role of performance evaluation and funding. There can be little doubt that whether intended or not, the abolition of fees formed the basis of establishing more centralised control of how funding is made and where or, perhaps more importantly, why it is channelled in a particular direction.

The green paper advocated a structural modification in the role of the HEA, expanding it to include responsibility for funding all the system and for the development of policy. It envisaged the introduction of performance indicators based on completion rates, research, plant utilisation and student care as measures of institutional quality. Moreover, it recommended that subinstitutional units should be evaluated at regular intervals and that an academic audit steering group should be established at the HEA. In many instances, and with only minor variations, most of these measures were implemented. In O'Buachalla's opinion, it represented the emergence of an evaluative state, intent more on central control and 'steering' higher education (O'Buachalla, 1992, p. 73).

If the 1980s were about meeting the 'new' demands of education, expanding provision and changing the nature of what was provided, the 1990s were about reforming how it was provided. Reform revolved around altering the supply side of education: a concern with inputs, rather than outputs. The first and by far the most important issue to address was finance. Mistakenly for many, the decision to abolish fees was heralded as a major breakthrough in the social democratic cause to reduce unequal representation in higher-level education. There was dissent from this move, albeit rather limited. The democratic left thought such arguments were spurious, largely because students from lower-income families remained under-represented at higher education levels and any move to abolish fees would disproportionately favour middle and higher income groups. In addition, the Advisory Group on Third Level Student Support opposed the move, favouring a phased abolition of income tax relief for covenants and use of the revenue to increase student support (Walshe, 1999, p. 127).

In one of the more surprising turn of events, the Department of Finance also expressed reservations, most notably about the fact 'that the quality of University education could be endangered if fees were abolished' (Walshe, 1999, p. 127). It warned that in the event of a tight budgetary situation universities might be tempted to take in more non-EU students to generate income at the expense of places for Irish students. Furthermore, it suggested that while there would be winners there would also be losers: most notably postgraduate students, of which there were 7,000 full-time, students in private colleges, students studying abroad and those on European structural fund grants (Walshe, 1999, p. 127).

A further area in which reform was introduced was that of quality assurance. A succession of ministers had voiced concern about drop-out rates and the veil of secrecy under which third-level institutions operated. The green paper was keen to assert the need to establish criteria for institutional quality. Three mechanisms for quality assurance were proposed: the development of performance indicators and internal quality review procedures, appropriate external monitoring, and an academic audit within the HEA. The HEA would be responsible for monitoring quality assurance, monitoring and promoting links between industry and colleges, receiving annual reports from each third-level institution and preparing subsequent yearly reports on the performance of the third-level sector. The Conference of the Heads of Irish Universities (CHIU) vigorously contested this role, arguing that that any academic audit unit should be located in the university system and not with the HEA. The CHIU pointed out that there was already a considerable role for external bodies in the areas of examinations, appointments, promotions and the peer review of publications. The CHIU argued that the HEA's role should be limited to one of monitoring.

If objections from the CHIU were to be expected, generated largely by the belief that sufficient mechanisms were already in place to ensure quality, the objections from the HEA came as more of a surprise to government. Under the 1971 HEA Act, the Authority had long held powers to impose decisions. However, the thrust of the green paper sought to specify these powers more closely. It was a move not welcomed by the HEA. In response it took the surprise decision to place an advertisement expounding the belief that over a period of 28 years its role in mediating between the state and universities had been successful because it had been conducted in a 'spirit of collaboration and dialogue' (Walshe, 1999, p. 148).

The Irish Federation of University Teachers queried the adequacy of the performance indicators, suggesting that they failed to consider the resource constraints under which teaching staff operated. Concerned that government would impose an evaluation process similar to that undertaken in the UK, the universities moved quickly to establish internal evaluation exercises.

Education in general, and higher education in particular, has become increasingly instrumental in its aims and purposes from the beginning of the 1990s. The role of universities in the transformation of the Irish economy has come under increasing scrutiny as policy makers perceive its function to be crucial in the construction of a flexible, high-tech, high-wage economy likely to be favoured by multinational capital. For those such as O'Buachalla (1992) the thrust of change can be explained in terms of the emergence of an evaluative state. In contrast this author would suggest that such moves form part of a wider political agenda to reorganise the relationship between higher-level education and the needs of the market. Reform has centred on the reform of educational regulation. Here the state has been keen to effect a fundamental reorientation of the role of higher education in line with developments that have taken place in the other Anglo-saxon public policy environments.

Pension reform

The issue of an adequate and comprehensive pension cover in Ireland has been debated on an ongoing basis for considerable period of time. Indeed, as a policy area it has remained largely fallow since the 1976 green paper *A National Income Related Pension Scheme,* which highlighted the pressing need to address then current and anticipated deficiencies within pension coverage. Innovative, and clearly in tune with the times, the green paper concluded that although social assistance (non-contributory) pension schemes, often referred to as the first pillar of pension provision, covered the whole population, they provided a flat-rate, means-tested allowance that at best catered for those in lower income groups. They were schemes that were 'structurally incapable of providing a variable pension related to past income' and aimed at preserving an established standard of living. The green paper argued that there was the very real prospect that those who relied exclusively upon this form of coverage (or indeed the marginally better contributory social insurance scheme) would experience a considerable reduction in income upon retirement (1976, p. 37). In addition, it pointed out that while occupational coverage in the public sector was adequate (79 per cent), there were reasons for concern over the lack of coverage both in the private sector and among the self-employed. Although accurate figures were difficult to come by it estimated that occupational pension coverage existed for only 183,00 out of 595,00 private sector employees (1976, p. 36).

In a far-reaching reappraisal of pensions policy the paper's observations extended beyond the simple issue of numbers. Indeed, it was keen to extol the need for legislation that would enhance the protection of pension rights in response to changes in household structures, labour markets and the increased tendency towards international takeovers and mergers. Here, for example, the green paper argued that there was a pressing need to redress the unequal treatment of women in pension schemes, ensure greater flexibility in the transfer of pension rights between schemes, and protect those funds that might be part of a takeover. While the paper was in many ways far-sighted, particularly on increasing flexibility in the transfer of pension rights, there was little in the way of political commitment to endorse reform, as the economy lurched into economic stagnation for the remaining part of the 1970s and throughout the 1980s.

It was to be an area of policy to which government would not return until 1985, with the formation of a new interim regulatory body, the National Pensions Board. In its first published report the Board maintained that legislation was required in a range of areas where deficiencies existed. In particular, the Board suggested that there was a lack 'of a comprehensive supervisory framework for pension schemes' and that while members might seek redress through trust law, there was a need to ensure 'greater accountability with regard to the management and operation of pension schemes' (1976, p. 36). To compound such problems the Board felt that there were a number of other areas that warranted attention. The failure of the system to cope with career changes, as well as the need to ensure adequate security of members' rights, were highlighted. Other issues raised were the monitoring and enforcement of minimum funding standards, the imperative to establish a system of control of pension fund investments to protect members' rights, and the creation of legislation that would deal with pension rights in the event of a company wind-up (1986, p. 51).

The report recommended a new Pensions Act that would safeguard the provision of minimum benefits for 'early leavers', establish the mandatory disclosure of information, introduce a minimum funding standard, require periodic actuarial valuations and annual reports, and set up a new permanent regulatory body: the National Pensions Board. This latter body would be responsible for monitoring and supervising the operation of the Pensions Act, issuing guidelines and codes of practice, encouraging the availability of appropriate training for trustees, and advising the minister for social welfare.

During the 1990s governments throughout western Europe were concerned with the long-term difficulties of welfare states faced with a potential demographic time bomb, a scenario in which the proportion of older people relative to those at work is set to increase rapidly. As the statistics provided by the National Pensions Board (1998) graphically illustrate, the median age of the EU increased by only four years (from 32 to 36) between 1960 and 1995. However, this was projected to increase by 9 years (from 36 to 45) between 1998 and 2025. In addition, the number of young people (under 20) was set to fall by almost 10 million and the number of retired people was set to rise by over 37 million. It is a situation compounded by the increase in atypical work patterns, which present problems for a coherent and well-structured path for pension contributions, and the fact that many social welfare pension schemes are paid out of current revenue. As such, it was anticipated that pension promises may well become increasingly difficult to meet.

Amid debate about the need to address such matters the department of welfare commissioned the Economic and Social Research Institute (ESRI) in 1995 to undertake a survey of occupational and personal pension coverage in Ireland. According to the survey, pension coverage among the self-employed remained low, accounting for only 25 per cent of 265,000 people. While coverage of the self-employed was better outside of agriculture, the report was concerned that it remained at best 'variable' (Hughes and Whelan, 1996, p. 18). Such disquiet at the level of coverage was unlikely to be allayed by the finding that less than 20 per cent of the self-employed had made other forms of financial arrangements (investments, stocks, shares or property) to provide for retirement (Hughes and Whelan, 1996, p. 25). In the private sector, coverage through occupational schemes was estimated to be 38 per cent. The picture in the public sector was rather different, with coverage estimated to be 83 per cent and most of those not covered being in part-time employment. While it is difficult to make comparisons with the 1980s the survey suggested that, as in other European countries, coverage had displayed signs of a slight decline (Hughes and Whelan, 1996, p. 43).

The survey's findings on the pension coverage among the 'not gainfully employed' sector made for uncomfortable reading. As the survey noted, only 51,000 of the 637,900 people engaged in home duties (8 per cent) and 25,300 of the 407,500 other inactive (6 per cent) had ever been in a pension scheme. Among the elderly, the survey observed that, while not all were in receipt of the full basic state pension, without it 'many would have no other source of income' (Hughes and Whelan, 1996, p. 27). The culmination of the debate that surrounded the National Pensions Policy Initiative was the publication of the Pensions Board report, *Securing Retirement Income* (1998).

The report confirmed many of the findings produced by the ESRI. Indeed, on the issue of coverage it reiterated the ESRI's conclusion that while many people could look forward to substantial occupational or personal pensions above social welfare levels, there was 'a significant proportion of the workforce' that could not (Pensions Board, 1998, p. 59). In a more optimistic vein, however, it noted that elderly dependency in Ireland would decline between 1991 and 2006 and, unlike that of most of its European counterparts, it was not projected to rise significantly. The Expert Group convened by the Central Statistics Office suggested that over the next 10 years the elderly dependency ratio would fall and then rise sharply.

Confirming that the early part of the new millennium offered an invaluable window of opportunity to initiate reform, the Board's report remarked that, of the 20 systems examined by the OECD, Ireland's was the most favourably placed to initiate successful reform. This was in no small part due to the fact that 'both contributions and benefits are lower than in most countries', which meant that 'the Irish Government should have fewer economic or political constraints than other governments in deciding how to manage pensions costs in the future' (Pensions Board, 1998, p. 70).

While the Pensions Board undertook an extensive review of a wide range of issues to do with pensions policy, its principal focus was on the need to explore mechanisms that would extend (and fund) pension coverage. In particular, the report emphasised that in the longer term reform was essential if poverty were to be alleviated and the burden on the welfare state reduced. Although the report fell short of recommending a particular target rate for first pillar pension coverage (industrial earnings), it did recommend the construction of a new social fund to finance the anticipated increased costs. As for second pillar pension coverage (personal and occupational schemes), the report recommended that the government explore a new pension account: a Personal Retirement Savings Account (PRSA). If the Pensions Board was concerned primarily with issues about regulation and the extension of pension protection rights, its report also highlighted the manner in which policy could assist with expanded coverage.

Adequate provision in the future will depend upon a combination of improvements to the social welfare old age pension (first pillar) and the development of supplementary forms of provision (second pillar) to simplify access and extend coverage. While the removal of poverty was a major objective of the initiative, it was hampered by the fact that this was not a task of simple calculation. Poverty is a relative concept and living standards change over time. The Commission on Social Welfare in 1986, for example, used no fewer than seven different approaches to estimate 'adequate' levels of income and recommended a figure of IR£50–60 per week. By 1995, the ESRI's figures were IR£68–96. Even at this juncture the ESRI remained reluctant to provide a definitive figure, since it was difficult to derive an 'unproblematic and objective' estimate of income adequacy which would be 'universally acceptable and convincing' (National Pensions Board, 1998, p. 86). Such difficulties were compounded by the fact that without active policies to encourage saving for retirement, coverage would remain limited in key areas (see Table 2.10).

The minister of finance's response to this initiative was to caution against a desire to establish targets or rates for future pensions. He argued that, 'subject to the uncertainties that attach to long-term forecasts in particular, the target rate may prove to be incompatible with the prudent evolution of both public finances and of the wider economic and employment needs of the country' (McCreevy, cited in National Pensions Board, 1998, p. 116).

Table 2.10 Supplementary pension coverage, 1995 (ultimate and interim targets by employment status and gender for 5–10 years after implementation of proposals: percentages

Status and gender	Age	1995	5 years	10 years	Ultimate
Overall targets					
All at work, of which:		46	53	57	60
	Up to 29	28	34	35	35
	30–65	54	62	66	70
self-employed		27	36	43	44
employees		51	58	61	64
public sector		83	90	90	90
private sector		38	48	53	58
Achieved as a result of subsidiary objectives					
Males. of which:		49	54	58	59
self-employed	Up to 29	24	28	32	32
	30–65	29	38	45	45
employees	Up to 29	29	35	35	35
	30–65	73	75	75	75
Females, of which:		40	51	56	61
self-employed	Up to 29	1	16	32	32
	30–65	20	33	40	45
employees	Up to 29	29	35	35	35
	30–65	54	65	70	75

Source: National Pensions Board, 1998, p. 93.

While the Pensions Board's report was far from ebullient there were grounds for optimism in its appraisal of the situation at hand. With government budgetary policy entering a three-year cycle and with a continued commitment to social partnership agreements, the Board was of the opinion that an opportunity existed to discuss and promote the importance of establishing improved pension provision. It was keen to endorse the view that funding would be a crucial issue. As the report noted, if the increase in Exchequer contributions and/or PRSI contributions was provided on a pay-as-you-go basis, then it would be the working generations of the middle years of the twenty-first century that would be paying for those working now but who would, by the mid-century, have retired (1998, p. 109). As the report notes, it would mean that the current generation 'will have got off lightly', accentuating intergenerational unfairness and raising the possibility that future generations might not be prepared to assume the burden.

In its detailed response the Board recommended establishing a fund that would be invested in a broad portfolio from the global financial markets in order to smooth over the burden between generations. This would enable Exchequer contributions to be capped for the foreseeable future and ensure that greater resources would be available for first pillar pensions in order to limit future costs. In the opinion of the Board, it was a measure that would ensure that costs would be spread evenly over time, ensuring greater scope to manage intergenerational transfers of pensions costs and retain the international competitiveness of the Irish economy (Pensions Board,1998, p. 110) (see Table 2.11). In its estimates of the required size of the fund, the Board recommended an annual Exchequer contribution of IR£250 million be made available for the first five years. This would rise to IR£500 million per year between 2004 and 2008 and be followed by an annual contribution equal to 50 per cent of the projected PRSI contributions for the remaining years.

Table 2.11 Total pension costs, 1996–2046 (as percentage of GNP showing effect of funding first pillar benefits)

Costs	1996	2006	2016	2026	2036	2046
1st pillar without funding	4.84	4.84	5.55	6.84	8.08	9.25
1st pillar using fund	4.84	5.61	6.39	6.39	6.40	6.24
Second pillar	4.18	4.56	5.02	5.43	5.18	4.76
Total						
Without fund	9.02	9.40	10.57	12.27	13.26	14.01
Using fund	9.02	10.16	11.41	11.82	11.58	11.00

Source: Pensions Board (1998, p. 113).

The Board recommended that the management should be undertaken by an agency established under statute, operating independently of government but under the supervision of representatives of the social partners (Pensions Board, 1998, p. 112). Under such regulatory arrangements, statute would provide for clarity of accounting and accountability, as well as define guidelines for investment. It was imperative that there were clearly stated mechanisms in place with regard to flows in and out of the fund and that its investment criteria be defined with the explicit intention of maximising long-term real rates of return. The Board was keen to note that it was essential to avoid the potential to confuse financial and social objectives. Innovative, far-sighted and technically adept, it was a policy that found favour, partly because the government was during the late 1990s awash with money. Measures that were likely to reduce inflationary pressure were seen in a positive light. Government was thus presented with an opportunity to place funds that would be politically and socially acceptable to the social partners (the other option was to reduce the national debt).

If the construction of a social fund formed the cornerstone of reform of the first pillar of pension provision, the introduction of the PRSA, a new type of pension vehicle, was intended to change the nature of second pillar pension provision. Designed specifically to meet the needs of the flexible labour market, the PRSA was intended to be a simple, portable product likely to appeal to those in atypical forms of employment or those likely to move between jobs. It is an investment account owned by an individual in which funds are invested and managed by an approved PRSA provider. Unlike previous pension products it is available irrespective of employment status and allows individuals to boost the fund with additional voluntary contributions. Previously, a change to an employee's status usually obliged the employee to cease contributing to a scheme. While this did not preclude moving to a new scheme there were costs to be borne. The PRSA was also intended to allow account holders to withdraw part of their accumulated fund (up to prescribed limits), thereby increasing its appeal and encouraging wider coverage.

On 16 December 1999 the Dáil debated and passed with apparently little notice a Bill to provide a temporary holding fund for 1 per cent GDP and IR£5 billion of the proceeds from the sale of Telecom Eireann. It would later establish permanent arrangements for a centrally managed fund for the state's future pension obligations with the intention of meeting future pension liabilities as Ireland's demography changes. It was envisaged that funds from the sale of any state assets in the future would be complemented by an ongoing contribution of 1 per cent of GDP to be invested each year.

Responsibility for managing the fund was assigned to the National Treasury Management Agency (NTMA). It was a move that met with disapproval from the Department of Finance, which argued that with the NTMA in charge the credibility and independence of the trustees would be undermined (*Irish Times*, 7 August 2000, p. 18). The department was of the opinion that unless the trustees could 'hire and fire' the managers of the fund, it could not be considered sufficiently independent. When discussions began in June of 1999 the department's view was that the fund should have its own trustees and that the 'NTMA may manage the fund on behalf of those trustees' without being the sole manager. Contrary to the advice given by the civil service advisory committee, the minister for finance,

Charlie McCreevy, opted for the NTMA to have responsibility for the fund. While the independence of the trustees was highlighted in the committee's decision, it also noted that the civil service unions might not fully support the fund unless it was completely independent of government (*Irish Times*, 7 August 2000, p. 18).

Some concluding remarks

If the dominant paradigm of the 1960s and 1970s revolved essentially around attempts to incorporate the socially disadvantaged, it has been a process largely reversed as governments have sought to abandon the level of commitments embodied within the political and institutional apparatus of the KWS. Put simply, the KWS is now viewed as an increasingly anachronistic structure within an era of flexible specialisation. It has been argued that business can no longer sustain the level of economic growth upon which both the economic and social rights of the welfare state were predicated.

The persistence of a combination of high levels of structural unemployment and increasing levels of poverty has made the search for alternatives to the KWS of paramount importance. Moreover, the changing structure of households, labour markets and the problem of immigration and/or a return of emigrants all pose serious questions about a purely 'national' response to the development of full citizenship. Social rights, as an attribute of citizenship, have been gradually eroded as governments have sought to reduce public expenditure, privatise public industry and reassert the primacy of individual self-help. Universality in welfare provision has been supplanted by a tighter grip upon entitlement policing, and policies have been underscored by supportive conditionality. What remains patently clear is that where reform has been marginally inclusive its principal motivation has rested firmly upon enhancing the flexibility of the labour market. It is in this sense that the reform in welfare has formed part of a strategy concerned with constructing a political discourse that champions greater flexibility in the labour market, the construction of a more active welfare regime and, ultimately, a redefinition of the relationship between the public and private sectors.

Notes

1   The metaphor was used by the minister of finance, Charlie McCreevy, to defend his decision to reduce the 'tax burden' on higher earners in the budget for 2000.
2   The political furore surrounding the strike by Dublin bus workers in March

2000 is an example of the clamour to celebrate the alleged virtues of the free market. It was a dispute about the low level of basic pay for drivers in Dublin. Alarm at the ability of the unions to bring the city to a standstill gave elements of the business community an opportunity to vent their opposition to the public sector and endorse the need to privatise all that moves.

3   Documents released to the *Irish Times* under the Freedom of Information Act. See *Irish Times*, 6 January 2000.

4   I would like to thank John Canavan for his insights on these issues.

5   When the first time buyers grant was reduced in the 2000 budget, the minister for finance was forced to do a U-turn and introduce alternative tax measures because of the political furore that broke out within his party and the wider media.

3

'Redefining the public': civil service reform in the era of the Celtic Tiger

Few would doubt that a new discourse on the execution of public policy has emerged from both inside and outside the Irish civil service. And yet, while the political scandals of the late 1990s may sustain an appetite for restructuring the public sector,[1] the origins of such change lie undoubtedly in the problems that emerged in the late 1970s and condensed towards the end of the 1980s. At the close of this period politicians were convinced that, if institutional sclerosis was to be avoided and Ireland's seat at the table of the global economic leaders secured, then it was imperative that the country's competitiveness should not be undermined by an inefficient public sector.

This attempt to 'redefine' the public has to a large extent been influenced profoundly by arguments surrounding the alleged onset of globalisation. However, more often than not this remains a sterile debate, dominated by financial commentators who see 'no alternative to neo-liberalism within the contours of the new global economy' (Hay and Marsh, 2000, p. 4). And yet, whether globalisation is taking hold at all may not necessarily in itself be that important to our understanding of civil service reform. As Busch succinctly observes, 'although there is little evidence for the much-vaunted hyper-mobility of capital, the *perceived* potential for capital flight in response to changing interest rates may, none the less, exert significant pressures on incumbent administrations' (Busch, cited in Hay and Marsh, 2000, p. 3, emphasis added). It is a view with which Hay and Marsh largely concur when they contend that 'a belief that expansionary measures may precipitate a flurry of capital flight may bear no relation to real economic processes. Yet such a bias may in turn serve further to entrench the impression that reflation is impossible and there is no alternative to neo-liberal economics in a context of heightened capital mobility' (Hay and Marsh, 2000, p. 9).

In other words, reform and change cannot be understood in terms of a simple, causal process: that globalisation leads to a particular trajectory of policy. Rather, what appears to be happening is more complicated. New directions in policy or political strategy are not necessarily informed by the processes of globalisation, or even globalising tendencies, per se, but by particular understandings and constructions of globalisation (Hay and Marsh, 2000, p. 9). Put simply, if there's a queue then it may be useful to join it, just in case. It is a perception, even a fear (whether justified or not may well be immaterial) that some form of change is taking place, and those who do not go with the tide may well be swept away.

We need to recognise that what demarcates the (failed) civil service reforms of the 1980s and their (partially) successful counterparts in the 1990s is not the content of policy, since in many ways they bear a striking resemblance to one another, but the change in the political and discursive landscape in which this reform took place. The policy interventions of the 1990s were made against a political backdrop increasingly predisposed towards neo-liberal political and economic solutions to public sector problems.

This should not be read as undermining an important role for high-ranking civil servants in this reform. On the contrary, I have a good deal of sympathy with Roche's view that the reform of the civil service in Ireland bears the hallmark of a 'mandarin revolution' (Roche, 1998, p. 5). However, while there has been a conspicuous lack of ideological zeal for such reform, it should also be stressed that attempts to redefine the role, function and performance of public service provision cannot be understood simply as an 'in-house' activity, isolated from the political and economic arguments taking place in the national and international political arena. Nor should we disregard the influence that a receptive audience at the EU level has had on this agenda. Certainly, these are issues with which civil servants are familiar: as one high-ranking official remarked, 'it is impossible to separate the public from the private sector in modern society as both are inextricably intertwined' (interviews, 1999).

It is also important to recognise that a political discourse, itself constructed in a period influenced by both national and international structural conditions (and not necessarily a crisis), will have a crucial bearing upon the content, nature and extent of reform. This should not be read as a straightforward causal process in which structural conditions determine a particular discourse, or for that matter as meaning that a set of structural conditions (often misread as simply an economic crisis) is necessarily conducive to a specific discourse and/or a particular policy strategy. There will always be resistance from the vested interests of the past order. We therefore need to explore how sets of structural conditions reproduce opportunities or constraints for competing political discourses.[2] The struggle between competing political discourses, and its successful resolution, will clearly impact upon the shape and trajectory of policy: what 'fits', what is recommended or rejected, and how it is 'pushed through' are all elements of policy choice which are profoundly influenced by the political, economic and discursive context.[3] There can be little doubt that on this matter the terrain of the 1980s was vastly different to that of the 1990s. Whatever pretensions to an inclusive social democratic project (or more accurately, a belief in state intervention) may have existed in the 1980s, it was progressively abandoned during the 1990s. This was a shift not simply in the political complexion of a particular coalition government, although this has undeniably taken place. Rather, it reflects the fact that a neo-liberal economic and political discourse has flourished as economic growth has spiralled.

The reforms undertaken during the 1990s were not exclusive to Ireland. On the contrary, at various stages throughout the 1980s a succession of states in the Anglo-saxon public policy environment initiated moves to overhaul 'antiquated' civil service structures, prompted by a desire to redefine the role, function and performance of public service provision. In Ireland, this manifested itself in a combination of legislative and policy change which strengthened the offices of the comptroller and auditor general (C&AG) and the ombudsman, initiated devolved budgeting, introduced the Strategic Management Initiative (SMI) and expanded the role for alternative delivery systems (agencies). While these were moves justified by the need to devolve responsibility, improve political transparency and enhance accountability, they were also undeniably motivated by the imperative to establish greater fiscal constraint and redefine the relationship between the public and the private. At the very heart of the Celtic Tiger lies a tension between state regulation and the incessant demand to expand the role of the free market.

An explosion in the public sector deficit during the 1980s provided the political backdrop to a quest for change from within both the civil service and wider government circles. In the short term, and amid increasing economic austerity, the preferred policy instrument was either to delay recruitment or to effect cutbacks in staff. In the longer term, as this chapter shows, the Irish state embarked upon a concerted attempt to redefine the role of public sector provision. Influenced by the new public management (NPM) initiatives undertaken by Australia, Canada, New Zealand and the UK, successive Irish governments installed devolved budgeting, introduced and increased the function of agencies, and sought to instil a managerialist philosophy in the civil service.

These are all issues that have figured prominently in debates about an alleged 'hollowing out' of the nation state. Depending upon which side of the political fence you sit, either it involves a loss of political confidence in government as it struggles to come to terms with increased scrutiny, or it refers to the impact of 'globalisation' upon the scope, form and function of the public sector (Saward, 1997). For those such as Rhodes, 'hollowing out' refers to a myriad of processes that entail a loss of functions in central government to agencies, supranational institutions (the EU), and/or a reduction in the discretion available to public servants subject to the rigours of NPM (Rhodes, 1996, p. 661).

In the longer term, it is a process likely to result in a smaller, more fragmented and less coherent public sector. It may well be the case that governments will continue to pass legislation and establish the overall trajectory of policy, but it will be a process circumscribed increasingly by interactions with public, voluntary and private sector bodies. In a subtle but none the less crucial fashion, the terms of reference in this debate have shifted from a concern with the nature of policy delivery (reducing costs, introducing new public management techniques or establishing greater accountability) to one with co-ordination. As Rhodes observes, it represents a shift from a concern with 'less government' (or rowing) to 'more governance' (or more steering) (Rhodes, 1996, p. 655).

The vocabulary of the new public management is infused with concepts that signify a shift from a preoccupation with inputs (bureaucratic regulation) to a concern with outputs: quasi-markets, consumer choice and empowerment. Citizens or clients now traverse a bureaucracy, armed with rights enshrined in mission statements that allow them to confront and challenge faceless bureaucrats. It is a debate not simply about modernisation but about establishing the need to overhaul public service delivery and, more often than not, it is about confronting the inefficiencies that are purported to exist in the public sector.

There can be little doubt that the most striking feature of the reforms of the 1990s has been the promotion of accountability, the underlying principle of which has been devolved management. It has been circumscribed by legislation that sought to alter the relationship between politicians and civil servants. This legislation was designed to 'surf' the tension between, on the one hand, the need to allow civil servants sufficient managerial autonomy to alter the supply-side nature of public service and yet, on the other hand, ensure that political authority continues to reside with the minister.

Civil service reform

It was the leap into a programme of central economic planning during the 1960s that initially raised doubts about the competence of the Irish civil service to perform and deliver. Influenced by events taking place in other

OECD countries, and the pressures emanating from Ireland's anticipated accession to the European Economic Community, the Devlin report argued that the dynamics shaping the modern Irish polity were everywhere producing 'demands for a renewal of the public service' (Devlin, 1969, p. 138).

For Devlin, the problems inherent in Irish public sector administration were synonymous with the concept of the 'minister as a corporation sole', an administrative mechanism he believed to be obsolete and responsible for frustrating innovation. Under the operating rationale of minister as a corporation sole, each minister had the arduous task of being accountable for all aspects of state administration. It was, in Devlin's opinion, an unnecessary burden compounded by a burgeoning welfare state and an increasing public sector. As a consequence, ministers had become so embroiled in the press of daily business that they had 'little or no time to participate in the formulation of overall policy' (Devlin, 1969, p. 138).

The nature of civil service employment was also considerably influenced by this administrative protocol, since civil servants were often dissuaded from entertaining initiatives not previously sanctioned by the minister. As many civil servants were only too well aware, there was always the possibility that a minister could experience a 'loss of face' in the event of any unanticipated political problem.

The solution for Devlin lay in the formal separation of policy making from implementation. Impressed by developments in Sweden, the Devlin group's final report suggested that the daily functions of government should be allotted to particular, designated executive units, allowing ministers to concentrate upon the task of long-term policy formation. Despite extensive research spanning three years, the final report failed to impact significantly upon the organisation of public service, due to a lack of political will on the part of politicians and stubborn resistance from within the ranks of the civil service.

Certainly, for some within the civil service there was a feeling that Devlin had placed far too much emphasis upon the organisational aspect of civil service reform, rather than balancing this with advancements in personnel practices. In the opinion of one senior civil servant, for example, the report's most significant weakness lay in the failure to recognise that 'you couldn't change the civil service by changing the offices, you had to change the civil service by changing the people' (interviews, 1999).

For those who sought radical change it had become increasingly evident that the principal barrier to reform lay with the antiquated system of promotion based on seniority above merit. If meaningful change were to occur, then treading the predictable route through the grade system would need to be altered. The fact that everyone knew when it was 'Boggin's turn' fostered resentment, complacency or apathy among staff. As one senior civil servant explained:

> This was to my mind a key issue, that people who are actually resisting change are given opportunities to get on more than people who would be hoping to change. There were one or two Secretaries still around at that time who had been appointed at a very early age and were still there, and I really found that they had a lot of opposition to any kind of change. (interviews, 1999)

During the early 1980s, and in a move designed to tap into the disenchantment evident in certain quarters, Garret Fitzgerald announced his intention to introduce a new system of appointments that would open competition for all top civil servant positions. It was not an initiative welcomed rapturously by all. Indeed, according to Fitzgerald, it led to an orchestrated campaign from the higher echelons of the civil service intent on virtually 'brainwashing' their respective ministers against the suggestion (Fitzgerald, 1991).

Despite such obduracy, Fitzgerald managed to lay the proposal to Cabinet, and a modified version of the initiative emerged in 1983/84, under the Top Level Appointments Committee (TLAC). Its objective was to promote interdepartmental competition for positions of assistant secretary and upwards. The aim was to erode the distinction between professional and non-professional staff, enabling candidates for positions to be considered on merit rather than seniority. Although it appeared only a minor success, given the raft of changes proposed during this period, it was, in the view of one high-ranking civil servant, 'a signal that things were changing. I think that it was very important in that regard' (interviews, 1999).

The move to create the TLAC had not been without controversy. Given that its impact would be far from uniform, and that it was largely uncharted territory for large parts of the civil service, division existed over its function. For some, the lack of representation from the Department of Finance (at least initially) was a source of consternation. This was compounded by the suspicion that the TLAC would become a 'vehicle for unloading people from the central departments' (interviews, 1999). To others, a clearer line of division could be defined. As one top-level civil servant explained, 'by and large a lot of the reservations [about the TLAC] were from the higher echelons themselves, the very senior people, but the younger members recognised that there was an opportunity emerging' (interviews, 1999). As a consequence, the TLAC provided opportunities for greater interdepartmental mobility and ensured a more prominent role for competition.

The Committee, which consisted of five civil servants and one member of the private sector, was empowered to make recommendations to the government for the post of general secretary and to the minister for other top civil service positions (Millar and McKevitt, 1997, p. 13). The decision to allow representation from the private sector in the form of John Boland, an ex-managing director of Esso, signalled a significant departure from previous practice. By 1987, the committee was able to suggest three candidates to government for the position of general secretary and was free to recommend open competition from outside the public sector at any stage.[4] In addition, a new seven-year contract for those at secretary level was introduced; upon completion they would be expected to step down.

The need for change in personnel practices during the 1980s should not be underestimated since many talented senior civil servants had been poached by the private sector with attractive packages (Hussey, 1993, p. 87). For the 'movers and shakers' within the Irish civil service the TLAC represented the single most important success to emerge from the wreckage of reforms advocated in the mid-1980s. Unlike Devlin, its central thrust lay in the transformation of process and procedure rather than structure. As one senior civil servant remarked, Devlin had been concerned with 'pigeon-holes', but the focus of change from here on in would be personnel and performance. In this vein, one of its more prominent and innovative legacies lay in the formation of the NTMA.

Established in 1990, the NTMA's origins lie in a combination of the onset of a public sector debt crisis and the construction of the TLAC. By the late 1980s, Ireland's national debt had reached traumatic levels. A figure of IR£11 billion (87 per cent of GDP) in 1980 had exploded to IR£23.6 billion (117 per cent of GDP) by 1987. The Exchequer's borrowing requirement increased substantially and, despite the fact that Ireland's economic growth was high during most of this period, the high level of nominal interest rates meant that the debt/GDP ratio had deteriorated significantly. In circumstances in which interest payments on the national debt were absorbing 66 per cent of income tax revenue, few would take issue with the sentiments of the NTMA's director when he described it as a 'proverbial albatross' (Hussey, 1993). It was a situation complicated further by the need to meet the economic criteria laid down for entrance into the single European market. Under the EU's guidelines an excessive budget deficit would preclude entry. A figure of 60 per cent was deemed a suitable benchmark, one clearly exceeded in the Irish case. However, the EU was willing to concede that providing the debt was in decline, Ireland's entrance would be assured (Hussey, 1993).

In the corridors of Leinster House it had been rumoured that prominent financial figures had the ear of the Taoiseach, Charlie Haughey, and that a private sector involvement in managing the country's debt would be pursued. Although this particular avenue was avoided, the government's response was to establish an agency outside of the immediate control of the Department of Finance. Officials argued that, in the light of the severity of the economic crisis, the NTMA would need to draw upon private sector expertise, where the requisite experience would not come cheaply and would certainly not materialise if the salary structure of the civil service dictated appointments. The formation of the TLAC was therefore an important precursor to the construction of the NTMA, since the single most important issue to resolve was the recruitment of personnel from outside the civil service. As one top-level civil servant noted, 'the Secretary of the National Debt Management soon found that within the constraints of the civil service he couldn't head hunt: basically, Finance had lost a lot of extra people and if he wanted to head hunt he'd have to pay them the salaries, but you can't head hunt in the civil service' (interviews, 1999). Elements within the Department of Finance were not particularly enamoured of this prospect, since it appeared to reflect poorly upon its management of debt. As if to compound this, the chairman appointed to the Agency was drafted from the Department of Defence and not from within the Department of Finance.

That the NTMA was a significant development in the history of the Irish civil service is undeniable. It broke with a tradition in which managing the national debt came under the watchful eye of the Department of Finance. There were also radical changes to the way in which recruitment of staff took place. Indeed, an indication of the importance of this latter point can be derived from the fact that no fewer than five sections of the National Treasury Management Act relate to the role of staff, superannuation, expenses and recruitment.

It would be churlish to suggest that the NTMA has not been an outstanding success. Indeed, its performance in reducing the national debt throughout the 1990s prompted the current minister for finance, Charlie McCreevy, to assign it control of the funds earmarked for a new public pension fund. However, it is also important to recognise that the formation of the TLAC/NTMA represents only a limited success against the background of a raft of reforms proposed in the 1985 white paper that failed to materialise.

The origins of the 1985 white paper, *Serving the Country Better*, lie in the formation of the National Planning Board in 1983, which was set up to formulate a new national economic plan. The result of collaboration between the Department of Finance, a ministerial task force and a group of independent experts was the document *Building on Reality*, which served as the basis for the white paper in 1985 (Millar and McKevitt, 1997, p. 42). The white paper's prognosis was clear: without reform, institutional sclerosis would ensue. From the outset the white paper was keen to identify the relationship between civil servants and ministers as central to 'any process of change or development of the public service' (*Serving the Country Better*, 1985, p. 3).

Acknowledging the changing nature of public service provision, particularly after Ireland's accession to Europe, the white paper argued that some of the central characteristics of the civil service could 'lead to a lack of concern with the cost and speed of delivery of services' (1985, p. 5). As the white paper noted, in a system where ministers are responsible to the Dáil, departments often place a higher priority on avoiding mistakes which would 'embarrass the minister' than on the efficient delivery of service to the public. If a managerial concern with getting results was to be instilled into the civil service, then this was an issue that would have to be addressed. Summarising the general nature of the problems facing the Irish civil service, the white paper observed that 'the best civil service managers manage well in spite of rather than because of the systems at their disposal. Too often *the real costs of programmes are not known to the managers responsible for them*' (1985, p. 11, emphasis added).

Serving the Country Better also argued that public servants were so entangled in a legal and bureaucratic administrative culture that the standard of public service delivery had ultimately suffered (1985, p. 5). Not surprisingly, the white paper returned to the theme of separating advice from execution, one clearly influenced by events taking place elsewhere in the Anglo-saxon public policy environment. Indeed, it recommended the introduction to 'all departments of management systems based on corporate planning and emphasising personal responsibility for results, costs and services' (1985, p. 6). It went on to identify two areas of immediate concern: financial management and the introduction of a total management system.

Prior to the publication of the 1985 white paper the Department of Finance had undertaken moves to improve financial accountability and consistency across departments with the introduction in 1984 of *Guidelines for Financial Management*. Under these arrangements, departments were expected to detail major expenditure programmes and identify those suitable for budgeting on an ongoing basis. The recommendation in the white paper to introduce a total management system was viewed as a move designed to complement this approach and extol further the virtues of identifying costs on a systematic basis. While the white paper was willing to concede that not all civil service outputs 'readily lend themselves to quantification' and the 'evaluation of effectiveness', it stressed the need to shift towards a culture which recognised the imperative of a results focus (*Serving the Country Better*, 1985, p. 12). With the introduction of a central guideline for all departments, the aim was to maximise efficiency and, in conjunction with formal structures for co-ordination, minimise unnecessary overlap and waste.

Although planning units had existed, the white paper's contention was that they had been 'limited in their effectiveness'. It was a problem exacerbated by the historic role of personnel and finance branches, which had tended to move decision-making out of the 'hands of line managers and [make it] become centralised' (1985, p. 16). If this centralisation were to be reversed, and the clutter of bureaucracy removed, then devolved management would need to be introduced.

Under the provisions of the white paper it was considered vital to devolve the power to hire and fire to departmental managers. However, under a legal provision, existing employment tenure in the civil service could be terminated only by means of a government decision, even in instances where an individual employee wanted to leave the civil service permanently. The over-riding problem concerned the continuation of these rigid channels for dismissal. As a response to this, the white paper proposed that the secretary of a department or another appointed official should have the legal ability to appoint, discipline and dismiss staff, without immediate recourse to the minister. Ultimately, this would reduce considerably the number of tasks dealt with by the minister, while devolving responsibility and accountability (white paper, 1985, p. 26). Although this suggestion was largely ignored throughout the 1980s, the argument later resurfaced in the 1990s when the Public Service Management Act, 1997, came into effect. This signalled a distinct move to devolve responsibility from the minister to the general secretary of a department.

As part of a drive to devolve power, the white paper also suggested that civil service managers should have greater levels of autonomy, an argument premised upon the belief that, providing civil servants and managers could be made formally accountable, executive functions could be transferred. For those advocating change it was a matter of simply identifying areas that could benefit from the agency format. For example, it seemed eminently reasonable to suggest that 'making contributions and giving out benefits could be screened off away from the minister's responsibility' (interviews, 1999).

Overall, the white paper of 1985 advocated the radical overhaul of the civil service, a course of restructuring that would be dominated by the principles of managerialism widely followed in the private sector. Certainly, there are those who saw the dismissal of the white paper proposals as detrimental to the modernisation of the Irish polity. Indeed, the pervading view amongst many of the 'movers and shakers' within the Irish civil service was that there was a failure to recognise the potential benefits to accrue from such reform. As one civil servant remarked:

I think the 1980s were a period of lost opportunity because there was no restructuring done. It was pure stripping out of people and a reduction in numbers, an embargo on recruitment and expecting the people who remained to pick up the pieces in the same way as had happened previously. We lost the potential to find new ways of working together. Normally in a situation like we had in 1987 it would be a signal for quite a major change of structure and that never happened. (interviews, 1999)

Serving the Country Better to the SMI: policy learning in the Anglo-saxon public policy environment

In choosing to ignore the recommendations of *Serving the Country Better*, the Irish governments of the late 1980s ensured that restructuring the public sector would remain peripheral to the political agenda. For those such as Barrington, it signalled the need for a new leadership in the civil service. In his opinion, the 'top brass' would have to be removed in order to drag the Irish system out of the dark ages and into the twentieth century (Barrington, 1980). Without reform of practise, stagnation of the public arrangement would remain.

By the late 1980s the prevailing view within the higher echelons of the civil service was that avoiding change would be costly. Economists and politicians alike were fully aware of the role the public service could play in enhancing international competitiveness. If Ireland were to pull itself out of financial crisis, then reform of its increasingly outdated system of administration would need to be undertaken. Issues such as the beef tribunal in 1990 and the contamination of anti-D blood supplies with hepatitis C sparked a furore of media attention, bringing to light the failings of Irish administration and heightening public awareness of the problem (Millar and McKevitt, 1997, p. 36). While the formation of the NTMA represented a uniquely Irish response to an Irish problem, many of the other developments in the late 1980s and early 1990s drew extensively upon international experience, particularly from events taking place in the Anglo-saxon public policy world.

The manner in which civil service reform has taken place throughout the Anglo-saxon public policy world has attracted increasing attention from political scientists interested in how policies become diffused among nation states (Dolowitz and Marsh, 2000, p. 5). For those such as Rose, the quest to secure an organised response to the demands of globalisation has meant that nation states have moved firmly into a phase where collective problem solving has become paramount (Rose, 1991). Access to information has become easier, and it is precisely the interaction this affords which has led observers to examine more closely the role 'policy transfer' plays both *in* and *between* nation states (Dolowitz and Marsh, 1996, 2000; Stone, 2000). It is a process that has had a profound influence on the pace and trajectory of civil service reform in Ireland and is therefore worth teasing out in a little more detail.

While those such as Dolowitz and Marsh concede that policy transfer is by no means a new phenomenon, they note that it appears to be on the increase. The ever more pervasive influence of international organisations in the dissemination of particular policies (EU, International Monetary Fund [IMF] and the widespread perception among advanced economies that it is now impossible to be isolated from the processes of globalisation are cited as reasons for the growing occurrence of policy transfer (Dolowitz and Marsh, 2000). While these remain largely exogenous reasons for policy transfer, often emphasising the incentive to pursue policy learning (or explain why policy transfer is coerced), the literature has also been keen to identify the endogenous conditions that have eased the passage of transfer. Here Dolowitz *et al.* have argued that the combination of similar political ideologies, language and administrative structures ensures that it is hardly surprising that there should be a flow of policy ideas and influence from one country to another (Dolowitz *et al.* 1999, p. 726). This is a move away from a preoccupation with the structural exigencies of global capitalism to the salient features of a polity which influence its receptiveness for transfer: culture, politics, institutions (administrative practices and policy styles) and ideology.

Yet, to this author at least, it seems that to understand contextual receptivity fully demands an examination of the manner in which a political discourse is constructed and evolves, and which in turn necessarily influences how and where we search and what we extract or borrow. Put simply, the question 'Why reinvent the wheel?' may capture an entire set of reasons for transfer (administrative symbiosis, similar language, etc.). However, when interviewed Irish civil servants were at pains to stress that while there were many reasons to examine policy in the UK, these declined substantially during Margaret Thatcher's period in office, because 'wild free marketers' drove it.

For some, the explanation would seem to rest on identifying a division between endogenous and exogenous reasons for policy transfer. While this has the virtue of remaining simple it may fail to capture a more detailed (and often more complicated) picture. In other words, what is often presented as an innocuous and hardly controversial split between endogenous and exogenous reasons for policy transfer may well undermine a more informed understanding of the dynamic at work.

In the case of Ireland it seems there has always been an intuitive recognition of contextual receptivity, and of a pre-eminent role for the UK in transfer. Fanning's research on the Department of Finance, for example, was drawn to conclude that the Irish administrative machine had been 'thoroughly overhauled by some of the best brains in the British civil service' (Fanning, 1978, pp. 7–19). While Fanning's work was published in the late 1970s some of the principal issues it raises, such as the political and administrative symbiosis between the civil services of the UK and Ireland, is particularly useful in the current context. It is certainly a picture with which contemporary civil servants are all too familiar. As one Irish civil servant remarked, we would be 'generally on the same side as the British . . . looking at it against the background of broadly similar administrative and implementation arrangements, and also legal arrangements'. When you look at it in detail 'our basic codes of law are similar' and 'even when you look at it objectively, we will find ourselves in the same camp' (interviews, 1999).

It is also plausible to suggest that if transfer is to be successful, and in the case of Irish civil service reform it certainly has been, it is a path made easier by similarities in policy style (see Richardson and Jordan, 1982). Irish policy style has always attempted to avoid confrontation with firmly entrenched interests and has displayed a penchant for adding on to existing policy directives, a process that has effectively circumvented the need for a radical departure from existing legislation. In a situation similar to that presiding in the UK it assigned importance to consultation. On the one hand, formal and informal contacts with organised interests are an important source of political legitimacy, offsetting the possibility of revolt. On the other hand, they also act as an invaluable source of information for policy judgements. In other words, such relationships are generally reciprocal and are often based upon the maxim that 'only the wearer knows where the shoe pinches'. Granting access to organised interest groups in this way simply makes the system more effective in supplying public needs (Richardson and Jordan, 1982).

The concept of policy learning over a period of time and subsequent transfer is viewed as a typical scenario amongst those involved in the process of policy making (see Taylor and Horan, 2001). As one Irish civil servant candidly remarked, 'we can obtain information on what is happening in other member states or not; the importance of what's being said and in more practical terms how they managed to achieve it; or what new difficulties they experienced; we look at that and see to what extent we can learn from that' (interviews, 1999). Clearly, while policy transfer (and particularly learning from the UK) has been a familiar feature of Irish civil service practice over the years, it is undoubtedly an element of policy formation that expanded during the 1980s. Irish civil servants were regular participants at OECD conferences and seminars on civil service change, forums where initiatives taking place in New Zealand, Canada, Australia and the UK could be discussed. It was this interaction that was to have a profound influence on the trajectory of change over the next decade. As one influential civil servant recalls:

> Yes, I certainly came back with new ideas in terms of the quality of services particularly from Australia, also in terms of management development and *making managers manage*; doing more with less was the 'in' term at the time. There was also another in-put there, which was coming from the Americans. I can't remember the time but I remember getting friendly with the chairman of personnel management in the Carter administration. Carter was committed to changing the civil service and they had lots of terms, lots of terms came in like downsizing and so on but they had lots of other positive ideas as well. (interviews, 1999, emphasis added)

One of the more prominent legacies of this international contact was the Auditor and Comptroller Act of 1993. Prior to the 1993 Act, the C&AG had two statutory functions: the control of all Exchequer finances on behalf of the state and the auditing of government accounts. Influenced by developments taking place in Canada, Ireland chose to extend the remit of the C&AG and shifted its focus to an examination of the effectiveness of public spending. As one senior civil servant explains, 'there was a new type of auditing going into efficiency and effectiveness. The Canadians were big into that. We still had our C&AG, but he wasn't doing any large investigation into public expenditure as to whether it was being effective or not' (interviews, 1999).

With legislation now firmly in place, the C&AG's powers to audit were extended to include a range of public institutions: health boards, vocational educational committees, harbour authorities, regional tourism authorities and para-state agencies. The emphasis was placed firmly upon assessing the effectiveness of expenditure, a change which transferred the terminology from spending public resources legally to spending public resources sensibly (Verheijen and Millar, 1998, p. 111). To date, the C&AG has published a succession of reports on value for money in public service delivery, a number of which have been critical of current practice. Of these, one of the more notable was that into university procurement procedures.

Financed largely through block grants from the HEA, universities had previously enjoyed considerable autonomy with respect to procurement and budgetary policies. While the HEA had tentatively encouraged co-operation in a limited number of areas of procurement, it was an issue left largely to the universities. The C&AG's examination thus represented the first, albeit tentative step into a territory once considered out of its remit.

The C&AG's report argued that savings of between 5 and 15 per cent could be readily achieved with the type of 'best practice procedures' employed in the UK. Indeed, the report argued that alteration to procurements policy, particularly the need to ensure that 'procurement activities are properly controlled and economically and efficiently operated', was essential (C&AG, 1996a, p. iv). It also stressed the need to identify shortcomings in management control procedures, without which it was not possible to 'evaluate the current position and monitor purchasing effectiveness' (C&AG, 1996a, p. iv).

In explaining the flaws it had identified, the report observed that purchasing was devolved to such an extent that no one person was in a position to identify potential savings from the type of collaborative arrangements used in the UK.[5] In the C&AG's view it was a difficulty manifest in areas such as the purchase of chemicals (where responsibility lay with technical staff in each department, subject to the appropriate authorisation) and where some remarkable variations were recorded.[6]

The report was not simply an exercise in cost cutting; rather it was intended to be an examination of practice. It was concerned with establishing the benchmark for 'best practice' procedures in procurement, a process it felt should involve proper planning, management review and the use of well-trained staff. On these matters the report noted that no Irish university had centralised monitoring of procurement by management. There was little or no reporting on the value-for-money achievements of purchasing operations, and staff involved in purchasing received only 'on the job training' (C&AG, 1996a, pp. 18–25).

Chastened by the critical tone of much of the C&AG's analysis, the CHIU commissioned Deloitte Touche to prepare a response. While the report from Deloitte Touche recognised that 'some savings may be made', it argued that they were 'nowhere near as large as anticipated by the C&AG report' (Deloitte Touche, 1997, p. 1). Indeed, the response from Deloitte Touche argued that 'collaborative arrangements are only suitable to specific types of expenditure', that a 'consortium approach may be difficult' and that 'significant savings did not appear to be available in the areas reviewed' (Deloitte Touche, 1997, p. 6). While the report from Deloitte Touche appeared to provide a robust defence of the CHIU's position, it did acknowledge that there was scope for improvement and that training courses should be introduced to establish agreed 'strategy and practices' (Deloitte Touche, 1997, p. 1).

A further area of reform, which bore the hallmarks of the Canadian experience, was the attempt to change appointment procedures. In Canada every post which arose in the public sector was advertised and applicants were examined by lengthy interview and assessment procedures, including tests conducted by psychologists employed in order to evaluate the suitability of the candidate. In Ireland, the idea of open competition had been mooted in the early 1980s. As a senior civil servant pointed out, 'we were thinking of going this way with all the recruitment – specify the job, specify the person and then have a proper selection process' (interviews, 1999). The most significant problem during the 1980s was that Ireland was experiencing a crippling level of cutbacks in public finance. In such austere economic circumstances a lengthy process of recruitment was clearly out of the question and, as one senior civil servant remarked, to adopt the Canadian process would have 'cost you an arm and a leg'. Drawing upon the Canadian experience, the final response was to take the 'general idea but adopt it to the reality of our financial position' (interviews, 1999).

The policies adopted from Canada clearly complemented the general thrust of the ethos underpinning the TLAC. It is therefore important to recognise that while the TLAC itself represented an important development within the Irish civil service, it was part of a wider process increasingly conditioned by international developments. The TLAC acted as a catalyst for change within the Irish civil service, a starting point from which ideas about performance assessment could gestate. It had certainly become clear that it was no longer acceptable for those in the upper echelons to promote civil servants on the basis of familiarity, since any unsuitable candidate put forward would reflect poorly upon that department. As one senior civil servant remarked:

> There was a spin-off in terms of performance measurement because we devised a very good process of assessment for principal officers and upwards and I think that had a lot of beneficial spin-offs as well; they found they had to be increasingly honest with the assessment because if you were on a practical task and if you were giving it to somebody who wasn't up to it and he appeared before the committee then you got a message back as to what the hell is going on. (interviews 1999)

The frequency and length of international meetings within the Anglo-saxon public policy world has changed significantly during the 1990s, permitting a reciprocal and ongoing exchange of information and experience. The dynamic of such meetings also altered, as one civil servant points out:

> The first one was '85 in Canada, the second one was '87 in London, the third one was in London in 1990. There were two more, one in Canada and one in New Zealand. I think the Australian influence has changed and they were more interested in involving the United States and other countries such as Japan. There was also developing in the 1990s a strong OECD public management reform where the Americans were very significant. It wasn't just

> Europeans. Certainly I found it of tremendous use, not just simply the meetings but the contacts as well, there was a flow of information in between meetings. (interviews, 1999)

As the financial situation in Ireland deteriorated, an embargo on new appointments and cutbacks on both staff and wage levels were made. Indeed, the Fianna Fáil government of 1987–89 chose to ignore the clamour for change, buttressed by reluctance on the part of both politicians and civil servants to embrace the idea of recruitment from the private sector. By the late 1980s frustration within the civil service had become increasingly pervasive, as is evident in the remarks of one senior civil servant, who observed that:

> The difficulties were apparent in the system in terms of getting anything done. Just the sheer bureaucracy; lack of clarity about who had responsibility for what and lack of accountability. It became even more obvious that the whole centralised way of doing business really was militating against efficient service delivery. We need to think more strategically. I suppose that was the big lesson that was learned. (interviews, 1999)

Despite the severity of the setback experienced in the mid-1980s there was still a handful of civil servants determined to push through a new agenda of change, one that both incorporated and drew upon the wreckage of the 1985 white paper. For those who had attended the OECD conferences it was impossible to ignore the fact that performance measurement was now firmly on the international agenda. As one civil servant recollects, a large part of the conferences was dominated by ideas 'about performance. I found that in Australia and certainly in the States it was seriously on the agenda; as it turned out not that successfully at that stage but it certainly was a whole new idea' (interviews, 1999). Such change at an international level fitted uncomfortably into the state of play in Ireland, where the pervading view was that reform lagged significantly behind its Anglo-saxon counterparts. From here on in, the focal point for the 1990s would be a *strategic* approach to better (financial) management procedures for public organisation.

Strategic management reform in the 1990s

If the TLAC had been pivotal to the introduction of 'new blood' and had formed the first, albeit tentative step towards instilling a new ethos into the Irish civil service, the Co-ordinating Group of Secretaries provided the structural platform upon which this vision could find expression. This Group was to have a profound effect upon the changing nature of public organisation in the 1990s. With the once powerful faction of internal opponents now in retreat, the space was created in which new ideas could flourish. For the first time in the Irish system of public administration, departmental secretary generals came together in order to outline and negotiate available options. More importantly, such meetings signified the new level of recognition assigned to cross-cutting areas of public policy.

In 1994 the SMI was launched, prompting a renewed interest in the restructuring of public sector organisation and, unlike previous initiatives, attracting media attention, sustaining the impression of a new direction being taken in Irish politics (Verheijen and Millar, 1998, p. 97). The principal components of the NPM came to the fore in the SMI: devolved administration, decentralisation, accountability, co-ordination, evaluation and the adoption of flexible work practices.

The *strategic* dimension to the new initiative included the incorporation of a 'strategy statement' for individual departments. These would be published every three years and were intended to mark a new era of clarification and demarcation within the civil service structure. Prior to 1994, there were no formal projections by individual departments, which had led to a situation where the planning of departmental business remained predominantly ad hoc and inefficient. The express intention was to clarify and filter down government policy to individual branches of the civil service and flatten the rigid hierarchical structure so typical of the Irish administrative style. Although it remains a precarious task to define a 'result' in public policy circles, the primary aim was to shift the significance away from inputs to outputs and, when complemented with the introduction of performance management, to regenerate a stagnant work culture.

While a full-scale overhaul of the Ministers and Secretaries Act of 1924 was deemed unnecessary, there can be little doubt that the lessons of the 1980s had been taken on board. This time, reform would be achieved *with* legislation. Thus the Public Service Management Act, 1997, sought to reconcile a desire to ensure that a minister's political authority would not be undermined with the release of civil servants to manage service delivery. Indeed, Section 3 of the 1997 legislation is devoted to addressing this issue. In particular, it attempts to 'surf' the tension between ensuring a prominent (and autonomous) role for civil service managers while retaining a minister's pre-eminent political position. This particular feat is achieved by defining more carefully those areas where a minister intervenes on a 'normal' basis (strategy statements, the allocation of resources, policy) and those where intervention would be viewed as 'unusual, unforeseen and infrequent developments'. This latter category is dominated by managerial concerns: the day-to-day business of a department; implementing and monitoring government policies, preparing strategy statements, progress reports and ensuring the proper use of resources (Tutty, 1998, p. 90).

Although it is a reform welcomed by many, there are those who remain sceptical, convinced that it could engender a 'distance' between the minister and his or her department, constructing a semi-detached authority who would be seen only when 'things were going well' (Tutty, 1998, p. 101). Tutty, however, remains more confident, suggesting that the Act expressly states that the 'minister is responsible for the performance of functions that are assigned to the department' (Tutty, 1998, p. 101). It is at this juncture that the role envisaged for strategy statements manifests itself as a crucial managerial tool. While the secretaries general have responsibility for the preparation of these statements, it is only with the express approval of the minister, who may at any time seek amendments through directions in writing.

Devolved budgeting

The traditional strategy for controlling the running costs of the civil service had always involved the close scrutiny of the Department of Finance and required individual departmental submissions to justify specific levels of expenditure. During periods of intense fiscal constraint, such as those which prevailed during most of the 1980s, expenditure would have been controlled principally through either stalling recruitment or reducing staff, a process which ensured that civil service numbers declined from a peak of 30,800 in 1981 to 25,600 in 1990. As the scale of expenditure rose during this period, and negotiations became more protracted and tortuous, the Department of Finance delegated the power to sanction in a number of areas, up to agreed limits and subject to central guidelines.

Influenced by events taking place in other OECD countries, where the trend had been to move away from centralised control, government sought to devolve decision-making to the operational level. Under this system, departmental heads would be responsible for fixed administrative budgets, agreed for a two-to-three-year timespan with the intention of establishing greater levels of managerial autonomy. Devolved budgeting, which by 1999 had completed three cycles, involved the delegation of decision-making with the express aim of establishing clarity, reducing the 'clutter' of bureaucracy and defining more effectively civil service spending procedures. By shifting the locus of decision-making towards the line management of individual departments, and providing incentives for creative responses to traditional spending practices, it was anticipated that costs would be reduced and an 'efficiency dividend' reaped.

The starting point of the administrative budget system was a set of bilateral agreements between the Department of Finance and individual departments, in which a budgetary allocation and a baseline figure would be decided. Under devolved budgetary arrangements, departments would control decisions on expenditure for staff recruitment and promotion (subject to the overall agreed budget). In addition, incentives to reduce expenditure were introduced and those savings that accrued could be 'carried over' from one year to another (virement).[7] The traditional practice had been framed by the maxim of 'use or lose it'. Not surprisingly, under such arrangements departments tended to 'hoard' during the early part of the financial year and 'gorge' at a later date. This 'within-year flexibility' was complemented by a 'between-year' flexibility whereby departments were allowed to carry over unspent balances from one year to the next. In practice, while most departments have used this facility, some have felt that there should be greater scope to transfer funds and others that a cash limit should be used rather than a percentage of funds.

By allowing greater departmental autonomy, devolved budgeting was designed not only to reduce costs but to alter the nature of spending practice. It was also envisaged that departments would transfer authority for spending to their line managers and, for the first time, the opportunity was afforded to establish quantitative indicators from which to assess the effectiveness of spending (C&AG, 1996a, p. 5). Monitoring was therefore an integral element of devolved budgeting. However, as the C&AG report noted, there was little in the way of consistent practice: no schedule for group meetings was arranged, there was often a 'confusion' over when meetings were to be convened, and there was little in the way of annual reports from monitoring groups. Indeed, in some instances groups did not produce a report in any shape or form. As if to compound such matters, those departments which produced reports expressed disappointment at a lack of response from the Department of Finance (C&AG, 1996b, p. 23).

A further area of weakness exposed by the C&AG's report into devolved budgeting was the omission of items such as pensions and maintenance costs, two of the more expensive items of the civil service. And yet, despite these omissions overall running costs continued to escalate during the 1990s. Indeed, between 1988 and 1996 overall running costs rose from IR£352m to IR£850m, an increase of 24 per cent above inflation for the same period. To those who had advocated the adoption of devolved budgeting, it was all the more disappointing to find that running costs did not appear to have been significantly affected by the shift to administrative budgets. As the C&AG's report pointed out, increases in those departments that operated administrative budgets and those that did not followed a similar pattern. More disturbing, perhaps, was the C&AG's finding that non-pay running costs increased faster than pay costs over this period. As a consequence non-pay costs accounted for 29 per cent of the total running costs in 1996 as opposed to 24 per cent in 1988 (C&AG, 1996a, p. 9). It was also envisaged that devolved budgeting would have a beneficial impact upon staffing levels. Between 1988 and 1990 staff numbers had been reduced from 27,900 to 25,600 (–8 per cent). However, by the beginning of 1995 numbers had risen to 28,400, prompting the government to introduce restrictions on further appointments. Under devolved budgeting agreements, authority had been delegated to departments but, as the C&AG report notes, there had been little in the way of any significant change in practice (C&AG, 1996b, p. 11).

The issue of staffing (or more commonly staff reductions) had been a source of consternation during the 1980s. Under the SMI, however, the issue would shift away from a simple and crude preoccupation with numbers to that of flexibility in work practice. In particular, issues such as grading would now become inextricably linked to the desire to flatten hierarchies and 'make managers manage'. To those who wished to defend 'traditional practice', it was essential that the civil service be 'seen in its entirety', until strategic objectives were rarely if ever being assigned to individual departments, and the career paths of civil servants facilitating the invaluable cross-pollination of ideas and experience between departments. It was felt that these were benefits that should not be sacrificed at the altar of political fashion or indeed the whim of the markets.

By the 1990s, however, such views were no longer in the ascendant. Spurred on by changes taking place in the Anglo-saxon public policy environment, where the philosophy of the NPM was to the fore, the idea of a unified civil service occupied by 'all-rounders and generalists' appeared dated. The introduction of new technology and a shift towards a more consumer-oriented focus meant that civil service tasks could no longer be seen as homogeneous.

In theory at least, grading systems are designed to provide internal relativity between jobs. While they may not accurately reflect 'market values' they should, nevertheless, provide an indication of the complexity of the job. In practice such issues are rarely, if ever, uncontentious. Within the civil service, grading affects pay, status and trade union affiliation (Buckley *et al.*, 1999, p. 9). Indeed, as Buckley *et al.* note, the political dynamic which underpin attempts to reconcile such conflicting agendas has meant that over time, whatever logic existed for a service-wide grading system has been systematically eroded, as 'a plethora of once-off arrangements have been put in place to sort out particular problems such as skill retention or solve or avert an industrial dispute' (Buckley *et al.*, 1999, p. 9).

Grading had been one of a number of contentious issues addressed in the 1985 white paper, which recommended that the distinction between staff officer and executive officer be abolished. At the behest of the Civil and Public Service Union, it was a move allowed to 'die quietly', largely because the union was concerned about the loss of representation rights for a supervisory grade (Buckley *et al.*, 1999, p. 13). A more significant attempt to grasp this particular nettle surfaced in a proposal from the Department of Finance to 'broadband' as part of the restructuring under the PCW framework. This initiative had included a new division of grades between paper keeper and assistant principal into three broad bands of clerical, executive and administrative (reducing ten to six levels). As Buckley *et al.* point out, progression within the broad band would be through increments on a very long scale or by way of accelerated progression on merit – the equivalent to a kind of promotion within the band (Buckley *et al.*, 1999, p. 14). It was certainly a move which sat comfortably with the findings of the Hay report, which had argued that it was difficult to conceive of any modern organisation which had more than 'four to six levels of complexity' (Buckley *et al.*, 1999, p. 12).

While the quest for a flatter structure also fits comfortably with much of the rhetoric that accompanies NPM, it is by no means a move without difficulty. There is, for example, a problem in reconciling the tension between flatter structures, where promotion is limited, and providing an incentive structure in the public service, where promotion remains the principal source of reward for good performance.[8] Moreover, as Jabes and Zussman's work in Canada confirms, it may well be the case that there is a need within public sector organisations to create a 'visible and objectively satisfying' climate in which the assignment to 'powerful committees', public recognition and task variety are to the fore (Jabes and Zussman, 1988; see Boyle, 1997a).

In Ireland there is clearly a potential problem in linking remuneration and performance in the SMI. As Roche has argued, there is considerable international evidence to suggest that in the public sector managers do not believe that pay is the single most important source of motivation among employees (Roche, 1998, p. 14). In Australia, for example, the Task Force on Management Improvement found that the rewards staff preferred were 'personal recognition' and more 'career development options'. Such views were confirmed in the wider OECD survey of 11 public sector agencies, where performance-related pay was constantly ranked lowest in managers' expressed preferences (OECD, 1997). In addition, attempts to introduce incentives have been persistently undermined by poor planning, design and management (Roche, 1998, p. 14). It may well be the case that performance-related pay is an important element of the SMI, but it is far from clear whether it will generate the efficiencies anticipated by many.

A further area in which it was anticipated that devolved budgeting would reap benefits was in the reduction of correspondence between the Department of Finance and other departments. Prior to devolved budgeting several sections of the Department of Finance had been responsible for setting budgets for all departments. Under such arrangements it was customary for these expenditure estimates to be 'settled' through protracted negotiations. One of the more prominent difficulties encountered in this arrangement was that while the Department of Finance might lack detailed operational knowledge of individual departments, it was still required to 'negotiate' cutbacks. The initial response was to reduce the 'constant' pressure to 'extract as much as possible' from these negotiations, prompting the emergence of the Expenditure Review Committee. By the 1990s salvation appeared to lie in the introduction of devolved budgeting.

Under the arrangements envisaged within devolved budgeting, a baseline estimate would be agreed, whereupon the onus would shift to the department to justify the increases sought. In such circumstances, those departments seeking additional staff resources would have to carry out a review of the existing staff deployment. However, while the C&AG's report confirms that a reduction in the amount of correspondence between Finance and individual departments has taken place, it remained far more circumspect on whether departments have changed entrenched practices and moved to a systematic appraisal of the use of resources (C&AG, 1996b, p. 18).

The administrative budgets system was also based upon the assumption that once introduced, an 'efficiency dividend' would be converted into savings on running costs (C&AG, 1996b, p. 18). The target set for the first two cycles was a reduction of 2 per cent in real terms in each of the years 1992 and 1993. It has been a contentious area, one that reveals further a disparity between the slogans of change and institutional resistance – a difference, if you prefer, between the rhetoric which often accompanies the publication of glossy brochures and the reality of implementing polices which challenge vested interests. Discussion, consultation, negotiation and ultimately compromise remain firmly the order of the day.

The Department of Finance argued that the efficiency dividend should be incorporated into the second cycle of agreements, a move resisted by the larger departments. As the C&AG report noted, of the 24 departments participating, 10 would agree further contracts *only* if no dividend applied. In its response the Co-ordinating Group of Secretaries argued that all departments should cede to an efficiency dividend, although even this was qualified with the proviso that it might take the form of 'demonstrable improvements in service' (C&AG, 1996b, p. 18).

The C&AG report was also critical of the manner in which administrative budgeting was promoted. While it acknowledged that the Department of Finance had initiated or collaborated in seminars, commissioned a number of studies and provided operational guidelines, the report was, nevertheless, critical of the fact that it had been left up to individual departments to see how administrative budgeting would be implemented. There had been no training for staff and no transfer of personnel, expertise or models from Finance to departments (C&AG, 1996b, p. 24). The response from the Department of Finance was that it was not expected to 'hand-hold' other departments that were pursuing much-needed reform. However, as the C&AG report noted, in other jurisdictions, devolved budgeting control has resulted in resources in the lead agency being freed up, which are then used to promote best practice and to carry out evaluations. In the UK, for example, the Treasury established a list of contact points for practical advice on particular topics in order to improve line management. In a similar manner, Australia developed a management improvement advisory committee to promote good practice and investigate the extent to which devolution occurred within departments (C&AG, 1996b, p. 24).

Devolved budgeting was clearly designed to complement performance measurement, since it would involve the introduction of quantitative indicators to assess the effectiveness of running costs in meeting programme objectives. Such indicators would form the basis of setting targets for new contracts. However, as the C&AG's report noted, 'little or no progress had been made in devising quantitative indicators' (C&AG, 1996b, p. 23). The Department of Finance conceded that it might have been overly ambitious to expect devolved budgeting to have made significant progress in the area of performance indicators and output measurement, given its focus on administrative resources.

Programme review

Programme review is by no means new. As Boyle observes, there has been a succession of specific reviews undertaken, ranging from the Telesis report in 1982 to the Culliton report in 1992. In addition, there have been department-based three-yearly reviews of industrial performance, a science policy review and the construction of the Salmon Management Task Force in 1996.[9] With the exception of the evaluation of European structural funds, however, they tend to be ad hoc and limited in scope (Boyle, 1997a, p. 8).

Mounting difficulties with the existing mechanisms for programme evaluation prompted the changes devised. The kernel of the debate was astutely articulated by the 1989 annual report of the C&AG, a report which exposed the failure of the Business Expansion Scheme to supply reliable information in relation to the actual effects of the investment. As a consequence the focus shifted towards the need to strengthen financial control of public sector operations, with the intention of ensuring that all spending programmes would be reviewed over a three-year period (Boyle, 1997a, p. 8). It is likely that this arrangement will be limited in scope and vary between departments depending on the size and range of programmes for which they are responsible (Boyle, 1997a, p. 11).[10] There are several different areas where this could be located: with programme managers, in a corporate staff group or in independent units. The issue of where to locate programme review depends upon what is being addressed and the skill required. The frequency of such reviews will also be dependent on resources and the size of the programme.

The slow pace of change to devolved procedures in Ireland has come under close scrutiny. Certainly, a framework to implement purchasing independence for departments was established in 1990, in which bulk budgeting procedures were introduced with the aim of permitting greater financial control for individual managers. An agreement was made with the Department of Finance concerning an advanced budget over a three-year period and in return, a genuine reduction in costs by 2 per cent per annum was expected. By 1991, three-year budgets were in operation in most departments, loosening the reign of central control over resources; and yet the initiative failed to include any significant reduction of bureaucratic control. It only incorporated expenditure in areas such as training, remuneration, travel and consultancy, and although the move was welcomed generally, considerable frustration exists within the civil service that it has not gone far enough.

There are also other areas of concern with regard to the thrust, pace and extent of change. Roche, for example, has been struck by the 'heady optimism' which envelops the change envisaged under the SMI and writes that even allowing for the fact that the picture has been painted with a 'broad brush', the discussion has been 'excessively theoretical and text bookish' (Roche, 1998, p. 4). Indeed, he goes on to suggest that the raft of changes entailed, ranging from coherent HR strategies at departmental, agency and company levels to performance-related pay and flexibility in the deployment of employees, has been presented as 'inherently unproblematic' (Roche, 1998, p. 4). And yet, experience from both the private sector and other countries in the Anglo-saxon public policy environment would suggest otherwise. As he notes, the introduction of HR management strategies in the public sector is arguably more difficult. Although politicians 'may be expected to sanction strategies when they are couched in broad and abstract terms, they nevertheless seem very likely to intervene on grounds of short-term pragmatism' (Roche, 1998, p. 8).

If reform is not to be mired in political wrangles, then it is paramount that it encompass the involvement of staff and trade unions. This represents a fundamental and dramatic change in the framework of Irish administration, and yet measures cannot be approved without constant negotiation and discussion with the trade unions. As one civil servant describes it:

> Performance management is such an enormous cultural change; it has to be managed. We haven't any hope of getting it successfully unless it is by partnership with the unions. I am absolutely certain that if we attempt to bring in a performance management system without partnership it would be exactly the same as the failed appraisal system that we've had over the last twenty years. (interviews, 1998)

If the problems which have beset other countries are to be avoided then the HR management strategies to be invoked will need to avoid becoming an exercise in 'head counts' or cost reductions. It is certainly plausible to suggest, as Roche does, that the conversion of existing civil servants with administrative expertise into HR managers is far from unproblematic (Roche, 1998, pp. 11–13).

Some concluding remarks

The most striking feature of recent public sector reforms in Ireland has been the promotion of managerial accountability, the underlying principle of which is a proposed increase in the capacity of managers to manage. It is a reform agenda that implies the creation of a framework in which designated units remain (principally, but not exclusively) under the control of departmental managers and in which information systems are linked to a new culture of audit. It also implies a revision in the terms that form the bedrock of the relationship between politicians and civil servants. Here, the legal tends to give way to arguments that justify practices on the grounds of economic efficiency. Indeed, the language of the civil service is now imbued with a glossary of terms once the concern of the accounting profession: audits, value for money and financial monitoring. As Boyle has observed, such a shift also implies a move towards a contract culture where the legitimacy of actions is defined in terms of the agreed exchange between the respective parties (Boyle, 1997a, p. 18). The arguments forwarded to defend such moves focus upon the (beneficial) role that financial incentives play. All too often, however, there is a tendency to downplay the limits to such arrangements, so that there may be a tendency to limit actions not directly linked to such financial negotiations. In many ways these initiatives are not new, and it is not inevitable that they will be successful.

Notes

1 A succession of political scandals rocked Irish politics. They were to result in a series of tribunals investigating corruption in the planning system in Dublin, the illegal use of offshore bank accounts in the Cayman islands, and controversy surrounding the award of mobile phone licences.

2 This is a position which clearly owes considerable debt to Ward (1993) and to extensive discussions with Professor David Marsh, University of Birmingham.

3 Hay and Marsh rightly caution against an over-emphasis upon, and a privileging of, the discursive, when they suggest that 'it is important to recognise that the social, economic and political context constrains, circumscribes and delimit the ideas held about [the policies] and the related extent to which ideas mediate, conditions and circumscribe the realm of the social, political and economic intervention . . . the material does not determine the discursive, just as the discursive does not determine the material' (Hay and Marsh, 2000, p. 9).

4 From the outset the Department of Foreign Affairs and the Office of Revenue Commissioners were excluded from this ethos of external competition.

5 For example, in the area of insurance, the report noted that thirty three Universities in the UK had arranged a combined agreement which reduced costs by 15 per cent. It also observed that in 1993 an Irish broker had approached the HEA with an offer which could produce savings in the region of 25 per cent (C&AG, 1996a, p. 8).

6 University College Dublin negotiated the purchase of 200 containers of dichlorothemane in 2.5-litre quantities, a total volume of 500 litres, at a cost of £1,444. A similar quantity purchased in bulk would have cost £284. See C&AG (1996a pp. 9–18) for its findings on costs of library periodicals, books, furniture, computers, photocopying, international travel, cleaning and security.

7 This was subject to revision in the second cycle, where the dividend could be waived if the Department of Finance was satisfied that the reduction would seriously impair existing services or if the department undertook not to seek additions to the agreed budgetary allocations, other than unit costs for the years 1994–96 (C&AG, 1996a, p. 6).

8 As part of a move to flatten hierarchies (and the rigid division of responsibilities between agencies or departments) further, *Delivering Better Government* suggested that there were a number of vital national issues such as childcare, drugs and employment where there was a need to introduce team-based working through cross-functional teams. Such teams would be given a specific remit and a prescribed time period in which to work. This was introduced to the Valuations Office in 1994, where the existing framework utilised three separate divisions of labour: management, clerical and administrative. Reform of this structure involved the realignment of individuals into specific teams, incorporating managers, administrative and clerical workers to create particular units. According to Boyle, it met with considerable approval, from the viewpoint of staff satisfaction, customer service and the level of flexibility incurred. It also led to the formation of specific groups assigned on a one-off basis to gain

a particular objective. For more detail on issues surrounding the use of team-based working, and potential pitfalls, see Boyle (1997b).

9 There are also instances where senior managers meet with line managers, for example, in the Department of Public Enterprise and Social welfare. Since 1988 there has also been the Efficiency Audit group with a brief to examine the workings of individual departments and in recent times the SMI Co-ordinating Group . . . there is also the value for money audit facility undertaken by the Officer of the C&AG . . . However, he cannot directly assess the effectiveness of policy' (Boyle, 1997a, p. 10).

10 In Australia, where this agreement has been most extensively used, it is organised into individual agencies and departments and is devolved to programme managers. There is still an issue of whether to use in-house or outside expertise. See Boyle (1999, p. 12).

4

'Contestation in the countryside': rural governance in the era of the Celtic Tiger

It should have surprised few of those who endured the long periods of high structural unemployment during the 1980s to see the issue of economic growth figure so prominently in the political discourse of the 1990s. However, in the early years of the new millennium debate seems focused on the need for change within the political structures of the Irish polity. Almost imperceptibly, politics has become inundated with demands for greater political transparency, enhanced political participation, and the construction of political structures capable of reconciling the accelerated momentum towards a flexible economy with the retention of a democratic impulse to reduce social exclusion. There are few areas in Irish politics where these issues have figured more prominently than in rural development.

That rural areas have undergone a dramatic transformation since the early 1970s hardly requires to be stated. Successive reforms to agricultural support at the EU level, and the free market ethos which pervades international agreements such as GATT, have ensured that the contemporary countryside has been reconstituted around new relationships of production, consumption and exchange (Marsden, 1999, p. 504). It also seems likely that the social and political processes associated with globalisation will largely define the future trajectory of this restructuring. It is against such a backdrop that those such as Marsden have argued that rural space will be reordered, as the forces of globalisation alter the relationship between the state and the private sector. Policies such as the privatisation of state enterprises, deregulation and attempts at re-regulation will ensure that state intervention is fundamentally reorganised (Marsden, 1999).

To others, the processes that contributed to the changing nature of rural governance are better understood in terms of an ongoing 'hollowing out' of the nation state. It is argued that the functions of central and local government have changed. The discretion available to public servants has been curtailed and the implementation of policy now resides with a variety of new agencies.

If there remains reason for informed scepticism about the process of 'hollowing out' and its alleged impact on the rural economy, there can be little doubt that changes to the Common Agricultural Policy (CAP) have had a significant bearing on the changing nature of rural governance. CAP consisted of an intervention system designed to provide internal price support and protection against external shocks to European agricultural markets. Integral to this regime was the desire to sustain ongoing increases in production. Yet reform was firmly on the agenda by the 1980s, as a succession of EU member states expressed deep reservations about escalating cost. The problems within this regime, however, extended beyond the limited parameters of public financing. The industrialisation of agricultural production and the move towards larger, more intensive farms had a dramatic (and often detrimental) effect upon the relationship between agriculture and the environment. It should come as little surprise that it was placed under the spotlight by an environmental lobby that sought to challenge an agenda that had persisted with financial inducements to increase agricultural production at the expense of the European ecosystem.

In the short term at least, the response was to put agricultural support in a framework that displayed a new ecological sensitivity, reconstructing the farmer as the custodian of the countryside. Indeed, one could be easily forgiven for thinking that the proliferation of regulations in agri-environmental policy (Special Areas of Conservation [SACS], the Natural Habitats Directive) signifies substantial reform and that the demands of environmentalists have largely been met. However, if new policies such as the Rural Environmental Protection Scheme (REPS) have undoubtedly brought ecological benefits to the countryside, it should be recognised that agricultural interests had largely circumscribed the thrust, content and pace of change. There are few areas that highlight this more clearly than that of farm waste.

The issue of farm sludge, or to be more accurate, whether farm sludge should have been subject to an integrated pollution control (IPC) licence, was a matter of some controversy during the passage of the Waste Management Act. The environmental lobby insisted that regulatory control of farm waste had been woefully inadequate and that slurry spreading should be subject to the EPA's IPC licensing regime. The minister of the environment remained far more circumspect, adamant that it would be neither 'appropriate nor practical' since the *agricultural community would not be able to bear that type of imposition*' (*Dáil Debates*, 1995, Vol. 460, p. 85, emphasis added).

It is an example worth drawing attention to because it confirms the enduring strength of the agricultural policy community. Despite waning public support for agricultural subsidy during the 1990s, the agricultural lobby remains well organised, well connected and, more importantly, institutionalised within the policy process. As one politician acerbically remarked, when difficulties arose, or when trouble was brewing, the buffalo could be heard running down the corridors of Leinster House.

This is not an argument that maintains that policy always involves occasional political favours to secure temporary political respite for a minority coalition, a feature synonymous with the political administration of the late 1990s. Rather, it is about granting 'privileged' political access to organised interests that regularly contribute to an agenda formed in a tightly closed 'policy community', one characterised by a limited number of participants, where members frequently interact and seek to establish a consensus. What remains important is how policy is both formed *and* sustained. The community will have an influence on, although it will clearly not determine, policy outcomes (see Marsh and Rhodes, 1992, p. 23). This is not to suggest that 'deals' are struck which *always* favour a particular group; rather, access allows participation to a policy-making environment which seeks to minimise political disturbance and establish (a favourable) continuity in policy.

Few would argue with the contention that the stability of this policy community contributed significantly to continuity in agricultural policy over a prolonged period of time, or that it profoundly shaped the nature of rural governance. And yet, pessimism has engulfed this policy community amid a sustained period of turmoil. Clearly, while waning public sympathy for agricultural support and an expansion in the membership of the EU have been two of the more prominent issues to have impacted upon rural governance, they have been accompanied by a succession of controversial food and public health scares. Although the media's gaze has fallen upon the political and social drama associated with the collapse of beef sales, it is a crisis that involves more than the haemorrhaging of a particular market. The political fallout of the bovine spongiform encelopathy (BSE) controversy has meant a shift in regulatory responsibilities, creating a new epistemic community charged with restoring public confidence in the regulation of food (see Taylor, 2003). One of the more important outcomes of change in regulatory procedures will be to bring into question the legitimacy of the privileged access previously enjoyed by bodies such as the Irish Farmers' Association (IFA) (see Richardson, 2000).

There can be little doubt that in the Irish case the agricultural policy community exhibited both stability and exclusiveness (see Adshead, 1996). However, there are also clear signs of instability emerging. In part, this can be attributed to the very success of the policy community, which has become a cause for concern. It seems plausible to suggest, for example, that the success of interest group involvement tends too encourage over-crowding and an unstable policy environment. In addition, such policy communities may also become destabilised as a result of 'shock' exogenous factors. As Richardson has noted, Epstein's work on French agricultural interest shows the difficulty the French government had in balancing the interests of agriculture and other sectors of the economy during the tortuous GATT negotiations. The result was the decision by the French government to abandon its close ties with the French agricultural policy community (Richardson, 2000).

Of more import to the arguments presented here is the fact that entrenched policy communities can become destabilised because of a shift in the policy-making terrain as the locus of decision-making shifts to an alternative policy venue. This is not to suggest that producer-led interests are not to the fore, or that consumer and environmental arguments have necessarily gained ascendancy. Rather, it is to suggest that the formation of agencies such as the Food Safety Authority of Ireland has altered the venue in which decision-making is located, undermining the once fabled stability of the Irish agricultural policy community.

While issues of pollution and animal welfare have become prominent elements of political contestation in the countryside, there have been other environmental issues that have served to frame and constrain rural development. For instance, the value placed upon rural areas for different types of tourism or recreation (landscape) have not only served as potential sources of new forms of employment but have acted as a new source of political conflict. Greer, for example, has noted that while government policy has been keen to promote the jobs potential in 'green tourism', it has often ignored the fact that changes to landscape have very often proved controversial, serving as a barrier to some forms of development (Greer, 1992).

These are sentiments that emerge quite forcefully in documents such as the Department of the Environment's report *The Countryside and the Rural Economy*. Here the government stipulated that its policy for the countryside was aimed at enhancing 'the quality of life in rural communities by conserving the nation's countryside heritage and sustaining the rural economy . . . to allow development with no regard for conservation would lead to the destruction of the countryside we value. The best protection for the countryside is a healthy rural economy' (cited in Greer, 1992, p. 99).

At best, it is a position that disregards the potential for conflict between a community's interpretation of what may be 'acceptable development' and that of a state agency or supranational body. At worst, it may ignore altogether the intergenerational dimension to (sustainable) rural development: what a community may find acceptable development today neglects consideration of future generations. These were certainly among the issues that arose in the controversies surrounding attempts to construct inter-pretative centres in fragile ecosystems such as that in the Burren, County Clare. In a very important sense, environmentalism in the countryside reinforces the view that rural space is far from a single, unified entity and that it is often riven with conflicting interests.

If these constraints have their origins in the emergence of environmen-talism in the countryside, non-agricultural forces such as the rise and decline of particular industries and service sectors have compounded them. In addition, problems have surfaced about the geographic pattern of employment concentration, which has often focused on large urban areas. This was stimulated largely by an industrial policy that resulted in high levels of unemployment, low incomes, poverty, low levels of service ameni-ties and population decline in rural economies (NESC, 1993, p. 5).

While such observations remain useful at a general level it is also possi-ble to identify variations across different sectors of the economy. Thus, for example, there are significant differences between the experiences of for-eign owned multinational capital, which tend to be grant-aided, high-tech and export-oriented, and of indigenous capital, which is largely (but by no means exclusively) concerned with domestic markets. For example, Tovey has succinctly observed that 'we need to start from a view of rural Ireland as the spatial and social manifestation of global capitalist development and that both rural and urban areas are shaped by the same broad develop-mental process' (Tovey, 1999, p. 101).

During the 1960s public policy in Ireland was marked by a significant departure from the protectionist practices associated with preceding decades. With policy circumscribed by the imperative to attract foreign investment, it was the national rather than the regional focus that was paramount (Boylan, 1992). By the late 1970s and early 1980s the struc-tural problems associated with uneven development prompted a shift towards a regional focus within public policy. As a consequence of this industrial policy most rural regions experienced the fastest level of growth. And yet, as Boylan observes, despite the Irish state's attempt to orchestrate development around growth centres, little in the way of sustained employ-ment opportunities was generated in small towns and villages (Boylan, 1992).

By the mid- to late 1980s the focus of policy had shifted once more, revealing a concern less with issues about economic justice or equity than with creating employment opportunities where the infrastructure was sufficiently modernised. Embracing the rhetoric of the free market, Irish governments of the 1990s eschewed the policy tools of state-led moderni-sation, focusing more keenly upon creating centres of excellence where clusters of internationally competitive high-tech sectors could develop (McGrath and Canavan, 2001). While multinational firms continue to have a predisposition to locate in less industrialised areas (because they either do not require specialised skills or do not need to be close to suppliers), they actually employ more in the east, south-west and mid-west regions (O'Malley, 1992; NESC, 1993). What also remains patently clear is that the pattern of international investment in Ireland continues to be insufficient to maintain employment in many rural areas (NESC, 1994, p. 43).

Of more import, perhaps, is the belated recognition on the part of policy makers that although agriculture may still dominate the use of land, it no longer dominates employment in rural economies (Marsden, 1999, p. 510). For example, the NESC has been moved to note that 'while it can be said that some rural areas display a high incidence of all these problems, almost all rural areas experience one of them: lack of sufficient employment opportunities' (NESC, 1993, p. 5). Indeed, in a more pessimistic light the report went on to comment that 'there is no conceivable improvement in competitiveness which would solve the problem of excess capacity' and 'that underlying trends in world markets point to the importance of looking for alternative farm enterprises as well as off-farm employment in order to maintain economic activity and population in rural areas' (NESC, 1994, p. 314).

In an attempt to create a policy framework that responds to a myriad of problems facing the rural economy, it is possible to discern at least two core principles. There can be little doubt that policy has made a sustained attempt to encourage diversification at the farm level (pluriactivity), thereby accentuating a feature of the restructuring of the rural economy since the early 1970s The concentration of agri-business among multinational companies has meant a shift to larger, more intensive forms of agricultural production. As a consequence, farming has witnessed an upsurge in the use of new technology and a corresponding bias towards a reduction in the use of labour. In other words, as farms invest more in new technology they have had to increase in size in order to offset the impact of increases in investment. Indeed, as Tovey *et al.* point out, Irish agriculture is now firmly embedded in the global system of agri-business, serving to underline the difficulty individual states have in regulating national markets (Tovey, 1996, pp. 17-18). In turn, agriculture becomes increasingly exposed to macro-level problems such as market volatility or interest rate movements.

There are now two critical strategic actors involved in the global food system: multinational capital and nation states. Moreover, it is possible to discern two types of activity in which multinational capital is involved.

First, there are those companies with established links with the chemical and pharmaceutical sectors (vertically integrated) where the aim is to replace elements of (traditional) agricultural production with mass-produced ingredients. Second, there has been a concentration in the businesses associated with food processing and transportation (Tovey, 1999, p. 103). In such a business environment farmers, as producers, are faced with the dilemma of whether to become vertically integrated in the chain of production (implying a diminishing level of control over input) or face becoming sidelined by a market dominated by larger players (see Tovey, 1999, p. 103). Clearly farmers are now increasingly constrained by events taking place at an international level, as multinational capital strives to reduce barriers to competition and release the forces of the free market (Curtin *et al.*, 1996, p. 19). In turn, government policy has become increasingly predisposed to securing food production methods that seek to 'add value' and attempt to find a niche within export markets.

Such difficulties are compounded by the varied impact of these issues across rural space. This is highlighted in the NESC's observation that increasing specialisation and concentration do not occur randomly, largely because tillage farms tend to dominate in areas around Leinster. Moreover, while cattle farming has declined in most areas this has been most pronounced in the Midlands, west and north-west, so that the most profitable system of farming in these areas has witnessed a relative decline (NESC, 1994, p. 39).

Despite the fact that Ireland has experienced an unprecedented period of economic growth since the early 1990s the number of people employed in agriculture has declined. Between 1993 and 1997 the number of farms fell from 159,400 to just under 148,000 (–7 per cent). If the projections from the Department of Agriculture, Food and Rural Development are anything to go by, the figure is likely to be reduced to under 100,000 by 2020 (Kinsella *et al.*, 2000, p. 485). It is not just that there has been a corresponding fall in employment, although this has clearly been the case. Rather, the nature of agricultural employment appears to have changed, revealing an increased dependence upon a part-time work and pluriactivity (Kinsella *et al.*, 2000, p. 485). Once again, it also has an important spatial dimension. The shift towards greater dependence on non-farm incomes varies across different counties and has been most pronounced in areas such as Ulster and Connaught (see Table 4.1).

It is hardly surprising therefore that policy at both a national and a supranational level should seek to encourage diversification at the farm level. Here, one of the more important features of the reform to the CAP has been the shift away from price support to direct payments, with schemes such as the farmers' Early Retirement Scheme. In addition, the reform agenda affords more autonomy to adapt elements of the CAP to national circumstances, so that in Ireland every effort has been made to reduce the movement of milk quotas from the western region (NESC, 1994).

Table 4.1 Distribution of two samples of farm households by sources of household income (%), 1994

Source	West	East
Farming only	12.7	25.5
Farming and non-farm work	19.2	42.7
Farming and state transfers	32.6	14.6
Farming, non-farm work and state transfers	29.2	4.3
Other	6.2	12.8

Source: NESC (1994, p. 40).

The impact of policies designed to encourage diversification has meant that between 1972 and 1998 farm diversification in Ireland rose from 32 per cent to 44 per cent, a phenomenon by no means exclusive to Ireland (Kinsella *et al.*, 2000, p. 481). In 1998 some 47 per cent of Irish farms were engaged in part-time employment, the importance of which can be gauged from the fact that income from sources other than farming accounted for almost 40 per cent of total household income.

There can be little doubt then that pluriactivity has been an important development in rural Ireland, particularly (but by no means exclusively) in areas such as Roscommon. Opinion remains divided, however, over whether pluriactivity is simply a short-term strategy to offset the ongoing and apparently interminable decline of agriculture, or if it is more than a transitory phenomenon, signifying a shift towards new life styles, in which part-time farming is viewed as part of a wider attempt to redress the diminishing quality of urban living (Eikeland,1999; Kinsella *et al.*, 2000). Kinsella *et al.* remain cautiously optimistic that pluriactivity forms part of a wider rural livelihood strategy to provide sustainable rural development. They suggest that farm diversification could form an integral element of a sustainable rural economy, in which agriculture is seen as part of a development strategy which seeks to enhance rural service and industry within an ecologically sensitive framework (Kinsella *et al.*, 2000).

If policy at both the national and supranational levels has been framed with the intention of increasing diversification at the farm level, it has also favoured a 'bottom-up' approach, where the accent is firmly upon aligning development with priorities set by the local agenda. Such moves appear to fit comfortably with the structural exigencies of global capitalism, in which rural space seems increasingly vulnerable to the rapid flows of capital and the reluctance on the part of the state to engage in intervention (see Harvey, 1996; Ray, 1999). With participation and empowerment to the fore, it also appears that bottom-up approaches to development offer the tantalising prospect of challenging the ubiquitous control of globalised capital. By thinking and acting locally, it is argued, citizens are able to reconstitute a sense of community, challenging the anonymity often associated with the global economy.

Much is made of this attempt to replace passivity with active virtue by those who call for such forms of endogenous development. Yet the arguments that underpin this endogenous development are not limited to the 'political', for they extend to a particular projection of how local economies should be organised. The size and diversity of employment possibilities are deemed essential, offering a more robust structure to the vagaries of the global economy. In turn, new technologies and the creation of new information superhighways offer potential ways out of the impasse of geographical isolation. It is clearly a set of ideas which borrows heavily from the mantra of green economic thinking, where the emphasis is firmly upon situating viable and sustainable forms of development within smaller geographical boundaries (see Harvey, 1996; Ray, 1996, p. 150). In general terms, then, endogenous development embodies a shift away from an approach which accords priority to 'sectors', to one that seeks to address the potential offered by new economic and cultural opportunities located within geographical boundaries (Ray, 1996, p. 153).

An endemic feature of such forms of endogenous development is the pivotal role of community involvement (a bottom-up approach). Such sentiments can be found in the 1996 Living Countryside Agenda for Rural Europe, put forward by the European Commission, which underpins the 1999 CAP reform and outlines the contours of a new European agriculture model. It distinguishes itself from previous policies in that it recognises the multifunctional nature of rural areas. Agenda 2000 (a series of reforms involving the enlargement of and changes to the CAP and the introduction of new agri-environmental policies) is based on a model for change that is very different from those being pursued by the EU's competitors in that it attempts to forge a new paradigm, one based on the creation of a competitive, sustainable, quality-oriented agriculture that meets environmental requirements (Kinsella *et al.*, 2000, p. 484).

To a large extent initiatives such as Agenda 2000 reflect a clear shift in the direction of policy, abandoning (at least partially) the central role of increased production that informed agricultural policy from the early 1970s. This is not to suggest that the fragmentation and inconsistency of policy have been replaced by coherence. On the contrary, as Allanson and

Whitby observe, inconsistencies remain in a policy framework that seeks to reconcile agricultural support and environmental protection through further rationalisation and intensification of agriculture (Allanson and Whitby, 1996, p. 9).

It seems ever more apparent that the political commitment to providing unqualified public subvention to further increases in agricultural production has been brought into question. What is more, we can anticipate that any expansion in EU membership is likely to shift the focus of publicly financed intervention eastwards, implying further retrenchment in the rural economies of western Europe. The cumulative effect of these processes is indicative of how rural space has been dramatically restructured so that it has become 'progressively less self-sufficient, self-contained and sectorally controlled' and thereby more exposed to the forces of globalisation (Marsden, 1999, p. 506). The problem for those concerned with constructing policy is the complexity and diversity of this new rural governance. As both Ray and Marsden have argued, it is no longer feasible to view rural space as a homogeneous entity, since it may vary markedly in terms of its economic structure or resources. If we are to understand the nature of change within this new, contested rural space, and construct policies accordingly, it is crucial we analyse both the endogenous and exogenous influences which have shaped change (see Ray, 1996; Marsden, 1999).

Rural development programmes

In Irish public policy there are few areas more prominent in debates about the appropriate role of the state than rural and urban development. It is not that the social dislocation associated with uneven development is a particularly recent phenomenon. Rather, the problem (in its new guise), and by definition the character of its political response, are shaped by debates which surround public policy in both a national and international setting. As the NESC report outlines, there have been a considerable number of policies that have attempted to improve farm competitiveness, agricultural diversification, rural tourism, enterprise and development, and marine enterprises. As Commins and Keane (1994) note, after the mid-1970s a regional and rural focus disappeared from many areas of public policy. It was a feature of Irish politics that materialised largely because of the strong tendencies towards centralisation and the adoption of policies which favoured moving resources to weaker localities, rather than utilising indigenous capacities (Commins and Keane, 1994).

The first sustained initiative to introduce integrated development emerged in the pilot programme administered by the Department of Agriculture and Food between 1988 and 1990 and operated in 12 sub-county areas (NESC, 1994, p. 68). The programme was essentially a tentative step in a new direction, was limited in its focus, and provided very little in the way of new funding for anything other than technical assistance. With the intention of organising a 'core group' of local leaders, the department appointed a number of rural development co-ordinators (NESC, 1994, p. 68). Although the programme ran for only two years, the evaluation of this exercise drew positive conclusions. In particular, the programme appeared to indicate that harnessing skills and enterprise at the local level could make a positive contribution to economic and social development. The exchange of ideas, the establishment of new networks and the stimulation of 'new' thinking were all features of these early programmes. Often referred to in the literature as animation, it figured prominently in rural development discourse throughout the 1990s.

The arguments surrounding the positive benefits of animation tend to coalesce around themes such as co-ordination, networking and the construction of information linkages. This suggests that if rural development is to be successful, it needs to draw upon the community's ability to stimulate action rather than simply relying upon further financial backing. As O'Malley's evaluation of the pilot programme of Integrated Rural Development noted: 'it became evident from many of the projects which emerged that, quite apart from the quality or spirit of enterprise of individuals, there are certain types of project activity which can be initiated and developed more effectively through the process of co-ordination' (O'Malley, cited in NESC, 1994, p. 68). For O'Malley, the decision to engage in a new venture may well be influenced by the acquired knowledge (via networks or contacts) that other people will also be embarking upon complementary activities (O'Malley, 1992).

The Operational Programme for Rural Development (OPRD) was in many ways a similar scheme, although this was financed through the EU's community support framework. While its mandate was to maintain and strengthen the rural community, much of its focus was on attempts to diversify local economies and improve rural infrastructure (NESC, 1994, p. 70). The OPRD consisted of five separate sub-programmes that attempted to encourage diversification in animal production, horticulture, agri-tourism, forestry and the co-operative pooling of agricultural machinery. In addition, the small and community enterprise element to the programme aimed to stimulate enterprises that could attain commercial viability and assist in the preparation of feasibility studies and business plans. The other three sub-groupings were research and development/ marketing, training in agriculture, and assistance to develop rural infrastructure. Between 1989 and 1993 the OPRD funded projects to the tune of IR£120 million, of which the EU provided 60 per cent.

With support across such a wide range of activities it was, in the opinion of NESC, difficult to draw firm conclusions on the programme's success. There were certainly areas that benefited, most notably investment in mushroom production (NESC, 1994, p. 68). However, many of the recipients of grants tended to be young adults with above average educational levels and a higher than average farm size. Few targets were established and while the cost per job (IR£3,600) compared favourably with mainstream projects, it was difficult to determine the level of 'dead weight'. Despite these reservations NESC remained up-beat in its assessment, suggesting that the programme provided invaluable 'experience of various instruments and incentives' which could be developed under other programmes such as LEADER or the PESP area-based partnerships (NESC, 1994, p. 74).

In 1991 the European Commission introduced a new policy (LEADER) that aimed to explore the benefits of endogenous rural development projects at the substate or subregional level. The programme ran from 1991 to 1994 and assisted over 200 projects. In Ireland it spawned spawned 16 groups which included representatives from farming organisations, community groups, co-operatives, local authorities and state bodies. LEADER leaned heavily towards economic development, with a self-funding requirement of 50 per cent. It was hardly surprising that groups already established were favoured for support (9 of 16). The programme was also dominated by projects that could be classified under rural tourism (50 per cent), of which 35 per cent was directed towards establishing bed-and-breakfast and self-catering accommodation (NESC, 1994, p. 74). In addition, an examination of the profile of groups that promoted LEADER reveals that those which benefited from expenditure tended to be agricultural enterprises of above average size for the area and those small enterprises which had sales in excess of IR£180,000. In other words, disadvantaged groups were under-represented in LEADER projects. However, it should be recognised that while LEADER was not intended to target these groups, a substantial proportion of those employed in LEADER projects were previously unemployed (50 per cent) (NESC, 1994, pp. 78–9).

If these were positive aspects to be gleaned from LEADER, there were also grounds for pessimism. As Kearney et al. (1995) note, the extent of dead weight in these schemes was a cause for concern, evident in the finding that 40 per cent of the projects surveyed indicated that they would have gone ahead without LEADER funding. In addition, evaluation of the schemes was hampered by inconsistencies registered in the reporting of employment levels (Kearney et al., 1995).

An evaluation of LEADER, however, should not be limited to a focus on employment targets or the levels of dead weight in the projects, since in many ways it represented an innovative programme that attempted to develop the contribution of voluntary groups in community development. Indeed, NESC has argued that it represented a serious and sustained attempt at animation in local development, bringing together LEADER groups and state agencies in a novel fashion (NESC, 1994). However, while the political rhetoric accompanying such programmes often extols the benefits to accrue from enhanced political participation and community empowerment, the picture on the ground often remains more obscure.

Thus, while Kearney *et al.* were willing to concede that partnership was an important element of LEADER, they were at pains to stress that this often involved more in the way of developing processes rather than structures (Kearney *et al.*, 1995). While it is always possible to identify exceptions, Kearney *et al.* were of the opinion that, in general, many of the projects suffered from inadequate training in local development. In areas such as capacity building, such training in community development or entrepreneurship are important long-term features of this process, yet only a handful of groups employed trained workers in these areas. As a consequence, projects were all too often overly dependent upon the skills or motivation of a limited number of individuals representing different agencies. Such difficulties were often compounded by the frustration LEADER groups experienced with state agencies that bordered on the 'inflexible' (NESC, 1994, p. 80).

Most agree that LEADER contained important differences from other forms of support. However, evaluation has indicated that while most agree that LEADER was more than just a grant-giving exercise, 90 per cent still believe that its most important function was financial support (NESC, 1994, p. 82). Evaluation also showed considerable difficulty with themes such as innovation and integration. While these concepts often have a high profile in the accompanying political rhetoric, the groups themselves often found such ideas difficult to operationalise. As NESC observed, these are important areas for consideration if projects such as LEADER are to avoid excessive levels of dead weight (NESC, 1994, p. 82).

Despite these reservations, NESC was able to make a number of positive recommendations. In particular, it felt that if LEADER was to make a 'distinctive contribution' to rural development then innovation and integration would need to come to the fore to avoid excessive levels of dead weight and displacement (NESC, 1994, p. 83). These were themes that figured prominently in its successor, LEADER II, where the role of community groups, capacity building and animation were to the fore. LEADER II contained a further innovative element which placed an emphasis upon the 'preservation and improvement of the environment and living conditions'

(Kearney *et al.*, 2000).[1] Moreover, in contrast to LEADER the second initiative operated alongside schemes such as the Operational Programme for Local and Urban Development, the area-based partnerships and the county enterprise boards, and so attention was drawn to the nature of local linkages (Kearney *et al.*, 2000, section 1.3).

While a range of sub-groups were created within this initiative, the largest benefactors were those which congregated around rural tourism, small firms, crafts and service measures. Here, of forty-eight applicants thirty-six were successful in securing funding, of which seventeen had taken part in LEADER (Kearney *et al.*, 2000, section 2.1). In general terms, the aims of most groups coalesced around sustaining and creating employment, diversifying the local economy, promoting alternative sources of energy, targeting service provision for those experiencing isolation, and enhancing the life chances of marginalised groups.

As in the evaluation of LEADER and other rural programmes, the ESRI had expressed concern about the potential for overlap across agencies, which was likely to be 'most pronounced between County Enterprise Boards and LEADER' (Kearney *et al.*, 2000, section 2.2). On a more positive note, Kearney *et al.*'s interim report argued that there 'continues to be a relatively even balance between businesses and voluntary/specific interest groups which are improved or created with the LEADER assistance animation activity' (Kearney *et al.*, 2000, section 5.3.3). Indeed, the interim evaluation pointed out that in rural tourism there had been a 'rapid return' on marketing efforts for the groups involved. To a lesser extent, this was confirmed in examples such as small firms, craft enterprises, agriculture, forestry and fisheries (Kearney *et al.*, 2000, section 5.3.6).

Area-based partnerships

As part of the 1990 PESP the government initiated the development of 12 area-based partnerships in urban and rural communities. Prior to 1993, all these partnerships benefited from finance secured from the EU in the form of a global grant issued under the auspices of the European Directorate-General for Regional Policy. On a national level, the Department of the Taoiseach took responsibility for negotiating the grant with the EU. An advisory unit within this department, with a board comprising of the 12 partnerships, national interest groups and staff seconded from the state and non-state sectors, was established to oversee the grant's administration. Following prompting from the EU, this unit was separated from the department and incorporated as Area Development Management Limited, a body which operated the programme on a contract basis from the Department of the Taoiseach.

The process of 'partnership building' was documented originally in what became known as the 'gold book', a text which outlined the proposed structure of the board and the purpose of the partnerships. Each partnership was to be incorporated as a legal entity (registered as a company limited by guarantee). While the Partnerships remained independent organisations under Irish company law, they consist of representatives of a set of divergent interests: the unemployed, the social partners (trade unions and business), and regional representatives of organisations for social welfare, training and education, and farming (Sabel, 1995, p. 4). Through this structure the partnerships had an extensive influence over a significant share of the local activities and resources of the agencies of both local and national government.

The PESP partnership companies were involved in a range of activities and developed contact with 11,000 people in 1992 and 15,000 in 1993. Partnerships also made contact with 1,588 persons placed in full-time jobs and a further 193 in part-time jobs. For the most part, partnerships were not executive agencies, so that many of their activities were undertaken by the appropriate agencies. A number of projects were undertaken with a net increase in places on training from 2,245 in 1991 to 9,642 in 1993, a growth in Vocational Training and Opportunities places from 200 to 1,073 and a doubling of places on another early school-leaves' scheme, Youthreach, in the same period. The role of partnership lay in the identification and assessment of needs, help in recruitment, and suggestions on how courses might be tailored to meet these demands. As Craig and McKeown note, the partnership structure helped bring together the main delivery agencies, to improve perceptions in the community of 'what they do and why they do it' (Craig and McKeown, 1994, p. 63). It is a view with which NESC concurred, observing that partnerships in this sense should not be seen as an alternative form of delivery as much as a mechanism through the effectiveness of which mainstream measures can be improved (NESC, 1994, p. 87).

The Community Employment Development Programme (CEDP) was a good example of how local partnerships could contribute. The proposal to introduce this programme was agreed by the managers of the PESP partnerships on the basis of models suggested by the Training and Employment Authority (FÁS) and tried in a small number of locations. CEDP was a pilot project intended to replace the SES but differed in a number of important respects. First, projects were typically 10–15 workers, thereby creating a work environment different to that normally associated with SES, where 1–2 workers were the norm. This was further emphasised by the workers' involvement with the project supervisor. Workers were also able to retain welfare benefits associated with previous unemployed status. The CEDP, SES and teamwork were later subsumed under CE.

The operational framework in the 'gold book' placed a great deal of emphasis upon the need to have a substantial element of local participation in the programme. It was anticipated that the community would have a direct input in decision-making at board level through six representatives. The document also envisaged a 'ladder' of developmental measures aimed at providing a means of 'progression' for those suffering from the effects of social exclusion. As such, policy would address issues as basic as personal development and literacy and expand into areas such as occupational training and further education. While some measures would encompass broader social problems in disadvantaged communities, the primary thrust of the partnerships was to alleviate long-term unemployment.

Few would deny that the stimulus to such policy developments originated in the failure on the part of successive central administrations to resolve what appeared to be the intractable problem of long-term unemployment. This tentative governmental commitment to local development schemes was extended in the 1994–99 National Development Plans and the 1993–96 PCW. The publication of reports by both the OECD (Sabel 1995) and NESC (1994) sought to place the area-based partnership schemes, initiated under the PESP programme and aimed at alleviating unemployment, at the very forefront of the Irish state's attempt to overhaul the character of its economic development. Sabel, for example, was moved to note that such schemes were at the 'core of the experiment' to 'address issues of social exclusion in a more flexible, decentralised and participative way' (Sabel, 1995, p. 3). Similarly the NESC argued that local area-based initiatives should be developed as a 'potentially effective strategy' in promoting greater integration in social and labour market policies. It went on to argue that 'the more closely involved' local communities were in the planning and delivery of area-based projects, the more they would reflect 'local needs and priorities'.[2] Confirming its support for such intervention the NESC envisaged an expansion of such schemes operating within designated areas, where policies designed at the local level would dovetail with those implemented on a national basis. This broader approach, the NESC believes, will encompass a 'localised process of interaction between labour market, education, housing and environmental factors' that will prove more effective in reducing social exclusion (NESC, 1994, p. 41).

For both the NESC and the OECD, the novelty (and anticipated success) of these ventures rested firmly on their capacity to transcend the traditional dichotomies of advanced capitalist economies: the public and private, local and national, and representative and participatory forms of democracy. Partnership schemes represented, therefore, one of a number of experiments aimed at alleviating the rigidities linked with the KWS and the social dislocations associated with the adjustments to a new flexible economy. Thus, for example, the OECD's report maintained that partnership initiatives served as a 'springboard' to an exploration of innovative responses to economic and social problems. Dwelling upon this theme Sabel suggested that, as well as improving the efficiency of public policy making, 'area-based approaches also permit policies to be more socially inclusive and help ensure the social stability and a social cohesion without which economic growth and structural readjustment will be obstructed' (Sabel, 1995, p. 3).

In its publication *A Strategy for the Nineties* THE NESC recommended that the potential role for area-based approaches in social policy should be explored more fully. The Council argued that previously social policies had operated largely on a functional basis, with little in the way of integration and coherence. The report maintained that a substantial number of communities were affected by services from a wide array of government agencies. It concluded that 'concerted, intensive programmes in small areas, containing elements of housing, environment improvement, employment schemes and health and educational projects' could have an 'impact over and above' separate programmes (NESC, 1990, p. 84). The NESC was therefore firmly of the opinion that area-based partnerships were an entirely distinct method of co-ordinating public policy, and that they could reduce the tendency towards compartmentalisation in moves to resolve the problem of long-term unemployment. Here, the accent upon policy (one which would present a formidable challenge to the new civil service structures) was to integrate the endeavours of area-based partnerships with wider educational, housing and labour market policies (NESC, 1994a, pp. 190-4).

Within such partnership-based approaches it is possible to delineate at least three crucial, complementary themes of import to understanding the contemporary Irish polity. First is the forceful assertion that these schemes offer the basis from which to establish a new set of relations between state and civil society in a flexible economy. This forms part of a wider series of arguments integral to the view that a new, global economic order is emerging, one that is impacting substantially (and differentially) upon rural governance. While most appear convinced that economic relations have altered significantly, more often than not they tend simply to allude to the impact such changes have on state–civil society relations. It is hardly surprising, therefore, that the area-based partnerships should appeal to those such as Sabel. Indeed, it is plausible to suggest that the attraction (and presumably any success) of these ventures offers tangible evidence of the way in which the Irish state is exploring attempts to engineer a set of social relations which are more appropriate to the new, emerging global economic order.

A second theme that has sustained the widespread interest in partnership schemes is to be found in the alluring prospect that they are somehow capable of delivering economic regeneration in areas stubbornly resistant to the benefits of the Celtic Tiger. For far too long economies such as Ireland's have struggled with the thorny issue of long-term unemployment. In such circumstances, it is hardly surprising that any success, however limited, should be welcomed. However, for those such as Sabel these innovations may also form the foundation 'for a new model for transferring marketable skills to vulnerable groups and communities, unexpectedly providing the opportunity for them to participate in the kinds of activity characteristic of the modern sector of the economy from which they are normally excluded, (Sabel, 1995, p. 4). It is not simply that these experiments offer new avenues through which the unemployed may participate in mainstream economic activity. Rather, their supporters anticipate, or at the very least envisage, a remodelling of the traditional relationship between the state and the unemployed as stakeholders. Few issues are more politically salient, and even fewer more important.

Debates about unemployment, and any measures designed to avoid its debilitating consequences, impinge inevitably upon issues that surround the cost, impact and function of the welfare state. In Ireland, as in other European states, the pace of efforts to find alternatives to the KWS has accelerated with the prospect of an emerging underclass. The clamour to 'celebrate' any short-term successes generated by the artnership schemes should therefore be qualified by an awareness of the temptation to present such experiments as a way out of the apparent political impasse which confronts the welfare state.

In this context, one of the features of the new schemes that has received attention has been the manner in which they have encouraged the relaxation of rules governing eligibility for social welfare payments. For those such as Sabel, such adjustments 'make participation in these programmes broadly affordable and attractive', removing disincentives which may 'deter the most needy from exploring these possibilities' (Sabel, 1995, p. 10). This desire to applaud moves to relax rules governing eligibility stems from the belief that it marks an important step in redefining relations between citizens and state bureaucracies. In this vein, the Area Allowance (Enterprise) scheme has also attracted favourable review. Under this measure long-term unemployed people can establish their own business while maintaining social welfare benefits for one year. By December 1993 there were 740 people availing themselves of this facility, a success that influenced the decision to implement a national scheme along similar lines: the BTWA scheme.

The final theme that figured prominently in discussions about the partnership schemes was the manner in which they offer greater political participation and empowerment in decision-making. Here, it is argued that the partnerships allow the possibility for local development groups to communicate their concerns about the problems of targeting, and to act as 'conduits for local involvement in formulating strategies' to deal with major national and international issues (Sabel, 1995, p. 4).

It would be misleading to suggest that Sabel's report does not identify important problems within these forms of institutional arrangement. In particular, he argues that weaknesses revolve around three main issues: institutional legitimacy, democratic legitimacy and calls for rationalisation. These schemes lie largely outside of traditional forms of administrative rules, are not sanctioned by any form of electoral mandate, and pose the problem of overlapping jurisdictions. moreover, it is not clear what, if any, lessons have been learnt by central administrative structures. Notwithstanding such doubts, Sabel feels sufficiently confident to conclude that 'the Irish experience demonstrates that the principles guiding current restructuring contain the means for addressing some of the dislocations that restructuring itself causes, and especially for combining active, decentralised participation and the achievement of autonomy' (Sabel, 1995, p. 13).

In Craig and McKeown's evaluation of PESP area-based programmes, one of the more significant features to emerge was the fact that they raised the awareness of the plight of the long-term unemployed. In addition, the programmes showed how such schemes could bridge the gap between local development groups, partnership bodies and the agencies of the state. However, the work of Craig and McKeown also identified a number of problems, most notably the fact that partnerships operate within a centralised and compartmentalised administrative structure that presents a 'major structural barrier' to local development initiatives (Craig and McKeown, 1994). The evaluation undertaken by these researchers also identified a number of problems, most notably the fact that partnerships operate within a centralised and compartmentalised administrative structure that presents a 'major structural barrier' to local development initiatives (Craig and McKeown, 1994).

The recognition of the shortcomings of partnerships is familiar to the literature in this field. However, while those such as Sabel (1995) and Murray and Greer (1993) are willing to concede that difficulties persist, they remain convinced that the explosion in community programmes, with a range of bodies providing an alternative interface between local communities and the state, constitutes a 'renaissance' in local development. It reveals an incremental perception of the role of partnership dominated often by 'prescriptive inventories' that outline how partnerships address the function of policy and the challenges of practice. Here, problems are always resolved with more resources, time or personnel. The structures remain sound, even if the components need to be tweaked. It is an argument that remains ultimately flawed. The issue that needs to be resolved is not one of funding but whether partnerships, as they are presently configured, can perform the enormous task that their supporters envisage. Here, for example, Tovey has succinctly observed that while rural development projects such as tourism may well generate wealth and employment, it is by no means clear that the gains will automatically go to rural people or within the rural population to those groups most in need of them. Resource development may produce changes in the ownership of the rural environment, or in the forms through which it is worked, which benefit some groups far more than others (Tovey, 1999, p. 109).

In contrast to the NESC (1994), Sabel (1995) and Murray and Greer (1993), this chapter argues that partnerships are necessarily riven with conflict, division and discord. Indeed, by denying the 'politics' of partnership-driven development these authors ignore the possibility that these new arenas may become venues in which established networks simply rehearse old grievances. What appears to have eluded these authors is the possibility that partnership-driven development reproduces existing divisions within rural communities, and that such structures may act simply to reinforce existing power differentials within local communities.

In this vein, Tovey has argued that attempts to tackle rural poverty that fail to include a 'struggle to change the broader economic system in which agriculture and rural activity are enmeshed are likely to have little success'. Any decision to endorse the 'local' within rural development appears to be generated 'at least as much out of ideological perceptions of the rural as of any objective analysis of the dynamic processes producing rural poverty' (Tovey, 1999, p. 111).

Problems also surround the democratic nature of such schemes. As Ray has pointed out, a transfer of power downwards may in turn lead to a crisis of legitimacy. While these are crises which may not be necessarily generated by the reactionary instinct of (traditional) power holders to retain the status quo, they reflect concerns of 'elected representatives with the principles of democracy' (Ray, 1999, p. 527). In programmes such as LEADER there is a tension between the shift upwards to the appropriate directorate and a downward movement to the local level (Ray, 1999, p. 527).

However, the most serious obstacle facing programmes such as LEADER revolve around the difficulty of sustaining structures which exhibit political participation while recognising that their implementation often demands the financial support of the state. It is an issue upon which such programmes have been subject to criticism, with groups often accusing the prevailing structures of being undemocratic. The difficulty rests in the fact that these programmes rely heavily upon a private sector that often downplays the mechanisms for representation and accountability. However, for those such as Ray, this may present opportunities as well as constraints, since the manner in which endogenous development takes place may challenge traditional forms of representation and invite 'alternative, often more radical forms of development' (Ray, 1999, p. 528).

It is not the argument of this chapter to suggest that partnerships have not contributed in some positive fashion to Irish society. Rather, it is that current analyses and the ensuing recommendations neglect consideration of the political dimension to decision-making in local development. All too often communities are presented as cosy idylls bereft of any serious form of political division. The development which takes place in these partnership schemes is associated simply with the view that communities define problems, assimilate responses, and undertake initiatives that are in the interest of the community. The community is here presented as a single entity, with a clear and concise definition of what is in *its interests* and how those interests can be secured.

The rhetoric of political discourse emanating from both governmental and non-governmental sources is replete with politically charged concepts such as empowerment, participation or the importance of locating decision-making at the community level. More often than not, its authors introduce such concepts in an idle fashion, to evince a series of alleged improvements upon previous institutional arrangements. Clearly, what has happened is that the NESC (1994) has been seduced by neo-conservative interpretations of alleged administrative failure: the claims that the central problem that has beset western capitalism has been the explosion in the administrative state apparatus. All too frequently there is a tendency to juxtapose a labyrinthine bureaucratic structure with a series of area-based partnerships which purport to offer a panacea to all our ills: the distribution of resources *by* the community *for* the community. Within this convivial view of the world it is all too easy to lapse into a romanticised projection of the course of local development. Few references, if any, are offered on the political nature of this development, recognition of which demands consideration of the possibility that some interest groups are able to secure preferential access to resources. In this sense, local development is misleadingly presented as a forum in which, provided discussion takes place, amicable decisions 'favouring all parts of the community' can be made. It fails to appreciate the importance of power relations within such forms of development: that these structures inhibit the active participation of certain groups and that certain forms of political discourse achieve more success.

Partnerships operate within a set of defined political structures, accept-able discourses and preferred practices that favour certain groups and exclude others. Local development discourse takes place amid an array of conflicting demands over forms of knowledge and agendas. The result of this process is the creation of networks of actors sharing common beliefs that reflect and assist their own projects. Reports such as those pre-sented by the NESC (1994) fail to consider the dilemmas that arise when critical questions are raised about the nature of development which takes place, the role of local groups and the democratic nature of the policy process.

For those such as Sabel the benefits of such schemes are made real by the fact that they empower sections of society which hitherto would not have participated in mainstream decision-making. The most significant problem with this argument is the failure to acknowledge those groups that do not take part, or, alternatively, those groups that, for one reason or another, resist the forms of development envisaged by the partnerships.

In a more sceptical light, it is possible to suggest that the 'optimism' with which these schemes are endowed should be tempered by the possibility that any short-term success may be the natural by-product of an economy in a period of boom. What the state may really be engaged in is an attempt to engineer consent around new definitions of poverty. At some future point such schemes may well perform a role in reconstructing definitions of the deserving and undeserving unemployed.

There is also a tendency to portray development and its attendant pro-grammes as an apolitical exercise in administrative management. Here, one of the alleged strengths of the partnership approach lies in its ability to create a participative democratic context in which conflicting groups can reconcile or establish common ground around 'the agreed goals of devel-opment' (NESC, 1994). And yet, the experience of local development con-trasts sharply with this. These programmes are, by virtue of their resources and structures, necessarily political. Many of the projects aim to redress the inequalities of disadvantaged groups, a process that often requires deci-sions that challenge the interests of powerful groups in their respective areas. In such instances, local groups face the predicament of balancing the democratic wish to include disadvantaged groups (which may be time consuming) and yet produce results which are quantifiable. It is a problem that has become more common as the tendency towards broad-based, multi-sectoral initiatives has become more pronounced. Such develop-ments raise increasingly difficult questions about the nature of democratic structures and the type and rate of participation. It is a situation compli-cated further by the pressing need to respond to budgetary deadlines if resources are to be secured.

A final, but none the less crucial, element of the problem of dissent relates to the tendency among policy makers to view opposition from legitimate groups in purely technical terms, as something which can be resolved through 'facilitation and training'. This raises the formidable question of whether we are creating strong local alliances, or merely generating a tyranny of consensus in which legitimate local dissent is portrayed as a lack of technical know-how, where those unwilling to accept the clearly defined agenda are shut out.

Locally based community development initiatives result from encounters between numerous actors on an ongoing basis. More importantly, these encounters involve negotiations and struggle through which actors strive to pursue strategies in line with their own strategic interests. The role that different types of knowledge play, and the discourses which actors deploy, are crucial. Furthermore, this suggests that within the field of community development a network of actors and/or interests utilise a common discourse both to define the policy terrain and to act as a mechanism for excluding others (see Marsh and Rhodes, 1992). The capacity for actors with privileged access to demand their own version of development or the ability of powerful local forces to subvert or capture new initiatives is an important consideration.

Some concluding remarks

There can be little doubt that since the early 1970s the rural economy has experienced a protracted period of retrenchment. The shift towards more intensive forms of agriculture has been accompanied by a convergence between the chemical and food industries and an industrialisation of agriculture that has accentuated a predisposition to apply new forms of technology to animal rearing, food production and distribution. It has also become increasingly evident that this industry has become organised around a declining number of influential multinational actors, resulting in a shift of power away from farmers to food manufacturers and retailers. If such global economic pressures have exacted important forms of change, they have been compounded by an emerging environmentalism in the countryside that has served to politicise further the problems facing the rural economy.

The policy response at both the national and supranational levels has been to experiment with new forms of policy delivery, seeking to adopt approaches that favour the use of endogenous forms of development. As Ray has observed, the thrust of this approach has been to replace the traditional dichotomies of economic development (economic expansion, jobs creation and competitiveness) with a paradigm which aims to create a sus-

tainable, quality-oriented agriculture that meets environmental requirements (Ray, 1999; Kinsella *et al.*, 2000). In Ireland, we have witnessed a
series of programmes such as LEADER and the area-based PESP partnerships that have emphasised the need to empower communities and
enhance the participative nature of the decision-making (and development) process. The logic behind such endogenous development lies in its
attempt to resurrect the territorial over the sectoral. That is, it seeks to cul-
tivate a local community's development repertoire and assumes that communities possess a stock of resources that can be selected 'according to the
requirements of the situation' (Ray, 1999, p. 525). For those such as Ray,
the term 'repertoire' neatly encapsulates the principles of endogeny,
embracing fully the idea of the local ownership of resources and a sense of
choice (local and collective) in how to employ those resources (physical and
intangible) in the pursuit of local objectives (Ray, 1999, p. 525). That such
arguments are increasingly in the ascendant is not in doubt. They certainly
fit comfortably with the structural exigencies of globalisation, which
demand that the focus be placed firmly upon establishing new forms of
intervention and regulation.

The issue of rural development has not been isolated from this convivial
perception of the Irish polity. Here, PESP-based programmes and LEADER
schemes have been welcomed as an institutional innovation capable of
alleviating unemployment and empowering marginalised groups. As if
this were not sufficient, research bodies such as the NESC have promoted
the idea that partnership is also capable of precluding the more common
excesses of clientelism. And yet, the most disconcerting feature of this
work on partnership is the tendency to downplay the politicised nature of
this form of development. All too often the process of partnership is presented as bereft of serious political division. Communities are upheld as
coherent, well-organised and unified entities, with a clear view of what is
in *their interests* and how those interests can be secured. In contrast to this
convivial image of partnership-driven development, this chapter has
argued that it is crucial to consider groups that do not take part or those
that for one reason or another resist the forms of development envisaged.
Perceived in such terms, the process of partnership is revealed as far from
the 'harmonious' exercise in technical competence often depicted. Rather,
it involves groups actively promoting their own agendas and lobbying the
state to secure advantage. It is a process ridden with conflict, division and
political antagonism. Moreover, it is by no means clear that the partnership
structures are capable of reconciling the differences that exist between
groups with vastly different political agendas.

Notes

1 The interim report was downloaded off the web. There were no page numbers so references from here onwards will be by section.
2 See the National Development Plans of 1988–93 and 1994–99 and the PCW for declarations on the fundamental role for local communities in realising economic growth through political participation.

5

Environmental governance in the era of the Celtic Tiger

In one of the more influential reports published during the 1990s the Culliton Group was moved to observe that pressures emanating from the EU were likely to intensify demands for more stringent environmental regulation of industry. Endorsing what many considered crucial to any new ecological modernity, the report concluded that, 'far from dragging our heels in the international movement for environmental protection, it was in Ireland's interest to promote a green image, and position Irish industry to cope with tougher regulations in the face of what seems an inexorable trend' (Culliton, 1992, p. 33). At the time of its inception in 1992, the EPA appeared to confirm the optimism which lay at the heart of the Culliton group's findings: that it was possible, even imperative, that Ireland construct a new regulatory framework capable of ensuring greater ecological protection without jeopardising economic growth.

That this new agency offered an invaluable opportunity to restructure environmental regulation in Ireland was undeniable. What has patently failed, however, is any serious attempt to overhaul its regulatory style. Indeed, the fact that the names of sites of environmental political protest, such as Luggala, Mullaghmore and Mutton Island, are so indelibly stamped upon the Irish political psyche is a serious indictment of the ability of the agency's environmental policy to respond to the challenges presented in the 1990s. The euphoria that accompanied the formation of the EPA has subsided amid concern among community and environmental groups that expectations far exceeded performance.

If we are to explain the environmental dimension of the governance of the 1990s, it is important to understand that this cannot be grounded in debates about the state of Ireland's ecology. This is not to suggest that the upsurge in environmental protest, be it concerned with mobile phone masts, genetically modified foods, roads or wind farms, has not been significant: far from it. Neither is it to ignore the varied and increasingly sophisticated nature of that protest. Rather, this chapter argues that the origins of regulatory change are to be found not in some belated move to modernise ecologically, but in an attempt to accommodate the environmentalist critique of the 1980s without threatening the economic growth associated with the Celtic Tiger. Put simply, environmental policy debate in Ireland is concerned no longer with the extent of ecological degradation, environmental justice, the quality of the environment or encouraging environmental sensitivity, but with the complicated process of organising consent around new definitions of the *extent to which pollution can be justified*.

In order to explore the emergence and subsequent failings of the regulatory framework, this chapter begins by examining briefly the politics of environmental regulation in Ireland during the 1970s and 1980s. It argues that decision-making in Ireland conformed to a policy style not too dissimilar from that of the UK, accentuating the importance of procedural regularity, the significance of administrative convention and the value of consultation. It was a style which recognised that, on the one hand, formal and informal contacts with organised interests are an important source of political legitimacy, offsetting the possibility of revolt, and, on the other hand, they act as an invaluable source of information for policy judgements. In other words, such relationships are generally reciprocal and are often based upon the maxim that 'only the wearer knows where the shoe pinches' (Richardson and Jordan, 1982). Few would be surprised to learn that environmental policy in Ireland suffered problems similar to those experienced in the UK, where policy was hampered by a lack of co-ordination and integration and by a parliamentary style in which a minister's allegiance (and ultimately political prestige) was defined by his or her success in defending a particular department.

The second section traces the development of the EPA and contends that its institutional configuration reflects the difficulty in resolving the tension between the needs to counter escalating environmental protest and not to compromise the free market ethos upon which the Celtic Tiger was predicated. It was a line of argument certainly not lost on the minister for the environment at the time, Mary Harney, who was keen to allay any fears on the part of business that the new agency would place it in an environmental straitjacket. Indeed, the minister was adamant that she would not be 'picking a group of environmentalists to review licences or issue new licences or to carry out a whole host of tasks which are being provided for in this legislation' (Harney, *Dáil Debates*, 1992, Vol. 418, p. 959).

In other words, while government was only too well aware of the clamour to reorganise environmental regulation, it was also fully cognisant of the imperative to avoid the (alleged) impact of excessive regulation on inward multinational investment. Government remained adamant that what was required was less, rather than more regulation. It was certainly an argument that resonated through planning reform in the early 1990s, where the pressure to improve the processing of applications met with criticism in some quarters because the rights of third parties to object had been undermined. While the minister was at pains to stress that such third party rights to appeal had not been curtailed, it was clear from her spokesperson's statements to the House that it was not these rights that were foremost in the minister's mind. Thus, while she recognised the need for a 'rigorous examination' of planning proposals she was conscious that a developer was entitled to expect a 'final and conclusive decision' within a specified period of time. Undue delay could, in the opinion of the minister, cause 'understandable frustration' for developers with a 'consequent loss of investment and employment opportunities' (Smith, *Dáil Debates*, 1992, Vol. 416, p. 73). As the narrative of this chapter reveals, while the formation of the EPA has ushered in important changes, particularly in the output of research and the dissemination of information, difficulties remain. This is most notable in its relationships with local authorities, the conflict of responsibilities between the agency and An Bord Pleanála, and the pervasive influence of the agricultural and business lobbies. The remaining sections of this chapter explore critically the problems that reside in environmental regulation in three areas in the post-EPA period: environmental democracy and planning, the EPA and the agricultural lobby, and waste management.

Environmental policy in the 1970 and 1980s

Until the 1990s, environmental law in Ireland consisted largely of legislation drawn up in the 1970s or earlier. Under this legislation the primary responsibility for the direction of environmental policy lay with the Department of the Environment, although it was the local authorities that were largely responsible for its implementation. It was a set of political arrangements subject to increasing public criticism as environmental pressure groups, which had assumed a more prominent political profile, voiced concern that Ireland's environmental legislation both lacked the relevant statutory powers and failed to provide adequate cover.

To a large extent the problems within this regulatory framework revolved around the pivotal and extremely contentious role of local authorities. On the one hand, they were charged with monitoring and regulating the environment while, on the other hand, they were in competition with one another to court the investment of multinational companies. It was a situation complicated further by the fact that they were exempt from many of the pollution controls they were enforcing on others. Scannell, for example, notes that the waste regulations of 1979 implementing EC Directive 75/442 did not refer to the obligations of the state authorities to promote recycling, carry out periodic checks on waste disposal facilities, respect the 'polluter pays' principle or forward regular reports to the commission. Equally, the toxic waste regulations of 1982 implementing EC Directive 78/319 did not refer to the requirement for all (public or private) bodies storing, treating or depositing toxic and dangerous waste to obtain a permit from the appropriate body (Scannell, 1990).

As if to compound matters, the conflicting tasks for which local authorities were responsible were hampered by a chronic lack of resources. It was hardly surprising therefore that on many occasions they should rely on outside expertise in complex areas such as waste management or air quality monitoring. More importantly, perhaps, given their pivotal role in this regulatory regime, local authorities did not possess the expertise to comprehend fully the technical implications of many of the control measures for which they were responsible. Keohane, for example, cites the case of an environmental officer who drew up planning permission for Penn Chemicals in 1975. The company, which was expanding the range of products to be produced at the plant, obtained an extension to the original planning permission without additional controls being imposed. This meant that either the environmental officer involved was not aware that methyl mercaptan was going to be a by-product of some of this new process or that she or he was unaware of the environmentally deleterious properties of methyl mercaptan. In either case, a serious lack of expertise was demonstrated (Keohane, 1987, p. 8).

The contradictory nature of this regulatory role intensified during the 1980s amid concern within the business lobby that further environmental regulation would undermine confidence in Ireland as an investment location. The threat, potential or otherwise, of undermining Ireland's image abroad was compounded by the 'spectre' of capital flight. In a global market in which trade controls have been relaxed, stringent environmental control was presented as a significant reason for multinational companies to relocate in more favourable political and regulatory climates. The impact of such veiled threats upon the local and regional economy should not be underestimated. There was, as Leonard has pointed out, always the prospect that a multinational company expressing the need to relocate production would focus attention upon jobs, often sufficiently to 'immobilise local officials' (Leonard, 1988, p. 187).

The prominent position enjoyed by the agricultural lobby in Irish politics also had a critical bearing upon environmental regulation in the 1970s and 1980s. Here, Adshead's research (1996) has shown that close political contact between the agricultural lobby and the Department of Agriculture, Food and Forestry (DAFF) often ensured that the former's views were aired in those political corridors that mattered. This contact was clearly a contributory factor in the agricultural lobby's success in retaining one of the more controversial elements of environmental regulation during the 1980s: the 'good defence' clause. This clause prevented the prosecution of farmers for water pollution as long as they were in accordance with 'good agricultural practice'. Of course, those who decided what constituted 'good agricultural practice' were in the agricultural policy network.

Certainly, the importance of this type of privileged access was not lost on those within the agricultural lobby who felt that formal meetings only served to 'tie up loose ends', the real decisions having been made at informal meetings held earlier (Adshead, 1996, p. 593). Moreover, its lobbying was not limited to politicians, since the lobby was acutely aware that while the minister may have been the political figurehead, 'the real substance of policy' lay with senior civil servants (Adshead, 1996, p. 593).

The decision by DAFF to resist any attempt to remove the 'good defence' clause in the Water Pollution Act, 1977, amply demonstrates the success of such lobbying and the way in which such networks and contacts have an important bearing upon the interpretation of legislation at the ground level. It was a practice familiar to many, as one TD described in the Dáil:

> There is a problem, in that before an officer from a local authority returns to his office or lab after taking a sample from a farm or an enterprise, some Fine Gael or Fianna Fáil councillor, or perhaps TD will have made representations by telephone not to proceed with a prosecution. Local authorities and the Regional Fisheries Boards are bombarded with political representations not to pursue pollution prosecutions. That is the political culture in which we live. (Gilmore, *Dáil Debates*, 1990, Vol. 394, p. 637)

In many ways, given the established links between the department and the farming lobby, the agricultural sphere became virtually self-regulatory. Thus, despite the signs of the disastrous effect of pig farming on the environment from the mid-1970s, epitomised by the severe pollution at that time of Lough Sheelin, there were few concerted efforts to control pollution from intensive livestock units. Such events were strongly influenced by the desire on the part of regulatory bodies to achieve a consensual policy style in which punitive forms of action were rarely adopted. It was also a feature of environmental policy that extended to the regulation of industry, where self-monitoring performed a significant role.

The nature of the regulatory environment in which industry operated during the 1970s and 1980s was influenced crucially by the role undertaken by the Industrial Development Authority (IDA). The IDA's function was to encourage and co-ordinate those investment projects that would attract labour-intensive industries in order to circumvent high unemployment. This preoccupation with labour-intensive production subsided in the early 1980s as the agency recognised the vulnerability of European producers to competition from those newly industrialised countries that could achieve lower wage labour costs (cited in Leonard, 1988, p. 17). Orchestrating a deliberate shift in policy, the IDA decided to court investment from those 'high-tech, high-wage' companies less vulnerable to the vagaries of the international economy. Its proffered choice was the chemical industry or, more accurately, its pharmaceutical division. It was a group of multinational companies which offered the tantalising prospect of being resistant to economic recession and, from a public relations point of view, could be projected as more environmentally friendly (Leonard, 1988, p. 130).

Whether the IDA's policy was designed to create a pollution haven is open to question. Critics suggest that while such a policy may have stopped short of being deliberate, it was nevertheless implicit in the IDAs overall aim (Leonard, 1988). Few would deny, even within the agency, that the perception among multinationals was that Ireland was unlikely to jeopardise potential investment through stringent environmental controls. There can be little doubt that politicians were fully aware of public sentiment on this issue. As one unnamed Irish politician remarked, 'all my life I've seen the lads leaving Ireland for the big smoke in London, Pittsburgh, Birmingham and Chicago. It'd be better for Ireland if they stayed here and we imported the smoke' (cited in Leonard, 1988, p. 12).

Critics of the IDA tend to ignore the complicated nature of the task it addressed. While this chapter sympathises with the general tenor of such arguments, it contends that the IDA was not involved in some form of duplicitous act designed to conceal the environmental impact of new investment. Too often the views of the IDA's critics lapse into little more than conspiracy theory, accusing it of a myopic disregard for Ireland's environment. It is as if the cumulative effect of the IDA's endeavours since the early 1980s have amounted to little more than a deliberate attempt to create some form of post-industrial landscape more commonly associated with the Mad Max movies (Taylor, 2001). In stark contrast this chapter suggests that the IDA was engaged in a far more complicated process of engineering consent around new levels of *acceptable pollution*. It is a debate that extends necessarily beyond the realms of environmental and industrial policy to embrace issues that resonate in arguments about unemployment, emigration and economic growth.

The IDA's appeal to foreign multinationals rested largely on the co-ordinated nature of the service it delivered. Those multinationals that wished to locate in Ireland were required to deal with a single organisation that did not have overlapping agendas or a conflict in political objectives (Barry and Jackson, 1989). Clearly, discussions with a single, unified organisation held considerable benefits to potential clients. In turn, the IDA would engage local authorities and act as an 'agent' for prospective clients. If the benefits remained clear, the drawbacks were to be exposed fully only at a later date when the IDA became embroiled in a series of controversies which surrounded the environmental record of some of its clients. Few were more contentious than that of Raybestos Manhattan in Cork. Despite fierce local opposition the IDA decided to support the company fully. It was a style of representation that continued in the cases of Merrell Dow and Sandoz and fostered the belief among environmentalists that the IDA and the multinationals operated a cosy cartel.

A further important feature of the IDA's relationship with multinational companies, and a source of consternation to many environmentalists, lay in the role of the Institute for Industrial Research and Standards (IIRS). The IIRS was set up under the authority of the Department of Industry and Commerce to facilitate industrial growth through technological research and development. It had no statutory function in the area of environmental policy, but in the absence of clearly defined environmental standards the IIRS advised a range of public bodies on acceptable norms for industrial practice in relation to effluents, emissions and hazardous waste.

The IDA commissioned the IIRS to report on the environmental implications of a number of projects subject to IDA grants. However, despite the fact that these reports were commissioned and carried out by a public body, the reports were never made public (Allen and Jones, 1990, p. 259). Given its prominent role in legitimating the actions of the IDA it is hardly surprising that the IIRS should have been subject to criticism from the environmental lobby. In particular, its decision to sanction operations at Raybestos, Merck Sharpe and Dohme, Merrell Dow and Sandoz raised eyebrows in many quarters. Ives, for example, was moved to remark that the IIRS was simply another state agency involved with the project of the toxic industry. Its primary function, she suggests, lay in its attempt to provide 'a scientific and technical veneer to state projects, designed to diffuse anger and fear' (Ives, 1985, p. 124). It was not the only criticism to which the IIRS was subject. Keohane, for example, accused it of being unscientific in its assessment of environmental risks. Citing the case of Penn chemicals, Keohane points out that the Environmental Impact Statement (EIS) undertaken by the IIRS noted the presence of a bird sanctuary next to the Penn plant as proof that no environmental damage had been caused (Keohane, 1987).

In the absence of more effective legislation it was evident that environmental regulation was increasingly dependent upon the Planning Acts, a function for which they were clearly not designed. As one civil servant explains, 'the planning conditions were being used to solve everybody's problems, because they provided a wide listing of conditions attached to planning permission. The problem was that they were never designed to provide continuing control' (interviews, 1999). How a plant operates on an ongoing basis, how it is managed, its air emissions or its water effluents, were all issues for which the Planning Acts were 'hopelessly unsuitable' because they 'were never really intended to provide the means for exercising that kind of control' (interviews, 1999). It was against this backdrop of eco-political turmoil that the editorial of the *Irish Times* was drawn to conclude that: 'there was a growing conviction . . . that the provisions for policing environmental controls are less than adequate, and that the industries are, in effect, left to police themselves' (5 September 1989).

Amid such escalating public concern the government sought to restructure environmental regulation, a move that ultimately led to the creation of the EPA. The agency's shape and operating ethos were, however, framed by a series of conflicting agendas. At the EU level it had become increasingly difficult to establish a consensus on the need for a further tranche of EU-wide regulation. Influenced by persistent British opposition to supranationalism, the EU gradually abandoned further moves towards binding legislation throughout the member states and opted for a site-specific approach. The British call for such an approach was expressly designed to avoid different national standards emerging that would threaten free competition between member states. Both the Single European Act and the Maastricht Treaty accentuated this penchant for greater pragmatism, reflected in a preference for framework Directives, soft law and voluntary codes of practice (Lowe and Ward, 1998, p. 24).

It had also become clear from the mid- to late 1980s that concern was mounting over the poor implementation record of environmental legislation. This was manifest in the increase in infringement proceedings against member states for partial compliance, non-notification and the poor application of EU legislation. Such difficulties were exacerbated by deficiencies within the institutional structures of the EU, where there had often been a failure to provide a sound scientific and legal basis to policy and to ensure adequate consultation (Collins and Earnshaw, 1992, p. 225). It was hardly surprising that the EU was reticent about engaging in a further tranche of regulations, given the lack of administrative capacity in some member states and the differences in the power structures operating at national and sub-national level (Collins and Earnshaw, 1992, p. 225). As if to compound matters, the requirement to achieve unanimity on EU decisions meant that all that was required to unravel the momentum of change was the objection of a single member state. Not surprisingly, public decision-making became a 'paradise' for private lobbyists seeking to persuade 'weak' governments to oppose legislation (Van der Straaten, 1994, p. 65).

Aware of these developments at the EU level, Irish civil servants constructed an IPC regime that anticipated many of the features to surface in the Integrated Pollution Prevention and Control Directive (IPPC) (96/61/EC). The agency's format also acknowledged the pervading influence of neo-liberal demands to release capital from the 'excessive' constraints of environmental regulation, as well as having to respond to the increasingly politicised nature of environmental protest.

Environmental policy in the 1990s: the role of the EPA

In the summer of 1989 the Fianna Fáil/PD coalition announced that it would create a new Environmental Protection Agency, a move welcomed by all the main political parties and, perhaps more importantly, endorsed fully by environmental pressure groups. However, despite the minister's assurance to the Dáil of a speedy introduction of the legislation, the EPA Bill was not published until the latter half of 1990 and did not reach a second-stage debate until the end of 1991. The EPA became operational only in July 1993, nearly four years after it was officially conceived. Its remit, however, would be ambitious, reflecting a new, positive embrace of environmental issues. The intention was to replace a myriad of previous legislative arrangements and individual institutional responsibilities with a single body to grant an IPC licence. The thrust of the legislative and institutional change was to develop coherence and integration where previously indecision and incoherence had reigned.

It was envisaged that the agency would provide guidelines and back-up to local authorities and other public bodies. It would also co-ordinate environmental monitoring and publish reports on the state of the environment. In addition, it would supervise the environmental performance of the local authorities, participate in environmental impact assessments and promote and develop environmental audits (*Dáil Debates*, 1991, Vol. 411, p. 1257).

While such an expanded portfolio received the seal of approval from government, the minister of the environment, Mary Harney, was extremely anxious to allay any fears that this new regulatory framework would restrict economic enterprise. Thus, she declared that the legislation would be part of 'a radical and progressive step forward. It will help to safeguard our environment and our *economic future*' (Harney, *Dáil Debates*, 1991, Vol. 411, p. 1263, emphasis added).

Given the raft of responsibilities assigned to the agency, and the increasingly politicised nature of this area of policy, it was hardly surprising that the EPA's institutional structure should have been subject to criticism. In particular, problems persist over its relationship with local authorities; the level of independence the agency enjoys from government; the voluntarist nature of its legislative powers; and the manner in which its environmental discourse is shaped by a fundamental belief in the ability to provide technocratic solutions to environmental problems.

While local authorities retain many of their environmental responsibilities under the 1992 legislation, a situation often misunderstood by environmental activists, the EPA was assigned a monitoring role. It possesses the power to fix criteria for the management of sewage treatment plants and landfill sites, and to perform a general supervisory role in the area of the quality of drinking water. In addition, and perhaps more importantly, the legislation also gives the agency powers of sanction over local authorities. It was a move designed to respond to the perceived deficiencies in co-ordination and monitoring previously undertaken at the local level. Thus, the act stipulates that where the EPA believes a local authority has failed in its statutory obligations, or where it feels these responsibilities have been carried out in an unsatisfactory manner, the agency *may* request a report from the local authority. In the absence of a 'satisfactory response', the EPA *may*, if it so wishes, implement the necessary changes and impose the costs on the local authority.

At a cursory glance it would appear that the EPA Act strengthened regulatory control over local authorities. On closer inspection, however, it is not as robust as it first appears. There is, for example, no compulsory obligation on the part of the EPA to request reports, thus ending a long-drawn-out process before it can even begin. However, a more damning indictment of the legislative control of local authorities lies in the fact that under section 63.3 a directive cannot be made unless a local authority possesses the requisite funds to comply. This clearly implies that regulatory control (or the use of punitive action) can be effective only if the local authorities are adequately resourced. More importantly, it offers an invaluable loophole for local authorities accustomed to operating with limited funds from central government. As one TD noted, in such circumstances it 'seems to me that smart local authorities will use their funds for everything except the requirements of the Bill and put the onus for its implementation on the minister' (Dukes, *Dáil Debates*, 1991, Vol. 411, p. 1711). It reaffirms, once again, the discretionary nature of the legislative arrangements and the insistence upon relying upon voluntary compliance, a feature of policy that was pervasive throughout the 1970s and 1980s.

In the build-up to the formation of the EPA, the government was faced with the unenviable task of ensuring that the agency would have the requisite level of regulatory power and would remain independent of government. On both counts the government was subject to criticism. The failure to establish definitive commitments on funding or provide an appeals structure for environmentalists, and the composition of the first advisory committee to the agency, all reveal a concern with the public's anticipated reception of the agency, rather than with the minutiae of its administrative and institutional aims.

The composition of the advisory committee was the first area to provoke criticism from the environmental lobby. The function of this committee was to select a list of candidates from which the director general and four directors of the agency would be selected. However, the EPA Act specified that some bodies should have permanent representation: the IDA, ICTU, the Council for the Status of Women and the heritage conservation body An Taisce. The presence of the IDA on the advisory committee was a particular source of consternation to many within the environmental lobby. Deputy Garland, for example, was moved to remark:

> How can the minister possibly have an organisation like the IDA on the Board of an independent environmental body when they are pro-development, pro-industry, and represent everything that is anathema to environmental policy? Politically, the IDA should not be let next or near the Environmental Protection Agency. There is no one in the IDA with an ounce of environmental sense or who knows anything about the environment. (Garland, *Dáil Debates*, 1992, Vol. 418, p. 953)

The government remained largely unperturbed. Harney defended the IDA's presence, insisting that if an 'inappropriate company' located in Ireland, it was the legislative framework that was at fault, not the 'body charged with the task of aggressively selling Ireland and promoting industrial development' (Harney, *Dáil Debates*, 1992, Vol. 418, p. 960). Furthermore, the choice of the IDA was, in her considered opinion, more apposite than an arbitrary decision between the Confederation of Irish Industry, the Federation of Irish Chemical Industries and the Federation of Irish Employers (Harney, *Dáil Debates*, 1992, Vol. 418, p. 959). The minister's more immediate concern lay in the need to reassure the agricultural and industrial lobbies that the agency would not be held to ransom by the environmental lobby.

From the outset, the government's concern was to instil a managerial ethos at the agency's helm. While this would not *necessarily* impose any undue constraints upon its environmental priorities, especially its scientific and research output, it would ensure that the agency's primary focus would be *managing* rather than *conserving* the environment. On this issue the minister remained adamant that the government's task was to choose:

> a Director General and a full-time board of Directors who will be given a very important role and function in relation to the way the agency will operate ...

some of them will have to have particular expertise. In addition, they will need *management skills* and be capable of making decisions. (Harney, *Dáil Debates*, 1992, Vol. 418, p. 959, emphasis added)

Integral to the debate generated on the advisory committee were fears over the level of independence the agency would enjoy from government. From the outset both the Green Party and elements within the environmental lobby voiced anxiety at the level of 'discretion' available to the minister on a wide range of issues. Section 21 of the Act, for example, specifies that the minister shall decide the organisations from which eligible candidates for the advisory committee would be selected. In the view of one opposition TD, this meant that the 'whole make up' of the advisory committee would be dependent entirely upon the opinion of the minister of the day (Garland, *Dáil Debates*, 1991, Vol. 412, p. 2433). There was understandable concern that the agency's independence would be compromised and that, ultimately, any decision to undertake a survey of politically contentious areas would be clouded by the conservative composition of its advisory committee and the discretionary nature of the tasks set out in the legislation.

Apprehension among opposition parties also extended to the issue of funding, where it was felt the EPA would effectively operate in a financial straitjacket. With regard to this, Deputy Howlin, among others, noted that there was the real possibility that the government would use its 'economic muscle to punish an agency who trawl in information or touch on issues about which the government are sensitive' (Howlin, *Dáil Debates*, 1991, Vol. 411, p. 1285). Such a fate had beset the body previously entrusted with environmental protection, An Foras Forbartha. This body had 'come a cropper when government decided that at a particular time they did not want an independent agency to deal with environmental issues and wiped out that body' (Gilmore, *Dáil Debates*, Vol. 411, p. 1297).

For those concerned with Ireland's environment a significant factor in the laggardly rate at which the EPA's functions became operational lay in the lack of funds it received. As one respected editorial was moved to observe: 'while care and thoroughness are necessary virtues, the slow pace at which the agency is being allowed to come to life is puzzling' (*Irish Planning and Environmental Law Journal*, 1994, p. 50). Although the agency was established in 1992, it was not until the latter half of 1994 that full licensing powers were transferred from the local authorities to the EPA. At the time it was alleged that the number of licences processed by the agency was such that many years could be expected to pass before all operations requiring a licence would come under its jurisdiction. As the editorial quoted above caustically remarked: 'the 21st century will have lost its gloss before the agency carries out the role which the public were assured it would be given when it was first mooted'.

In the original legislative framework the EPA was conceived and marketed as a modern super-agency that would tackle the environmental problems facing Ireland with a skill and expertise matched by no preceding state body. Certainly, few were in doubt of the enormity of its task. In the ensuing debate, government maintained that the agency would receive IR£8 million per annum. This proved to be rather optimistic. In 1994, the EPA's funding stood at IR£4.4 million, a figure that did not include potential income from licences (Browne, *Dáil Debates*, 1994, Vol. 444, p. 573). Even with this additional revenue, however, the shortfall was not met, since income from licence fees accounted for a miserly IR£340,000 in 1994 (Howlin, *Dáil Debates*, 1995, Vol. 452, p. 337). It is hardly surprising that the parlous state of the EPA's finances did little to allay the fears of an environmental lobby concerned that government lacked the political commitment to ensure the protection of Ireland's environment.

The EPA's remit was to be ambitious, befitting an agency fashioned to embrace more positively the green issue. Under the 1992 Act, the EPA was given a number of statutory functions, the most important of which was the introduction of IPC licensing. The intention was that IPC would supplant the practice of multiple permitting, serving to compress the application procedure and condense a range of licences (and responsible bodies). In addition, the EPA would play an active role in the promotion of environmentally sound practices through a wide range of advisory, support and supervisory functions, provide guidelines and back-up to local authorities, co-ordinate environmental monitoring, publish reports on the state of the environment and undertake environmental research.

Among a wider audience, it was the agency's punitive powers that attracted the headlines, *apparently* confirming the government's pledge that it would no longer tolerate damage to Ireland's 'green image'. Offences under the 1992 Act, for example, carry penalties which are markedly more severe than previous environmental legislation. A maximum of IR£1,000 and/or six months' imprisonment accompanies a summary conviction, while a conviction on indictment *could* lead to a maximum of IR£10 million and/or imprisonment for 10 years (EPA Act, 1992, p. 14). The idea of integrated pollution control had been debated at the European level, where the Fifth Environment Action programme of the Community had designated it as a priority field of action. Indeed, the programme envisaged that IPC licensing, when linked to improvements in the management and control of production processes, would give a 'new sense of direction and thrust to the environment/industrial policy interface, (EPA, 1996, p. 2). The IPC licensing regime was therefore designed with the express intention of resurrecting public confidence in environmental regulation. It was, after all, widely acknowledged that the regulatory framework was bureaucratic and unwieldy and had failed to regulate industry. The government had expressed concern about the lack of expertise among local authorities, the difficulties experienced by developers and industry in obtaining multiple authorisations, and the need to establish clear national environmental standards (Scannell, 1995, p. 513).

What remains novel in the IPC regime is not so much the political endeavour to improve environmental standards as how this will be achieved. In applying for an IPC licence the onus shifts to the operator to justify and defend the types of technology and practices to be used, a process it was hoped would encourage a new level of environmental awareness among management. It was anticipated that the IPC regime would also restrict the capacity for companies to cut corners and would simultaneously encourage a new, more holistic managerial approach to environmental protection. The EPA's objective was not only to ensure a reduction in pollution, but to implement an ongoing programme of environmental management and control that would focus on *continuing improvements* aimed at prevention, elimination and *progressive* reduction of emissions' (EPA, 1996, p. 2, emphasis added).

The main environmental objective of IPC was to prevent or solve pollution problems rather than transferring them from one medium to another, a situation that tends to create an incentive to release pollution. The EPA guidelines suggest that the aim was to 'eliminate or minimise the risk of harm to the environment'. In so doing it goes beyond the traditional framework of pollution control by encouraging the *anticipation* of the environmental effect of emissions. This is not just in the environmental medium into which they are released, but also the *potential* for the emissions to cross over into other environmental media (EPA, 1996, p. 2).

From a managerial point of view there were benefits to be gained. A new and more focused timescale for (un)successful applications was put in place and, with a single agency, there was the prospect that decisions would be consistent. Above all, business wants to avoid 'unnecessary delay', or tie up ventures in a protracted legal wrangle. Better a decision is made quickly, even if it is unsuccessful, so that business can move on (Taylor, 2001).

In the process of granting an IPC licence the agency's decision would be underscored by assessing whether the best available technology not entailing excessive cost (BATNEEC) has been used. The EPA's guidelines inform us that the technology (which extends to production techniques) should be 'best at preventing pollution, and available in the sense that it is procurable by the operator of the activity concerned'. BATNEEC would set out the 'balance between environmental benefit and financial cost' (EPA, 1996, p. 2). In order to familiarise business with this new regime the agency published a series of guidance notes that identified the types of technologies considered suitable to form a decision on the grounds of BATNEEC. The agency then sets the relevant emission limit values. As its guidelines state, the principle of BATNEEC emphasises pollution prevention techniques, cleaner technologies and waste minimisation, rather than end-of-pipe treatment (EPA, 1996, p. 3). It certainly appears to represent a quantum leap from the instruments available in the 1980s, and yet, on closer inspection, significant difficulties remain.

That the agency prefers a soft regulatory style is revealed in the extent to which it has resisted attempts to impose new regulations on existing operations, thereby reducing the potential for discord. The EPA is of the firm belief that the economic dimension to BATNEEC – the burden of costs imposed by the introduction of new technology or environmentally friendly practices – should weigh less heavily on existing companies. Thus, when questioned on how the agency would deal with the 'best available technology' requirement proposed in the draft Integrated Pollution Prevention and Control directive, a director of the agency declared that, while the definitions of BATNEEC and best available technology were fairly similar, existing activities in Ireland would not have to meet the requirements of BAT for about *another eleven years* (MacLean, 1994, p. 82).

While the distinction between 'new' and 'existing' facilities received rather less attention it was, nevertheless, important. As far as new facilities are concerned, the BATNEEC equation should have regard to 'the current state of technical knowledge, the requirements of environmental protection and the application of measures which do not entail excessive costs' (EPA, 1996, p. 4). However, the equation alters significantly when we consider existing facilities. Here, an *additional* regard should be had to the nature, extent and effect of the emission concerned, the nature and age of the activity and the period during which the facilities are likely to be used or continue in operation. The decision to impose conditions on the licence will depend on the 'costs which would be incurred in improving or replacing these existing facilities' and 'in relation to the economic situation of activities of the class concerned' (EPA, 1996, p. 4).

It is clear that the EPA is at pains to avoid stipulating absolute standards or emission levels. Despite the view promulgated by the EPA that 'scientific rigour' underpins the determination of what is an acceptable level of pollution, it is evident that the *economic* circumstances of an operator have an important bearing upon what emission level is stipulated and how it should be achieved. The picture becomes fuzzier when we recognise that the agency only *envisages* that existing facilities will *progress* towards the attainment of emission limit values similar to those of new facilities (EPA, 1996, p. 4).

To environmentalists, one of the more appealing features of the new IPC licensing regime was that it would produce reasonably accurate figures for pollution releases and their environmental impact. It was assumed that such information would perform a dual function: restricting the ability of companies to persist with 'cowboy practices' and simultaneously encouraging a new, more holistic managerial approach to environmental protection. In practice, however, these aims have been partially undermined by the EPA's reliance upon self-monitoring and its preferred option of relying on voluntary compliance. The problem with a soft regulatory style such as this is that when it is coupled with a persistent level of non-compliance it undermines confidence in the regulatory regime, serving to reinforce a culture that does not take environmental issues seriously.

Although this is by no means conclusive, the EPA's operating ethos can to some extent be gauged by the rigour with which it has been prepared to pursue breaches in environmental regulations. Contrary to popular belief, not all breaches necessarily lead to prosecution. On this matter the EPA has declared that its role is not to document all breaches of licence conditions; rather, minor variances are *noted* and the company is then informed. It is only in cases of larger variances that an investigation is pursued through inspection, and only in circumstances of *significant* variances are prosecutions sought (MacLean, 1994, p. 82). Given the prominence of licence enforcement in the EPA's role, it seems disturbing that it has summarily failed to establish what constitutes a minor, large or significant variance from the regulations. It is a situation in which ambiguity prevails, allowing a potential regulatory vacuum to emerge in which the EPA acts as judge, jury and executioner on the issue of whether to pursue a breach of environmental standards. More disconcerting, perhaps, is the responsibility the agency places upon individual companies to undertake self-monitoring, a position that raises an interesting conundrum: why notify the company at all, since, presumably, the company is already aware of any breach in the regulations.

From both its legislative framework and its operating rationale it is clear that the EPA does not perceive its role as being simply to enforce stringent environmental standards. Its preferred practise is to rely on voluntary compliance, cajole those who operate under its licences to practice 'good environmental management' and, where necessary, encourage more environmental awareness. As its record amply demonstrates, punitive action is pursued only as a last resort. Indeed, as one of its directors has revealed, the agency is prepared to concede that if variances lie within an area which can 'still be considered consistent with the concept of good environmental management', then 'these can be tolerated if the overall environmental performance is good' (MacLean, 1994, p. 82). Not surprisingly, the agency has displayed a marked reluctance to accept the rate of prosecutions as a useful indicator of performance. While it recognises the need to encourage good environmental management it has argued that this should be measured not in terms of prosecutions, but in reductions in the level of pollutants emitted to the environment. Further, while it has declared that it is fully aware that non-enforcement 'cannot be seen as constituting good environmental management', it is at pains to stress that '*actual enforcement comes in a number of differing forms*' (MacLean, 1994, p. 82, emphasis added).

The EPA's determination to sustain congenial relations with industries operating under its licences is also confirmed in the fact that it is prepared to accept an individual company's interpretation of the BATNEEC principle. This principle is enshrined in the 1992 Act and has been an extremely contentious issue. Critics of the legislation were convinced that the EPA's interpretation of what constitutes 'best available technology' or 'excessive cost' would be compromised by its insistence upon accepting the company's view of BATNEEC. Indeed, as one of its directors has acknowledged, the agency has a desire to go as far as possible to accept the interpretation of what an applicant company believes entails excessive cost. It is a relationship that depends largely upon accepting the company's version of whether certain practices will or will not be financially viable.

The imperative of sustaining cordial relations with its licensees also extended to the agricultural community, where the EPA believes that 'the challenge is to *encourage* an environmental ethos in the *minds and hearts* of farmers so that they will make the right choices for environmental protection' (Sherwood, 1994, p. 66, emphasis added). Such caution on the part of the EPA needs to be set against the backdrop of the EPA's own report on the quality of water in Ireland, which identified the agricultural sector as the largest single contributor to water pollution. And yet, the agency has been keen to allay any fear that its messages should be perceived as a threat to vested interests (EPA, 1996). Rather, its preference is for relying upon a system of voluntary compliance in which agriculture continues to be largely self-regulatory.

Finally, one of the more novel features of the EPA Act was the introduction of an environmental audit. While this move provided an environmental gloss to the legislation, it remained flawed from its inception. There is, for example, no statutory obligation for the EPA or any other public body to undertake such an exercise. In many ways this appealing area of environmental legislation highlights the flaws at the very heart of Ireland's environmental regime: the discretionary nature of much of its legislation. It is a problem replicated in areas such as environmental quality objectives, codes of practice, eco-labelling and access to information.

As if to compound matters, the legislative framework pays little heed to environmental protest. Channels for the improved dissemination of information have been put in place, there is even the possibility that an oral hearing may be conducted, but the general emphasis of the Act is upon establishing 'procedural regularity', closing the loopholes exposed by the environmental disputes of the late 1980s. This is most evident in the procedures adopted for licence applications, which were profoundly shaped by regulations adopted in the planning arena. It was legislation that sought to reduce the number of vexatious appeals and curtail excessive delays to major projects. There are specific obligations imposed on third party objectors (what constitutes a 'valid submission' and the timescale allowed for submission). For an application to be valid, the developers must submit information on the types of technology to be used, production procedures involved and costs). Finally, the directive ensures that the agency makes a decision as expeditiously as possible.

As a consequence, the sequence of events from the publication of the intention to apply for a licence to the decision on whether to grant or refuse a licence is tightly controlled. If all goes well a licence application can be completed in as little as two months, provided that the agency is content with the quality of the application and finds no grounds for refusal after submissions from interested parties. However, if objections are received, then the agency may (or may not) decide to hold an oral hearing, which sets in train a process that may then take up to four months to be completed.

The issue of procedural regularity, and the subsequent impact of new legislation on the nature of environmental protest, came to the fore in the controversy surrounding the EPA's decision to allow trials on genetically modified crops. The principal argument in the case brought by Genetic Concern (an environmental protest group) was that the EPA should not have consented to trials for genetically modified crops because it could not ensure that the 'risks to the environment were effectively zero'. Genetic Concern was of the opinion that the EPA recognised this when it publicly conceded that the risks involved were only 'very low'. The final judgement, delivered by Mr Justice O'Sullivan, stated that in deciding whether to consent to a deliberate release of a genetically modified organism, the EPA was not required to be satisfied beyond reasonable doubt that the risk of adverse effects has been reduced to an effectively zero level (*Irish Times*, 14 December 1998, p. 26). He argued that the 1992 Act, the 1990 EC Directive, and article 33(4) of the 1994 Regulations in relation to the release of genetically modified organisms provide that the agency 'shall not consent to a deliberate release unless it is satisfied that deliberate releases will not result in adverse effects on human health or the environment' (*Irish Times*, 14 December 1998, p. 2).

Mr Justice O'Sullivan observed that the 'standard' required by these instruments could only be read in the light of the 1992 Act, the 1990 Directive and the 1994 Regulations. The closest the 1992 Act comes to establishing a standard was in the phrase 'prevention of danger to health or damage to property or for the preservation of amenities' (section 111 [1]). He noted that section 111(2) allowed for the assessment of 'possible risk to the environment' from a potential release, and that 'if the possibility of risk was eliminated, then it was unlikely the Act would make provision for the assessment of risk and the study of such risk' (*Irish Times*, 14 December 1998, p. 26). He concluded that these sections, read together, assume a 'step by step' approach, whereby trials are conducted and evaluated before further measures are taken. In this context, interpreting the word 'avoid' as being 'effectively zero' renders pointless the study of risk and the anticipated further steps in this exercise. In other words, the possible risk of release is inherent to such evaluation, otherwise why bother to prepare for assessments in the first place.[1]

A further issue raised that is of importance to our discussion relates to the nature of a 'valid submission' and the shift in recent legislation (in planning as well as in the EPA Act) to constrain the time period allowed for objections to be constructed. The contention of Genetic Concern was that in a situation where supplemental material had been provided by Monsanto to the EPA in response to a questionnaire, the third party objector should have been given extra time (more than the 21 days stipulated) to make further submissions. The findings of Mr Justice O'Sullivan on this matter are revealing. He stated that a considerable amount of the opinion evidence would have to be ignored, as it was the EPA's function to assess the scientific evidence and the court's to determine the legal issues. It was, moreover, clear that the 1994 Regulations did not 'provide for further representations from members of the public after the 21 day period had expired, even where further material had been supplied by the party seeking consent.'[2] (Taylor, 2001, p. 108) (see below).

Environmental democracy and planning

The EPA became operational in July 1993. In its first month a fire broke out at Hicksons Pharmachem which led to an estimated IR£12 million's worth of damage and, in Irish terms, a significant level of water pollution. For supporters and critics alike the incident was seen as providing an acid test of the agency's competence and commitment to enforce its new regulatory powers. While the dominant interpretation of events was that the EPA had 'responded fittingly', it was by no means an incontestable one. Indeed, the case offers a valuable insight into the operating philosophy of the agency.

In its report the EPA declared that, with the exception of the pollution of the ground water, no significant environmental damage had occurred. More controversial, perhaps, was the finding that Hicksons Pharmachem had conducted its business in an even more unacceptable fashion than previously thought, and that over the preceding year and a half management had repeatedly breached the conditions of its licence. More bizarre was the evidence it uncovered that Cork County Council had recorded even lower levels of licence breaches than the company itself.

In the immediate aftermath of the Hickson disaster, the most strident demand from environmental protest groups was for a sworn public inquiry, principally because the groups had found multinational companies to be obsessively secretive (Peace, 1993, p. 18). Although it was within the statutory ambit of the EPA to hold an inquiry, the requisite legislation was not adopted. It was not the only source of discontent among the environmental lobby. There were three other areas of the investigation that drew criticism: first, the level of ambiguity and imprecision in the report; second, the technicist manner in which it was compiled; and, finally, the failure of the investigation to open democratic channels through which the voice of environmental pressure groups could be heard.

In the spring of 1996, the EPA granted a draft IPC licence to Syntex Ireland to operate a IR£12 million toxic waste incinerator. This licence was to become the subject of the first oral hearing in which the agency was engaged, and it provides a crucial insight into the dynamics of one of the most politically contested areas of decision-making. The purpose of such hearings is to allow public participation, thereby enhancing the democratic nature of environmental policy. When the company involved decided to build an incinerator, two applications were necessary: one to the county council for planning permission and the other to the EPA for a revised IPC licence to allow incineration. By early March, both applications had been successful.

The response from local opposition groups was to lodge appeals to both An Bord Pleanála and the EPA. The local opposition group, the Clare Alliance Against Incineration (CAAI), were supported by Greenpeace and the Green Party. In its opposition to the incinerator Greenpeace Ireland claimed that new research on dioxins, one of the by-products of the proposed incineration process, suggests that they are potent hormone disrupters, and by granting this licence the EPA was 'flying in the face of reason' (*Clare Champion*, 17 May 1996). In defence of its decision, the EPA pointed out that the Irish standard for dioxins is one tenth of the British standard, and that in 1995 the British government had announced that any incinerator operating within the UK limits posed no threat to the environment. Furthermore, the agency noted that surveys indicated that Irish levels of dioxin are very low and its presence in Irish milk was only one fortieth of the British standard (*Clare Champion*, 17 March 1996). The CAAI countered that while the level of dioxins in Clare was currently quite low, it was not acceptable to argue from there that more dioxins in Clare would be tolerable. Furthermore, they pointed to the investigations carried out into the unexplained livestock deaths in nearby Askeaton, County Limerick, which had been a cause for concern. While these investigations proved inconclusive it would be foolhardy to allow emissions of dioxins that were also known carcinogens (*Clare Champion*, 17 May 1996).

At the oral hearing in September 1996, three main issues emerged: the question of incineration as opposed to waste minimisation; the scientific debate on the effects of dioxin; and finally, the legitimacy of the oral hearing itself. A key objection raised by the environmental lobby to the proposed incinerator was that in so far as it hindered waste minimisation it was in direct contravention of government policy on sustainable development. Moreover, as Greenpeace Ireland noted, Roche Ireland had not produced a comprehensive register of all the anticipated emissions from the factory. Neither had it produced a waste reduction plan (*Irish Times*, 30 September 1996).[3]

To a large extent the debate on the scientific evidence centred on the contentious issue of dioxin release. In its quest to delay the licence application the CAAI argued that any prudent judgement should wait for the new guidelines on toxic emissions to emerge from the EU and the US EPA (*Irish Times*, 30 September 1996). Not surprisingly, Roche Ireland contested the 'scientific' findings of the CAAI, claiming that there was already an identifiable level of dioxin in Clare with no observable side effects (*Clare Champion*, 4 October 1996).

The case highlights the problems of adjudicating in complex areas that often entail appeals to 'objective' scientific evidence to establish the validity of a given position. This is compounded by the fact that the onus is upon the environmental lobby to prove that the incinerator is environmentally damaging, rather than the polluter to justify that it is environmentally benign. With regard to the latter issue at least two further critical observations can be sustained. First, oral hearings function not as a forum for the discussion of how to prevent pollution, but rather to establish criteria for an *acceptable level* of pollution within a defined set of parameters that do not impede economic growth. Even at this crucial juncture the agency is willing largely to accept the company's interpretation of the excessive economic burden imposed by adopting a particular form of work practice or new technology. In a subtle but none the less crucial manner, therefore, oral hearings tend to favour the industrial lobby in the way in which they shift the terms of debate away from environmental *protection* towards environmental *management*. This is clearly revealed in a statement from a spokesperson for the EPA, who acknowledged that 'where process wastes are unavoidable, the best available technology not exceeding excessive costs (BATNEEC) must be used to ensure that emissions are *reduced to as low a level as practicable, taking account of the sensitivity of the environment into which an emission is being discharged*' (EPA, 1996, p. 198, emphasis added).

Second, the hearing focused upon objective questions of scientific truth and economic viability, rather than any discussion of principles of environmental justice. It became clear in the course of the hearing that there was not a single unified scientific position on dioxins, undermining the view that science can always be the source of objective knowledge. Finally, the environmental lobby were alarmed at the procedures adopted at the hearing, in which a single person acted as 'chairman, recorder of all evidence and indeed assessor of the evidence to be given at the four day hearing' (*Clare Champion*, 4 October 1996). As the spokesperson for Greenpeace Ireland noted, that the decision should end in an 'oral hearing, presided over by one man with a notebook, is an insult to the people of Clare and testimony to the major inadequacies of the EPA Act' (*Clare Champion*, 4 October 1996).

The paucity of representation from the EPA and the absence of any formal record of the hearing combined to produce a perception of the agency as hostile to environmental democracy. Either way, the hearing into the Roche incinerator in Clare serves to reinforce the view held by many environmentalists that the formation of the EPA has not provided a check on the practices of multinational companies and that it has served to marginalise environmental and community groups. Although it may appear that the option of an oral hearing provides a framework for public participation, it seems clear from the conduct of such hearings that they be more symbolic than substantive.

The issue of environmental democracy is one that has recently come to the fore in the arena of planning and formed a major element of reform in environmental regulation. The construction industry has persistently sought changes to a planning system perceived to be excessively protracted. It should come as no surprise, then, that amid a speculative property boom arguments for further deregulation have become commonplace. And yet, it is an arena that has witnessed some of the most sophisticated and politicised forms of environmental protest in Ireland. In the planning arena, for example, we have seen bodies such as Lancefort (a non-commercial company which aims to raise crucial issues on the role of the planning process) challenge a number of prominent planning applications through litigation. Such moves sparked the comment that developers were 'apoplectic at never knowing when they were going to be ambushed' (*Irish Times*, 27 March 1998). Protests of this type contrast sharply with those that have taken place in the Glens of Wicklow, where eco-warriors have opposed the extension of the road network.

The introduction of the Local Government (Planning and Development) Act of 1992 was a government response that aimed to 'streamline' the appeals stage of the development process by focusing on the need to reduce the time period for a Bord Pleanála decision on an appeal. In its appraisal of Irish planning procedure the Culliton group (1992), which submitted detailed evidence to the minister prior to the Act, argued that while Irish planning procedures stood up well to international comparison in terms of processing, there were still difficulties with third party objections. In particular the group felt that recourse to the courts should only be through 'judicial review'. The group also made recommendations on the role of the EPA *vis-à-vis* planning. Its aim was not simply to highlight the need for co-ordination and integration between the EPA and An Bord Pleanála, but to ensure that the legislation for the EPA recognised the need to dovetail the timing of decisions over planning and licensing (Culliton, 1992, p. 48).

The EPA Act introduced two significant changes that have had an important bearing upon the democratic nature of environmental regulation. First, it extended the time period in which third parties could lodge appeals. Second, and perhaps more importantly, it stipulated that objections would have to be made *in full* during this time period (a 'one shot' appeal system).

At a cursory glance the extension in the time period would appear to have improved the democratic nature of the process. It is an illusion soon exposed when we consider that no extensions to the original objection are permissible in the light of new conditions after the time period has elapsed. In other words, in complex cases, where (additional) information is either required or not readily available or where experts need to be consulted, the quality of the objections (and presumably their potential success) are severely curtailed. The minister insisted that the existing rights of third parties to appeal would in no way be diminished and that the aim was to 'create a more orderly and effective procedural framework' (*Dáil Debates*, 1992, Vol. 416, p. 72). In response to its critics the Bord argued that while it was fully aware of the pressure to process appeals more efficiently, it should be noted that:

> many appeals are probably cases that have raised difficult issues at local level arising from the implementation of the provisions of the Development plan, the protection of amenities and the need to reconcile proposals with the

proper planning and development of the area. A number raise contentious third party issues. These cases by their nature require more time for processing and careful consideration, a factor which is sometimes overlooked in criticisms of the system. (Galligan, 1996b, p. 5)

It was a situation complicated further by the absence of any new funding or staff for An Bord Pleanála. Although appeals to the Bord had increased by 35 per cent in the period 1988–89, staff had been cut by 20 per cent, and the crucial grade of inspectors reduced by 50 per cent (Howlin, *Dáil Debates*, 1992, Vol. 416).

While the 1992 Planning Act does not legally remove any right of appeal from third parties, there is no doubt in the minds of most commentators that the ease with which this right can be exercised has been diminished. The argument that the 1992 Act eroded public participation in the system was compounded by the substantial (and ongoing) increase in the appeal fee for third party objections. By 1998 this position had been eroded further, so that while the number of appeals rose steadily from 1994 (2,434 in 1994 to 3,927 in 1997) the number of specialist planning personnel declined.

In a situation such as this, the new appeal stipulations clearly leave only sufficiently resourced developers or communities as players in the planning process. There is the very real fear that in an attempt to dismiss frivolous or vexatious appeals the impact of the legislation will be to undermine the role of protest from individual citizens, resident associations or communities. If the enthusiastic welcome the legislation received from the Irish Construction Industry Federation is anything to go by, then the balance has tilted firmly towards the developer. Certainly, as far as government was concerned planning was an issue inextricably linked to measures designed to create an environment in which multinational capital should seek to reside. As the minister was only too keen to point out, it could no longer be regarded as a purely local or regional matter. Delays in the 'planning system, or any perception that our system is ponderous or dilatory, would put us at a serious competitive disadvantage in seeking to attract internationally mobile projects' (Smith, *Dáil Debates*, 1992, Vol. 416, p. 73).

The EPA and the agricultural lobby

The EPA has both *direct* and *indirect* responsibilities for regulating the contribution made by agriculture to pollution in Ireland. Indirect responsibility arises in the form of monitoring water pollution, to which agriculture is a significant contributor. It has a direct involvement in the agricultural sector through its role in licensing large-scale pig and poultry operations. The introduction of agricultural licensing meant that farmers who wished to set up pig or poultry units above a certain size must apply to the EPA for an IPC licence, as well as applying to the local authority for planning permission. Licensed operators are then expected to have a self-monitoring plan that is checked on a random basis by the EPA.

For many environmentalists, a more rigorous form of control of agriculture was well overdue. It was a sector subject only to limited forms of environmental control under EC (Environmental Impact Analysis) Regulations (S.I. 349/1989) that require large-scale pig and poultry operations to submit an EIS with the planning application. Byrne's research has shown, however, that the standard of the EISs submitted was in many cases highly unsatisfactory. In many instances, for example, there was little or no consultation with local authorities as to what was required in an EIS; none of the EISs submitted mentioned the construction phase and only one attempted to describe the site. Many of the applications related to units currently in operation but did not mention the impact of existing operations. Moreover, few of the EISs referred to any data on surface water quality in the area, and those that did relied on data at least two years out of date. Very few surveyed the impact on ground water, and none presented any data on the subject. And yet, remarkably, of 32 applications, 26 were successful (Byrne, 1996).

The study also revealed serious deficiencies on the part of the planning authorities. Of the three planning authorities visited, none had kept records of environmental monitoring. More startling, perhaps, was the fact that one local authority, which did not make a practice of inspecting units after construction, was unaware whether or not some of the units for which permission was granted had ever even been built. The other two said they did inspect, but did not assess whether work undertaken had complied with planning conditions. In its defence, one local authority claimed that it was in the interest of the developer to build the unit properly. The other two authorities claimed that monitoring was required if it was part of the planning conditions, but both failed to provide documentary evidence of this. Such deficiencies were compounded by the fact that there was considerable variation in the number and severity of conditions imposed on planning permission across local authorities (Byrne, 1996, p. 128).

There can be little doubt that control of the pig and poultry sector was in urgent need of reform, a process in which it was anticipated the EPA would play a significant role. In its first set of forecasts the EPA suggested that new pig and poultry operations would be licensable by the end of 1994, and that existing operations would be brought into the system within 12 months (Sherwood, 1994, p. 62). As in other areas of responsibility the EPA's forecasts proved rather optimistic, perhaps because it had underestimated the trenchant opposition of the farming lobby. The introduction of IPC licences for pig and poultry units finally emerged in September 1996 and it was expected that licensing for existing operations would commence within a year.

From the outset, the agricultural community was openly hostile to the introduction of the licensing scheme. In order to reassure the IFA, the minister for the environment accepted that the licence would be open-ended with no need for renewal after a specified period (*Farmers Journal*, 10 August 1996). The IFA also strongly objected to the failure on the part of the minister to negotiate changes with the industry. In a desire to resist the fees associated with the introduction of licences, the IFA sought to bring the issue within the remit of negotiations for the successor to the PCW. As a consequence, the IFA was successful in delaying the extension of the 1997 ministerial order to existing pig-farm operations until March 1998.

The EPA is also involved in regulating the environmental consequences of agricultural activity in the area of water pollution, in which agricultural is the most significant culprit. The principal cause lies in the excessive use of fertiliser, leading to nutrient run-off and eutrophication. In this field the EPA undertakes monitoring with the assistance of the local authorities. In instances where the quality of water is found to be deteriorating, the agency is expected to take action to rectify the situation (Sherwood, 1994, p. 63). However, all local incidents of water pollution continue to be the responsibility of local authorities, the Fisheries Boards, and the affected parties (who can prosecute under existing legislation). As a result, the arrival of the EPA has not precipitated a notable change in the regulatory regime at this level.

As in other areas of responsibility, the EPA's preferred regulatory style is to avoid stringent environmental controls that are reinforced by prosecution. Thus, while possible options to reduce the excessive use of fertilisers and the spread of slurry exist, the EPA favours moves to coax farmers into adopting new practices (Sherwood, 1994, p. 63). It has argued that: 'it is far more important that farmers should become fully aware of all the circumstances under which nutrients from agriculture reach water and that they should *voluntarily adopt practices to prevent it* . . . it may take time but the prize is worth working for' (Sherwood 1994, p. 66, emphasis added). Despite the finding in the EPA's report on water quality in Ireland 1991–94 that agriculture was the largest cause of water pollution, the agency sought to reassure the agricultural community that this should not be taken as a threat. Rather, the EPA felt that this was an early warning signal designed to allow minor changes in policy that will prevent serious, and perhaps irreversible environmental and economic damage at a later stage (EPA, 1996).

This emphasis upon voluntary compliance is one that permeates the response of the EPA to environmental regulation. It was endorsed by the minister for the environment, who stated that we were still 'depending on the goodwill and vigilance on the part of every user of the natural environment, *particularly farmers*, to ensure that accidents ... do not recur' (Howlin, *Dáil Debates*, 1995, Vol. 453, no. 8, p. 1981, emphasis added).

The exclusion of the agricultural sector from the legislation on waste lends further support to the validity of this contention. When questioned on why farm sludge was not included in the Bill, the minister replied that 'the Bill is not meant to be a comprehensive one and that farm activity and its potential to cause pollution is covered under the licensing regime of the Environmental Protection Agency Act' (Howlin, *Dáil Debates*, 1996, Vol. 460, p. 11).

In an effort to demonstrate the government's willingness to tackle the threat to water from agricultural waste, the Waste Management Act of 1996 includes an amendment to the Local Government (Water Pollution) (Amendment) Act of 1990. This amendment provides local authorities with discretionary powers to oblige farmers to submit a nutrient management plan. A partial incentive to farmers to submit such a plan voluntarily rests on the fact that it can represent part of the 'good defence' clause in the water pollution legislation.

Attempts to reject the discretionary dimension of this legislation were rejected by government, which argued that a regulation requiring all farms to have nutrient management plans was not necessary. After all, the EPA's report *Water Quality in Ireland* showed that the input of chemical fertilisers could be reduced by an amount worth IR£25 million per year without adverse effects on production, thus demonstrating that a good nutrient management plan would actually save farmers money (EPA, 1996b, p. 121). More disconcerting is the likelihood that DAFF and Teagasc would strongly influence the specifications for nutrient management plans, as these organisations possess the power to define the parameters of acceptable farm practice and ensure that they remain firmly within the grasp of the agricultural policy community.

Given the combined incentives of the 'good defence' clause and financial benefits accruing from a nutrient management plan, the minister appeared convinced that all farmers would voluntarily comply. However, such compliance raises the crucial question that if a farmer follows an *effective* nutrient management plan, how serious would the pollution need to be to warrant punitive action from the local authority? It is clear that the agricultural policy community has been successful in maintaining a largely self-regulatory environmental regime. Even where this regime has been challenged it has successfully resisted attempts to overhaul the system in any radical fashion, sustaining a situation in which voluntary compliance predominates.

REPS was a further feature of Ireland's agri-environmental policy, and forms part of a wider package of reform that operates in tandem with the CAP. The pre-reform CAP with its price control mechanisms had fulfilled a key objective of the Treaty of Rome: providing adequate food supplies at reasonable prices. The accent was firmly upon the construction of incentives to increase production, which had a deleterious effect upon the environment. Both wildlife habitats and water quality were impaired as intensive agriculture increased its use of fertilisers and pesticides. Simultaneously, the intervention system produced huge quantities of surplus produce which had to be stored at the tax payers' expense. By the mid- to late 1980s the level of opposition to this system had become formidable, as a range of political groups argued that the CAP was in need of serious reform (Regan, 1994). From within the agricultural lobby suggestions for reform attempted to reconstruct the farmer as both producer and custodian of the countryside (Regan, 1994, p. 75). The simplicity of this vision was clearly persuasive. Certainly, for one minister, it seemed incomprehensible that anyone could disagree that 'farmers are the custodians of our natural environment, because they are so directly affected by it, they are more attuned to its protection than most people' (Howlin, *Dáil Debates*, 1996, Vol. 465, no. 2, p. 370).

To a large extent REPS is the policy expression of this duality in the farming function, serving to reconcile the needs to maintain income transfers to farmers and to assuage the environmental lobby's demands for greater regulation of the environment. Under the auspices of an 'environmental conservation' programme, government intended to reduce the burden on agriculture, a move made all the more meaningful when placed against the backdrop of a European political climate increasingly hostile to agricultural support.

REPS has a number of important elements. One of its principal aims is to introduce farming practices that emphasise conservation and landscape protection. The protection of wildlife habitats and endangered species of flora and fauna therefore figures prominently. In addition, REPS seeks to promote quality food production in an environmentally friendly way. The nutrient management plan is pivotal to this regime, attempting to ensure that nutrients are used in a more effective, environmentally conscious manner, and operates in tandem with measures designed to improve the collection, management and disposal of farm wastes.

It is clear cut and simple. And yet, on closer inspection, there are a number of problems that militate against its success as an effective form of environmental protection. For instance, payments under this scheme are made only up to 40 hectares, which acts as a disincentive for the larger, more intensive farmers. Perversely, it is these operations which need to embrace new agri-environmental practices. Further, although aid is available for additional conservation measures, payment for only one measure is allowed. There is little incentive, therefore, for farmers to develop a range of environmentally sound working practices. Finally, participation in the programme is entirely voluntary.

From its inception REPS was beset with problems. Initially, DAFF had predicted a participation level of about 40,000 farmers, covering about 1.3 million hectares (Regan, 1994, p. 25). At the close of 1996 agricultural consultants had declared that participation would have to double for the scheme to reach this target (*Irish Times*, 28 December 1996). Such a low level of participation undermined the potential success of the scheme, since a strongly positive contribution from REPS could be realised only if there were a good response to the scheme among qualifying farmers (Regan, 1994, p. 77).

The inspection level of participants in REPS also casts doubt on its credibility as a bona fide pollution control programme. In 1996, all cases were checked for compliance, with the minister for agriculture, food and forestry declaring that such an inspection rate was in the best interests of the Irish farmers. He noted that 'the enhancement of the agri-environment can be served only by operating effective control and monitoring arrangements' (Yates, *Dáil Debates*, 1996, Vol. 467, no. 6, p. 1870). It was a move that raised the ire of an agricultural lobby opposed to the stringent nature of the intended regulation. The IFA called on the minister to halve the rate of inspection in order to speed up the payments to farmers (*Farmers Journal*, 5 October 1996). In performing a U-turn, the minister withdrew his insistence that all cases be checked, given that those under investigation had confirmed that most farmers were complying with their obligations under the scheme. DAFF subsequently reduced the level of inspection by half (*Irish Times*, 26 November 1996).

A key problem which also undermined the credibility of REPS as part of an integrated environmental protection package was that it sent out conflicting signals to farmers, since as part of the CAP they were encouraged to maintain or intensify farming operations by price supports and annual payments. The Ewe Premium Scheme was typical of this initiative. It was a payment on the unit of livestock rather than by hectare, and so made overgrazing financially beneficial to certain farmers. The principal problem facing REPS was that it was viewed largely as one of a number of competing programmes of income transfer, rather than as an environmental protection scheme. In this light the comments of the minister for agriculture, food and forestry are particularly pertinent, when he observed that 'we see

REPS as a real money spinner for farm families' (Yates, *Dáil Debates*, 1996, Vol. 462, no. 4, p. 1046).

As an environmental protection scheme REPs also had an interface with the programme for the protection of Natural Heritage Areas. This scheme, which came under the jurisdiction of the Department of Arts, Culture, and the Gaeltacht (DACG), stipulates specific conditions which farms must operate under to qualify for payments. At first, the conditions drawn up for participants provoked a strong reaction from the farming lobby, particularly on the issue of stocking densities. Once again, after consultation with the relevant minister, in this case for arts, culture and the Gaeltacht, the severity of the rules relating to the stocking densities were reduced (*Farmers Journal*, 12 October 1996).

The DACG was also responsible for the implementation of the 1992 EU Habitats Directive. This Directive, which should have been implemented in 1994, was still under consideration as late as 1996. The delay was due largely to the resistance on the part of the agricultural lobby to regulations prescribed for SACs, which would have entailed a reduction in loss of income due to changes in farming rules for these areas. Under pressure from the agricultural lobby, the minister told the press that the delay in implementing the Habitats Directive was due to his efforts to secure adequate consultation and ensure that no group felt left out (*Irish Times*, 3 January 1997). However, it was clear that not all interest groups in the Irish political milieu were able to secure the access to and influence over policy granted to the agricultural lobby. The Irish Peatland Conservation Council, for example, claimed that the level of consultation they experienced was limited to one meeting with the DACG before Christmas 1996, at which they were simply shown a draft copy of the regulations and told that these could not be changed. On the other hand, the *Irish Times* reported that almost two days of the Partnership 2000 talks were devoted to discussions with the agricultural lobby, primarily on the issue of compensation (*Irish Times*, 3 January 1997).

Negotiations with the farmers continued until mid-February, when the farming press reported that the agricultural lobby had succeeded in securing a major breakthrough on the issue of compensation negotiations. Two packages were agreed: one for REPS participants in SACs and one for farmers in SACs but not in REPS. For those in REPS, the 40 hectare ceiling on payments was raised. Those not in REPS followed a special arts, culture and Gaeltacht plan and were required to follow the details of *agreements already reached with agricultural organisations* on National Heritage Areas (*Farmers Journal*, 22 February 1997). It is worth noting that when the minister announced that the SAC Order had been signed, he declared that apart from protecting habitats, *it would put much needed income into the pockets of smallholders* (*Irish Times*, 27 February 1997). Again, it is clear that the agricultural policy community secured its own terms for the implementation of a programme essentially geared towards environmental protection and conservation.

The latter part of the analysis of REPS illustrates how an agri-environmental scheme interacts with other policies in the sector in such a way that the existence of an environmental element in agricultural policy making cannot be substantiated. This failing is compounded by the conspicuous lack of a fully integrated approach to environmental policy, most evident in the controls on afforestation and the debacle surrounding the collapse of the Control Farmyard Pollution Scheme (CFYPS).

The minister of state at DAFF declared to the Dáil in January 1995 that environmental considerations would not be forgotten in the state's afforestation programme. A review of planning controls on large-scale forestry projects would be carried out in co-operation with the Department of the Environment (Deenihan, *Dáil Debates*, 26 January 1995, p. 539). Details of this co-operation were made public in May 1996. The environmental dimension to this policy focused largely on changes to planning permission, where new controls would reduce the threshold for which planning permission and Environmental Impact Assessments (EIAs) are required from 200 hectares to 70 hectares.[4] From May 1996, it stipulated that Coillte must notify local authorities of any application for grant aid for projects over 25 hectares, and consider the views of the local authority in any application. Furthermore, local authorities would designate areas considered sensitive to forestry development. While the reduction in the threshold at which planning permission and EIAs were required was a welcome move, particularly given the poor record of local authorities in this part of the environmental arena, difficulties persist.

These were not the only problems to be found in a forestry sector riven with ambiguities, most evident in the low level of integration between government departments. Indeed, in many ways it is by no means clear what the respective regulatory responsibilities of DAFF and the Department of the Environment are in this area. For instance, the minister for the environment informed the Dáil that the decision on the type of trees planted was primarily a matter for DAFF, while the environmental impact and planning requirements were in the jurisdiction of the Department of the Environment (Howlin, *Dáil Debates*, 1996, Vol. 465, no. 2, p. 458). When asked who would be responsible for environmental impact and planning controls of forestry, the minister of state at DAFF declared that the Forestry Department would be responsible for *all matters* affecting the forestry programme. When the suggestion was made that the Department of Environment saw elements of the forestry programme as falling within its remit, a spokesperson for DAFF replied that 'our Department will be responsible for *all matters that we deem affect the implementation of our programme*' (Deenihan, *Dáil Debates*, 1995, Vol. 454, no. 6, p. 1334, emphasis added).

Such a failure to achieve co-ordination between departments should come as little surprise to those conversant with the processes of Irish politics, where political prestige is won by those who successfully secure or defend the territory of their respective departments. It had been intended that the formation of the EPA would reduce such deficiencies in policy implementation. Indeed, at one stage the minister for the environment had gone so far as to declare that 'all state agencies will dovetail with the EPA to ensure that we strive for the pristine environment which is our common objective' (Howlin, *Dáil Debates*, 1995, Vol. 452, no. 2, p. 337). And yet, as a spokesman for the minister of DAFF candidly remarked, this element of the EPA's remit had not seeped through the labyrinthine structures of the Irish civil service sufficiently to be brought to his attention:

> my department has to date not found it necessary to consult the Environmental Protection Agency in relation to our forestry programme, nor has the Environmental Protection Agency found it necessary to approach my department requesting information or offering advice and/or recommendations on our forestry policy and practices. (Deenihan, *Dáil Debates*, 1995, Vol. 454, no. 6, p. 1332)

The reaction of the Department of the Environment to the collapse of the CFYPS attests further to the lack of any genuine spirit of institutional integration on environmental policy. The CFYPS was a central part of the government's effort to address agricultural pollution, and its subsequent collapse had a deleterious effect on REPS. When questioned about this collapse the minister for the environment claimed that questions in this regard should be addressed to DAFF and that they had 'no implications for my department' (Howlin, *Dáil Debates*, 1995, Vol. 453, pp. 2000–2022). The position held by DAFF was markedly different. As far as the minister for agriculture, food and forestry was concerned, the collapse of the CFYPS would impact upon the ability of farmers to reduce pollution. His response was that, in the absence of any direction from the Department of the Environment, he would exert the power of DAFF on local authorities, inhibiting them from prosecuting farmers for water pollution offences. The level of support the minister was willing to extend was conveyed in his speech to the Seanad when he argued that 'In view of the overall situation, *I am anxious that local authorities will be sensitive to this matter and I will ask my officials to communicate to them in this regard.*' (Yates, *Seanad Debates*, 1996, Vol. 143, no. 8, p. 956). Clearly, while the minister for the environment claimed that the collapse of the CFYPS did not come within his remit and therefore did not require comment, it was evident that the sentiments of the minister for agriculture, food and forestry were rather different.

Waste management

The problem of waste management has emerged as one of the most contentious areas of environmental politics in Ireland. Disputes such as those at Kill dump in Kildare and the controversial closure of the landfill site at Carrowbrowne in Galway have ensured that landfills, Not in My Back Yardism and debates about recycling remain an increasingly common feature of the Irish political landscape. With little attention given to location and more often than not poorly managed, landfills have been a consistent source of local protest. As if to complicate matters further, it now seems that a 'generation' of landfills, extended beyond their anticipated operational lifespan, are on the verge of closure, a situation that could rapidly precipitate a crisis in waste disposal.[5]

It is a debate both politically charged and complex, one that certainly does not revolve simply around the estate agent's old adage that what is important is location, location, location. Few would disagree that a policy vacuum has emerged, largely because of a failure on the part of central government to define the parameters of policy. Local authorities are faced with the prospect of making decisions not only on the location of landfills, or on whether to transport waste to other areas (super-dumps), but also on how to finance waste disposal. Contentious though this area of environmental regulation is, it is depressing to note that the EPA's role remains far more circumscribed than many had anticipated. Indeed, it is an area of policy that reveals, once again, that grey areas persist, and that integration has been a term loosely defined and often inappropriately adopted in describing the EPA's role.

During the 1970s and 1980s waste management was largely controlled through public health statutes and ministerial regulations implementing relatively undemanding EU legislation (Scannell, 1995). However, from the mid-1980s onwards it attracted the attention of EU environmental policy makers. The government responded with the Waste Management Act, 1996, which attempted to draw together many of the objectives of EU policy. The Waste Management Act accords the EPA a central role in regulating waste, places a duty upon it to produce a national hazardous waste plan, and grants the agency powers to issue and monitor licences for the disposal and recovery of waste (Meehan, 1996, p. 59).

The Waste Management Act contains many policy developments in line with recent EU directives and incorporated into the EPA Act, 1992: a preference for management plans, licensing, compliance monitoring, and significant discretion on how to achieve the goals set. The Waste Management Act thus affords regulatory bodies a variety of options, ranging from charges and taxes to the dissemination of information and operation of voluntary agreements. To date, the most prominent development in this regard has been the agreement struck with IBEC over waste recycling, whereby the minister set up a voluntary agreement. It is one of several avenues available to the minister, who may stimulate recycling by providing financial assistance, imposing mandatory regulations, establishing voluntary programmes or a combination of all three.

In the case of packaging waste, successive administrations were prepared to give industry the opportunity to organise voluntary approaches to the problem, suggesting that in the absence of satisfactory progress, mandatory schemes would be imposed. IBEC responded with a recycling and packaging initiative that set modest, comfortably achievable targets. However, by far the most significant area of change in the area of waste management in Ireland has been the introduction of waste licences regulated by the EPA. Here, section 98 of the Waste Management Act redefined the relationship between the EPA and the local authority. It stipulated those operations that require an IPC licence for the incineration of hazardous and hospital waste, waste with a capacity of more than one tonne per hour, and the use of heat for the manufacture of fuel from waste (Brassil, 1996). It would be churlish to suggest that the Waste Management Act is not a significant improvement on previous regulations. However, this should not detract our attention from problems that persist, particularly with regard to landfill charges and the designation of sites.

One of the more controversial aspects of waste management in Ireland has been the dependence upon landfill, a method of disposal that accounts for 70 per cent of commercial waste and 98 per cent of domestic waste. This preponderance of landfill is aggravated further by a failure to establish a national waste policy. Successive administrations chose to leave decisions to local authorities, defending this position on the grounds of the EU's preference for the principle that the polluter should pay. This means that the cost of collection and disposal of waste, from either industrial, commercial or domestic sources, should be met as close to the source as possible. How local authorities are supposed to devise the financing of these schemes remains unresolved. Landfill charges have been mooted, a policy option favoured in some quarters (see Barrett and Lawlor, 1996). However, politicians are innately conservative creatures and are haunted by the spectre of being the harbinger of an 'Irish poll tax'.

In theory, such a charge should stimulate a diversion of waste up the hierarchy, encouraging composting, recycling, waste minimisation or incineration with an element of energy recovery. To date, a range of systems for recycling, composting or waste minimisation has emerged. However, as Barrett and Lawlor point out, price volatility in this area presents a significant chalenge to its economic feasibility. The average price of recyclables in September 1993 was IR£17 per tonne, a figure which increased to IR£60 per tonne in June 1995 but then returned to IR£30 per tonne (Barrett and Lawlor, 1995). Barrett and Lawlor estimate that aluminium recycling is profitable in its own right, whereas the recycling of bottles and textiles depends on large volumes and sustained prices (Barrett and Lawlor, 1996, p. 76; Barrett *et al.*, 1997).

Traditionally, planning authorities and An Bord Pleanála have been involved in environmental protection in the assessment of land use. Prior to 1994, issues of environmental pollution associated with proposed or existing developments were assessed by local authorities and controlled through conditions attached to planning permission. Appeals were taken to An Bord Pleanála. However, section 98 of the EPA Act shifted the terms of responsibility so that where an IPC licence was required, the EPA was the competent authority. However, this was only in so far as it related to environmental pollution matters; all other considerations (landscape, visual effects, traffic implications etc.) remained within the ambit of the planning authority and An Bord Pleanála.

This division of responsibilities between the EPA and the planning authorities on projects that require an IPC licence caused considerable confusion. The outcome of the changes contained in the EPA Act was that neither the planning authority nor An Bord Pleanála can consider matters relating to *potential* environmental pollution from a project where an IPC licence was required. Pollution generated during the development phase may be considered, but not pollution which is likely to occur once the plant is up and running. The impact that this subdivision of responsibility can have came to light most prominently in the inspector's report on Masonite.

The proposal by Masonite to construct a fibre-manufacturing plant in Leitrim was opposed by numerous parties who argued that, while issues of water and air pollution may not be considered by the Board (following section 98, EPA Act), they felt that such matters were subjective perceptions regarding pollution risk and, therefore, were relevant planning matters (Brassil, 1996, p. 21). However, the Inspector concluded that 'perception' was a matter relating to the risk of environmental pollution once the plant was up and running, a factor that could be considered only by the EPA.

In a further issue raised in this case, Masonite suggested that the Board and the EPA must take a balanced view of the proposed development with regard to 'environmental protection and infrastructural, economic and social progress' (Brassil, 1996, p. 22). The inspector's response was to point out that 'the sub-division of responsibilities resulted in two separate balancing acts, in which the benefits of the development are weighed against separate sets of drawbacks or disadvantages' (Galligan, 1996a, p.2). Given that the two bodies may utilise different criteria in terms of costs and benefits, it was quite possible they might reach 'two conflicting recommendations' (Brassil, 1996, p. 22).

In part, this subdivision of responsibilities has clearly taken some of the teeth out of An Bord Pleanála, restricting its capacity to impose planning conditions. However, it is also worth pointing out that in the event that the planning authority or An Bord Pleanála find in favour of a particular development, it is likely to increase the pressure upon the EPA to recommend the proposal, no doubt with conditions, but recommend nevertheless. Government is unlikely to be too enamoured if a major project is accepted by An Bord Pleanála and then turned down by the EPA. After all, the EPA's function essentially is to engineer a situation in which compromises can be reached, to ensure that firms *become* compliant, and not to prevent development.[6]

While it is plausible (if not entirely convincing) to suggest that the 'grey areas' that materialised in the EPA Act were an 'oversight', no such defence can be offered with regard to the Waste Management Act. It was an issue raised extensively at both the committee stage of the bill and at the final stages in the Dáil. Trevor Sargent, for example, moved an amendment which stated that 'a planning authority will consider a planning application for a development that requires a waste licence *only after that licence has been granted*' (*Dáil Debates*, 1996, Vol. 460, p. 88, emphasis added). The intention of the amendment was explicitly to avoid the problems raised in the Masonite case, where 'grey areas' emerged over responsibility between An Bord Pleanála and the EPA (see Taylor, 1998b).

The minister, while 'mindful of the arguments advanced', conversant with the possibility 'for confusion' and aware of 'anomalies', chose to reject the amendment. Presented with an opportunity to address a serious deficiency in the EPA Act, the government stalled, sheepishly looked around and found cover in the bemusing phrase that it wanted to establish an 'expert body on the environment. It argued that it did not want to alter sub section (3) of the Act which delineates the respective roles of the planning authorities and the EPA' (*Dáil Debates*, 1996, Vol. 460, p. 88). Why? The government's abject response was that reversing the EPA's position in the 'queue to assess' would unnecessarily crowd the planning arena.

The tensions that exist in the subdivision of responsibilities between the EPA and the planning authorities reappear in the area of mineral extraction, which has been designated a schedule 1 activity and is subject, therefore, to EPA licensing. Mineral extraction and storage are unique among list 1 activities in that the conditions of the licence may never lapse; the mine may have closed, but the storage of waste and post-closure care present innumerable difficulties for future environmental management (Derham, 1995).

While the scarring of the landscape is undoubtedly the most visible environmental intrusion, one which usually attracts the more animated forms of political protest, policy also needs to address some of the more complicated issues which surround mining, and which are aired only rarely in the public domain. The pollution problems that surfaced during the mid-1990s at Silvermines, County Tipperary, is a case in point, where waste storage, acid generation and the release of toxic substances into ground water supplies emerged as important features of a lapse in post-closure care. The problems presented to the EPA were born largely out of the subdivision of responsibilities with the planning authorities, and from the complexities surrounding the transfer of mine ownership and post-closure care. To most people, it would have appeared appropriate to include the developmental work of the mine within the environmental evaluation for licensing undertaken by the EPA. However, the EPA emerges as the competent authority only when the company is up and running or, in this case, when a product is being extracted. An important distinction needs to be drawn between cases such as Masonite and that of mineral extraction, since mining carries the potential to raise pollution matters further down the road. Excavated material has to be stored, and disposal therefore needs to be controlled (Derham, 1995).

It is not the only area in which the EPA has experienced difficulty. The legislation has struggled to come to terms with the complexity of changing ownership and post-closure care, issues that came to the fore in the investigation surrounding problems at the Tailings Management Facility at Silvermines, where mine tailings waste was produced. This was a waste from a metal ore processing mill after the extraction of metal concentrate from finely crushed rock. The risk posed from such waste depends to a large extent on the management methods and standards applied. The primary ores extracted at Silvermines were lead, zinc and silver (which contained pyrite and chalcopyrite). The latter two are high sulphide minerals and when incorporated into tailings waste have the potential to become acidic and produce acid rock drainage. Such waste storage requires perpetual maintenance (EPA, 1999).[7]

The matter of waste storage in cases such as that at Silvermines presents considerable difficulties to the EPA, who consider that 'storage of mineral waste is only subject to a IPC licence where *related* to IPC'd extractive and processing operations' (Derham, 1995, p. 129). 'Related' in this context could either mean 'part of the same operation (carried out by the same company operating the processing plant) or it could mean waste storage by a separate company on contract where the waste originates from an IPC'd extractive operation' (Derham, 1995, p. 130). Put simply, it becomes an issue of establishing responsibility for the site and, ultimately, who pays.

In certain areas of planning there is legal provision that creates a financial guarantee or bond, operated by the Department of Trade, Energy and Communications and the planning authorities. However, planning bonds of this type tend to be finite and are usually exhausted or returned to the operator on the completion of the project (Derham, 1995). It is one thing to set aside a fund to deal with a defined closure plan, where costings can be confidently approximated; it is quite another where remediation is required in the event of unforeseen circumstances. It is a matter where the EPA has made important strides, rectifying previous policy failures, and upon which it should be commended.

At the European level, the issue of environmental liability emerged as a logical extension to the phasing in of the 'polluter pays' principle. The intention was to put in place a liability regime that would encourage the implementation of environmental rules. As the EU commissioner on environmental liability stated:

> it is essential we have a system in place which will force the people who cause pollution to clean it up. Even more important, we must ensure that everyone engaged in potentially dangerous activities knows about the risks of being liable in this way, so that they have a strong incentive to prevent pollution happening in the first place. (Bjerregaard, cited in Derham, 1999, p. 2)

One of the obstacles to developing a policy on environmental liability is that public liability policies have a clause that exclude coverage in areas thought likely to incur large costs. As Derham notes, generally what is covered is the 'big bang event', rather than long-term environmental damage. However, under regulations from 1996 the EPA is empowered, where it thinks necessary, to require IPC licensees to furnish information on financial security to meet commitments or liabilities which may arise after the operation has ceased production (Derham, 1999). It is a welcome development and should reduce the possibility of incidents such as that at Silvermines.

There can be no doubt that the EPA's role in many areas of waste management represents a distinct improvement, most notably in the introduction of monitoring and IPC licences for landfill sites. However, the persistence of grey areas of responsibility presents significant hurdles. It is a reflection not so much of any shortcomings in the EPA as of the unwillingness on the part of government to create a legislative framework that could have resolved these difficulties. It is a political issue, an omission that has its roots in the ability of the planning lobby to persuade government that a 'streamlined' planning appeals system was essential to the health of the Celtic Tiger

Some concluding remarks

That the institutional structures of environmental regulation in Ireland have undergone change in recent years is not in dispute. What remains a far more important source of consternation is not so much the inadequacy of any specific element of the legislation as the failure to overhaul a regulatory style that has more often than not made significant concessions to the agricultural and business lobbies. It would be churlish to suggest that positive developments have not been achieved or improvements sustained. The new regulatory powers available to the EPA, the development of new monitoring techniques, and a welcome zeal to allow access to environmental information surely represent more than simply a 'political gesture' to an increasingly politicised environmental lobby. And yet, such progress should not be allowed to conceal the flaws that remain. In particular, the legislative framework is replete with opt-out clauses, features which sit comfortably within the Irish style of policy making. Indeed, it is the persistence of this soft regulatory ethos that remains the hallmark of this new framework, revealing rather more in the way of continuity with than of change from its discredited predecessor.

Above all else the restoration of order was essential. The accent of reform was firmly upon imposing uniformity in licence conditions, compressing the timescale for authorisations to be granted and 'calling time' on vexatious appeals. The origins of the EPA lie therefore not in any systematic overhaul of administrative convention but in an attempt to reconstruct a new form of environmental governance, one that demanded it meet the criticisms of the environmental lobby without threatening the free market ethos that underpinned the Celtic Tiger.

Notes

1 For a discussion of the changing nature of risk and how it impacts upon regulation see Taylor (2004).
2 For more detail on this see S. Gillane, Law Report, *Irish Times* (14 December 1998, p. 26).
3 Prior to the hearing, the Syntex plant in Clarecastle had been taken over by the Swiss pharmaceutical giant Roche.
4 This includes cumulative afforestation, i.e. within 500 metres, by or on behalf of a single developer over a three-year period where the afforestation would result in a total area planted exceeding 70 hectares.

5   This emerged as a serious concern among residents in Silvermines, County Tip-
    perary, where a subsidiary of Waste Management Inc. (a huge American
    multinational company) proposed to develop a disused barytes mine contain-
    ing 1.6 million cubic metres of toxic waste into a landfill. The *Irish Times*
    reported that a number of local authorities were 'waiting to see' whether the
    company would get a licence before deciding what to do with their waste (*Irish
    Times*, 25 January 1999).

6   It is common in cases such as this to pursue the possibility (where objections
    arise) for alternative sites to be considered, an avenue that was taken by the
    third party objectors. However, it was an instance in which the subdivision of
    responsibilities between the Board and the EPA raised further issues for con-
    cern. Masonite had argued that an adequate body of water for the disposal of
    effluent was necessary in its site selection, a point on which the Inspector con-
    curred, noting that once again these considerations no longer remained in the
    ambit of An Bord Pleanála and were the responsibility of the EPA. It has
    undoubtedly been a source of consternation among the planning authorities,
    since it effectively precludes 'the Board from consideration of the entire range
    of site selection criteria, thereby obviating the possibility of a comprehensive
    and fully informed assessment by the authority ultimately charged with loca-
    tional considerations' (Brassil, 1996, p. 23).

7   In instances where underground storage is preferred, and where ground water
    has been lowered, consideration should be given to the potential for a 'shock
    load' of contamination arising from back-filled waste when the mine is
    reflooded (EPA, 1999). Once flooded, the ongoing risk of acid generation is
    reduced and thus enhanced mobility of priority contaminants is inhibited.
    Attention should be paid, therefore, to removing any potentially polluting
    process chemicals from the tailings waste prior to back-filling; otherwise there
    is a high risk of migration (Derham, 1995). Tailings waste is usually stored in
    varying proportions between underground disposal and surface impound-
    ment. The principal driving force behind the agency's approach to mining
    waste is the EU Groundwater Directive (80/68/EEC), which prohibits certain
    list 1 substances and requires the limitation of others (list 2) from entering
    ground water. The agency is required to ensure that all technical precautions
    are taken to prevent the discharge of list 1 substances. The regulations (Local
    Government and Water Pollution), 1992, contain a zero-polution quality stan-
    dard in respect of list 1 substances. However, this presents the 'EPA with a legal
    difficulty in that there is no laboratory that can determine a zro value in any
    analysis' (Derham, 1995, p. 130). Where surface storage is chosen, water sat-
    uration of the waste has to be maintained and presents a residual and long-
    term pollution potential long after the mine has stopped producing. In the case
    of the Tailings Management Facility at Silvermines, which the EPA reported as
    being 'a perpetual risk to health and the environment', the pollution stemmed
    from a tailings pond which had been rehabilitated in the mid-1980s. The mine
    was formerly owned by Mogul Ireland and closed in 1982. The company itself
    was taken over by Ennex International in 1984, and the Tailings Management

Facility was later sold to a farmer with no mining or waste management experience, a move which the EPA believed contravened the Waste Management Act, 1996, Section 32(2) (EPA, 1999).

Conclusion

There can be little doubt that the last two negotiated agreements between the social partners, Partnership 2000 and the PPF, have succeeded in embedding national agreements firmly in the Irish political psyche. The political furore that accompanied a severe currency crisis in the early 1990s has been weathered, political and economic stability maintained and the problem of long-term unemployment 'eased'. Few politicians would now subscribe to the view that national-level agreements have not contributed significantly to Ireland's economic regeneration.

This book maintains that amid a period of bewildering economic success the Irish state has attempted to engineer a form of governance capable of reconciling the demand for the level of economic growth of other major European countries with ensuring at least a modicum of social inclusion. In contrast to those countries such as the USA or the UK, where a neo-liberal political strategy has been dominant, Ireland has opted to pursue a neo-corporatist approach to the restructuring of its economy. As part of a wider attempt to remain competitive within a new global order, it has increased the number of political actors now involved in the construction and implementation of policy.

The negotiated agreements of the late 1980s and 1990s formed the bedrock of the creation of a stable political environment in which management was encouraged to innovate and reduce productive rigidities. In such circumstances it is palpably clear that it is no longer credible to view political concertation as simply an incomes policy, a form of compensatory state action and/or a belated attempt at crisis management. In turn, an explanation of the shift in the fortunes of the Irish polity demands that we abandon the claustrophobic idea that negotiated forms of governance are the outcome of a social democratic political vision, or that they necessarily impart an increased role for the state and/or a commitment to the redistribution of wealth. Only then can we begin to see that a political project that extends over a period of time may contain a confusing and contrasting myriad of (inconsistent) ideological arguments to support a particular trajectory. The waters are often muddier than commentators would prefer, and political views are prone to deviate in the event of political illwinds. All will not be plain sailing. In the aftermath of an unprecedented economic boom the trade unions remain perturbed at escalating house prices and the failure to redistribute more evenly the economic gains of the Celtic Tiger.

This book has argued that it is crucial we place recent developments within an international context. The forces of globalisation (or at least the perceived need to take cognisance of these alleged forces) and the influence of supranational institutions continue to stimulate moves towards further deregulation and privatisation, curtailing a range of mechanisms for governance. This does not necessarily mean an end to national politics or the assertion of the national interest in the international arena. New relationships of governance emerge and are necessarily contested. The policy developments that emanate from the international arena, and that are shaped by its attenuated processes, are refracted in politics at the national level. This is a position that contrasts sharply with those that assume that nation states will have little autonomy in the global order. In areas such as civil service reform and rural governance these issues have been particularly prominent.

Within European public policy circles the reform of public service delivery is purported to signal a wider process of 'hollowing out' the state. Policy is no longer the outcome of simple directives from central government. Rather, government interacts with a myriad of organisations charged with providing public services. The kernel of this debate can be found in the influence that international reform has had upon the Irish civil service. For those employed within the civil service it has involved the adoption of flexible working practices, new forms of accounting, greater transparency, reductions in cost and the introduction of measures designed to enhance 'client services'. It is reform that has sought to reduce bureaucratic rigidity. What remains quite clear is that Ireland has followed a succession of states that have demanded greater control of civil servants, reducing the level of discretion available to them.

The issue of whether the modern state is 'hollowing out' has been particularly prominent in the area of rural and urban development. In such a context the book has argued that the Irish state has been at the forefront of moves to develop innovative responses to alleviate the types of social division often associated with the drive towards a modern, flexible economy. While such concerns are far from new, the response has been influenced by reforms in public policy at both the national and international levels.

Similarly, the changing nature of environmental governance has been shaped by developments that extend beyond national boundaries. During the late 1980s a protracted upsurge in environmental protest had enveloped the Irish state in its struggle to construct a new political discourse on the environment. It was a discourse shaped not simply by 'green issues' such as the eutrophication of lakes, fish kills, the loss of blue flags or a sprawling road network. The formation of the EPA was the outcome not of a concerted desire to construct a new ecological modernity, but of the need to accommodate the environmentalist critique of the 1980s without undermining the free market ethos that pervades the rhetoric of the Celtic Tiger. It is not ecological degradation, environmental justice or the quality of the environment that is at the forefront of debate. Rather, government appears concerned more with the complicated process of organising consent around new definitions of acceptable pollution.

That the Irish economy has experienced an unparalleled period of economic growth remains incontrovertible. And yet, almost imperceptibly, a few are now willing to question the nature of this economic and social development. It often appears that the critic stands alone, vulnerable to the heinous charge of begrudgery. From environmental protest at property development to union 'intransigence' over low pay, the prevailing view is that we should not question, let alone resist, the mantra of the free market.

As a succession of budgets during the late 1990s testifies, political discourse in Ireland is increasingly concerned with the cost, impact and function of the welfare state. Once viewed as a component crucial to the completion of any democracy, the institutions of the welfare state are now the subject of intense scrutiny. Irrespective of one's political persuasion, it is evident that the final curtain has been drawn on the KWS: charged with being a monolithic institutional apparatus ill-suited to the prevailing conditions of contemporary capitalism, it has been fatally wounded by persistent unemployment and increasing poverty.

While a succession of negotiated national agreements have framed public policy since the early 1990s, the political and ideological nature of those agreements has not remained static. On the contrary, during this period we have witnessed a discernible drift in the ideological complexion of the coalition governments as they embrace more willingly the strictures of neo-liberal economics. Since 1994 there has been a sustained challenge to the social democratic arguments used to justify a role for political concertation. Indeed, emblematic of this political revisionism is the fact that more often than not the origins of the Celtic Tiger are (allegedly) to be found in the dynamism of the free market and not in political intermediation. Irrespective of the policy candidate, the sterility of the public sector with its incumbent monopolies is counterposed to a new modernity, in which the entrepreneurial spirit remains the driving force.

By contrast to the experience of our counterparts in New Zealand and the UK, it often seems that this transition has been seamless, possible largely because of the startling nature of economic growth. It would be churlish to suggest that many elements of Irish society have not benefited from this growth. It would be misleading, however, to deny that those who have gained most have been the employed, and those who have gained inordinately have been those on higher pay.

It is important to recognise therefore that while the negotiated governance constructed during this period of extended accumulation may prove successful, it will not necessarily be predicated on a redistribution of wealth between active and inactive members of the labour market. An improvement in public finances may have ensured that a calculated assault upon the welfare state has been largely absent, but few would argue with the fact that it remains incongruous, indeed obscene, that poverty persists in modern Ireland.

Bibliography

Adshead, M., 1996. 'Beyond Clientelism: Agricultural Networks in Ireland and the EU'. *West European Politics*, Vol. 19, No. 3, pp. 583–608.

Allanson, P. and M. Whitby, 1996. 'Prologue: The Rural Economy and the British Countryside', in P. Allanson and M. Whitby (eds), *The Rural Economy and the British Countryside*. Earthscan: London.

Allen, R. and T. Jones, 1990. *Guests of the Nation: People of Ireland versus the Multinationals*. Earthscan: London.

Bacon, Peter, and Associates, 2000. *The Housing Market in Ireland: An Economic Evaluation of Trends and Prospects*. Stationery Office: Dublin.

Barrett, A. and J. Lawlor, 1996. 'Solid Waste: Should We, Can We, Continue Relying on Landfill'. *Irish Planning and Environmental Law Journal*, Vol. 3, No. 4, pp. 73–9.

Barrett, A., J. Lawlor and S. Scott, 1997. *The Fiscal System and the Polluter Pays Principle: A Case Study of Ireland*. Ashgate: Aldershot.

Barrington, T., 1980. *The Irish Administrative System*. Institute for Public Administration: Dublin.

Barry, U. and P. Jackson, 1989. 'Women's Employment and Multinationals in Ireland: The Creation of a New Female Labour Force', in D. Eleson and R. Pearson (eds), *Women's Employment and Multi-nationals in Europe*. Macmillan: London.

Beck, U., 1995. 'The Politics of Risk Society', in J. Franklin (ed.), *The Politics of Risk Society*. Polity: Cambridge.

Black, B., 1994. 'Labour Market Incentive Structures and Employee Performance'. *British Journal of Industrial Relations*, Vol. 32, No. 1, pp. 99–111.

Black, W. A., 1993. 'The Contraction of Collective Bargaining in Britain'. *British Journal of Industrial Relations*, Vol. 31, No. 2, pp. 189–200.

Block, F., 1987. *Revising State Theory: Essays in Politics and Post-industrialism*. Philadelphia, PA: Temple University Press.

Boston J., 1999. *Redesigning the Welfare State in New Zealand: Problems Policies and Prospects*. Oxford University Press: Oxford.

Bottomore, T. (ed.), 1992. *Citizenship and Social Class*. London: Pluto Press.

Boylan, T. A., 1992. 'Paradigms in Rural Development: From Critique to Coherence?', in M. O'Cinneide and M. Cuddy (eds), *Perspectives on Rural Development in Advanced Economies*. Centre for Development Studies, Social Science Research Centre, University College Galway: Galway.

——, 2002. 'From Stabilisation to Economic Growth: The Contribution of Macroeconomic Policy', in G. Taylor (ed.), *Issues in Irish Public Policy*. Irish Academic Press: Dublin.

Boyle, R., 1997a. 'Developing an Integrated Performance Measurement Framework for the Civil Service'. Committee for Public Management Research (CMPR) discussion paper 2. Institute for Public Administration: Dublin.

——, 1997b. 'Team Based Working'. Committee for Public Management Research (CMPR) discussion paper 3. Institute for Public Administration: Dublin.

——, 1997c. 'The Use of Rewards in Civil Service Management'. *Committee for Public Management Research (CMPR) discussion paper 4*. Institute for Public Administration: Dublin.

——, 1999. 'Regulatory Reform: Lessons from the International Experience'. Committee for Public Management Research (CMPR) discussion paper 12. Institute of Public Administration: Dublin.

Brassil, D., 1996. 'The Interface between Planning and IPC: After Masonite'. *Irish Planning and Environmental Law Journal*, Vol. 3, No. 1, pp. 20–3.

Brown, W. A. and J. Walsh, 1991. 'Pay Determination in Britain in the 1980s: The Anatomy of Decentralisation'. *Oxford Review of Economic Policy*, Vol. 7, pp. 45–59.

Buckley, J., J. Corcoran, J. Devlin, J. Feehily, F. Flanagan, D. McNally, M. O'Grady, J. Walsh and M. Whelan, 1999. 'Integrating Performance Management in the Irish Civil Service: Performance and Human Resource Issues. *Administration*, Vol. 47, No. 3, pp. 3–31.

Busch, A., 2000. 'Unpacking the Globalisation Debate: Approaches, Evidence and Data', in Hay and Marsh, 2000.

Byrne, D., 1996. 'Environmental Impact Statements: Their Role in the Process of Pig and Poultry Units in Ireland 1990–93', *Irish Planning and Environmental Law Journal*, Vol. 1, No. 3, pp. 123–9.

C&AG (Comptroller and Auditor General), 1996a. *Report on Value for Money Examination: Procurement in Universities*. Stationery Office: Dublin.

——, 1996b. *Administrative Budgets in the Irish Civil Service*. Stationery Office: Dublin.

——, 1998. *Consultancies in the Civil Service.*Stationery Office: Dublin.

Callan, T. and B. Nolan, 1999. *Tax and Welfare Changes, Poverty and Work Incentives in Ireland*. ESRI: Dublin.

Calmfors, L., 1993. 'Centralisation of Wage Bargaining and Macroeconomic Performance: A Survey' 3. OECD Working Papers 131. OECD: Paris.

——, 1994. 'Active Labour Market Policy and Unemployment: A Framework for the Analysis of Crucial Design Features'. OECD Economic Studies 22, pp. 7–47. OECD: Paris.

Calmfors, L. and J. Driffel, 1994. 'Bargaining Structure, Corporatism and Macroeconomic Performance'. *Economic Policy*, Vol. 6, pp. 118–37.

Clarke, S., 1992. 'What in the F****'s Name is Post-Fordism?', in Gilbert *et al..*, 1992.

Collins, K. and D. Earnshaw, 1992. 'The Implementation and Enforcement of European Community Environment Legislation'. *Environmental Politics*, Vol. 1, No. 4, pp. 213–49.

Collins, N. and T. Cradden, 2001. *Irish Politics Today*. Manchester University Press: Manchester.

Collins, N. and M. O'Shea, 2003. 'Clientelism: Rights and Favours', in M. Adshead and M. Millar (eds), *Public Administration and Public Policy in Ireland*. Routledge: London.

Commins, P. and M. Keane, 1994. 'Developing the Rural Economy: Problems, Programmes and Prospects'. In NESC, 1994.

Coolahan, J. (ed.), 1993. *Report on the National Education Convention*. Stationery Office: Dublin.

Craig, S. and K. McKeown, 1994. 'Progress Through Partnership: An Evaluation Report on the PESP Pilot Initiative on Long-term Unemployment'. Combat Poverty Agency: Dublin.

Culliton, J., 1992. 'A Time for Change: Industrial Policy for the 1990s'. Industrial Policy Review Group. Stationery Office: Dublin.

Curtin, C. and T. Varley, 1997. 'Take Your Partners and Face the Music: Community Groups and Area Based Partnerships in Rural Ireland', in P. Brennan (ed.), *L'Irlande: Identités et Modernité*. Centre de Question des Revues, Université Charles De Gaulle: Lille.

Curtin C., T. Haase and H. Tovey, 1996. *Poverty in Rural Ireland: A Political Economy Perspective*. Oak Tree Press: Dublin.

D'Art, D. and T. Turner, 1999. 'An Attitudinal Revolution in Irish Industrial Relations: The End of Them and Us?'. *British Industrial Relations*, Vol. 37, No. 1, pp. 101–16.

Deloitte Touche, 1997. 'Report for the University Chief Financial Officers' Group: Procurement of Universities Value for Money Report'. Dublin.

Department of Labour, 1991. *Department of Labour Annual Report, 1991*. Stationery Office: Dublin.

Derham, J., 1995. 'IPC Licensing of Mining Activities'. *Irish Planning and Environmental Law Journal*, Vol. 2, No. 4, pp. 127–31.

——, 1999. *Providing for Environmental Liabilities in Integrated Pollution Control Licensed Operations*. EPA: Wexford.

Devlin, J., 1969. 'Report of the Public Service Review Group, 1966–69'. Dublin.

DoE (Department of Education), 1984. *The Programme for Action in Education, 1984–7*. Stationery Office: Dublin.

——, 1992. *Education for a Changing World*. Stationery Office: Dublin.

——, 1995. *Charting our Educational Future*. Stationery Office: Dublin.

Dolowitz, D. and D. Marsh, 1996. 'Who Learns What from Whom: A Review of the Policy Transfer Literature'. *Political Studies*, Vol. 44, No. 2, pp. 343–57.

——, 2000. 'Learning from Abroad: The Role of Policy Transfer in Contemporary Policy Making'. *Governance*, Vol. 13, No. 1, pp. 5–25.

Dolowitz, D., S. Greenwold and D. Marsh, 1999. 'Something Old, Something New, Something Borrowed, but Why Red White and Blue?'. *Parliamentary Affairs*, Vol. 52, No. 4, pp. 700–730.

Dore, R., 1988. 'Rigidities in the Labour Market'. *Government and Opposition*, Vol. 23, No. 4, pp. 393–412.

Eikeland, S., 1999. 'New Rural Pluriactivity? Household Strategies and Rural Renewal in Norway'. *Sociologia Ruralis*, Vol. 39, No. 3, pp. 359–76.

EPA (Environmental Protection Agency), 1996a. *Integrated Pollution Control Licensing: A Guide to Implementation and Enforcement in Ireland*. EPA: Wexford.

——, 1996b. *Water Quality in Ireland*. EPA: Wexford.

——, 1997. *Report on IPC Licensing and Control*. EPA: Wexford.

——, 1999. *Report on an Investigation of Recent Developments at Silvermines Tailings Management Facility, Co Tipperary*. EPA: Wexford.

Fahey, T., 1998. 'Housing and Social Exclusion', in S. Healy and B. Reynolds (eds), *Social Policy in Ireland: Principles, Practice and Problems*. Oak Tree Press: Dublin.

——, 1999. *Social Housing in Ireland: A Study of Success, Failure and Lessons Learned*. Combat Poverty Agency: Dublin.

Fanning, R., 1978. *The Irish Department of Finance: 1922–58*. Institute for Public Administration: Dublin.

Farnham, D. (ed.), 1999. *Managing Academic Staff in Changing University Systems*. Open University Press: London.

Faughnan, P. and P. Kelleher, 1993. *The Voluntary Sector and the State*. Conference of Major Religious Superiors: Dublin.

Finn, D., 1989. *Training Without Jobs: New Deals and Broken Promises: From Raising the School Leaving Age to the Youth Training Programme*. Macmillan: London.

Fitzgerald, G., 1991. *All in a Life: An Autobiography*. Gill and Macmillan: Dublin.

Friedman, M., 1969. *Free to Choose*. Penguin: London.

Gallagher, M. and L Komito, 1999. 'Dáil Deputies and their Constituency Work', in J. Coakley and M. Gallagher (eds), *Politics in the Republic of Ireland*. PSAI and Frank Cass: Dublin

Galligan, E., 1996a. 'Editorial: Masonite Inspector's Report'. *Irish Planning and Environmental Law Journal*, Vol. 3, No. 1.

——, 1996b. 'Editorial: An Bord Pleanála's Report, 1995'. *Irish Planning and Environmental Law Journal*, Vol. 3, No. 3, p. 142.

Gamble, A., 1996. *Hayek: The Iron Cage of Liberty*. Polity: Cambridge.

Gilbert, N., R. Burrows and A. Pollert, 1992. *Fordism and Flexibility: Division and Change*. Macmillan: London.

Gobeyn, M. J., 1993. 'Explaining the Decline of Macro-political Bargaining Structures in Advanced Capitalist Societies'. *Governance: An International Journal of Policy and Administration*, Vol. 6, pp. 3–22.

Goldthorpe, J. H. (ed.), 1984. *Order and Conflict in Contemporary Capitalism*. Clarendon Press: Oxford.

Government of Ireland, 1993. *Ireland: National Development Plan 1994–1999*. Stationery Office: Dublin.   .

Green, R., 2001. 'Structural Reform in Ireland: Deregulation and the Knowledge

Based Economy'. Mimeo. National University of Ireland: Galway.

Greer, J., 1992. 'The Rural Environment: Asset or Constraint', in M. O' Cinneide and M. Cuddy (eds), *Perspectives on Rural Development in Advanced Economies*. Centre for Development Studies, Social Science Research Centre, University College Galway: Galway.

Habermas, J., 1989. *The New Conservatism*. Polity: Cambridge.

Hardiman, N., 1988. *Pay Politics and Economic Performance in Ireland 1970–87*. Clarendon Press: Oxford.

Harvey, D., 1996. 'The Role of Markets in the Rural Economy', in P. Allanson and M. Whitby (eds), *The Rural Economy and the British Countryside*. Earthscan: London.

Hay, C., 1999. 'Crisis and the Structural Transformation of the State: Interrogating the Process of Change'. *British Journal of Political Science and International Relations*, Vol. 1, No. 3, pp. 317–44.

Hay, C. and D. Marsh (eds), 2000. *Demystifying Globalisation*. Macmillan: London.

Hayek, F., 1960. *The Constitution of Liberty*. Routledge: London.

Healy, S. and B. Reynolds, 1993. 'Work, Jobs and Income: Towards a New Paradigm', in S. Healy and B. Reynolds, *New Frontiers for Full Citizenship*. Conference for Major Religious Superiors: Dublin.

——, 1994. *Towards an Adequate Income for All*. Conference of the Religious in Ireland (Cori): Dublin.

Hirst, P. and J. Zeitlin, 1991. 'Flexible Specialization Versus Post-Fordism: Theory, Evidence and Policy Implications'. *Economy and Society*, Vol. 20, pp. 1–56.

Hoggett, P., 1994. 'The Politics of Modernisation of the UK Welfare State', in R. Burrows and B. Loader (eds), *Towards a Post-Fordist Welfare State*. Routledge: London.

Hughes, G. and B. J. Whelan, 1996. *Occupational and Personal Pension Coverage, 1995*. ESRI: Dublin.

Hussey, G., 1993. *Ireland Today: An Anatomy of a Changing State*. Viking: Dublin.

Hyman, R., 1988. 'Flexible Specialisation: Miracle or Myth?', in R. Hyman and W. Streeck, *Industrial Relations and New Technology*. Blackwell: Oxford.

IDA (Industrial Development Authority), 1998. *IDA Industrial Plan 1978–1982*. IDA: Dublin.

Ives, J., 1985. 'Hazard Export in the Developing Irish Republic', in J. Ives (ed.), *Export of Hazards, Transnational Companies and Environmental Control*. Routledge and Kegan Paul: Boston.

Jabes, J. and D. Zussman, 1988. 'Motivation, Rewards and Satisfaction in the Canadian Federal Public Service'. *Canadian Public Administration*, Vol. 31, No. 2, pp. 204–25.

Jessop, B., 1990. 'Regulation Theories in Retrospect and Prospect'. *Economy and Society*, Vol. 19, pp. 153–216.

——, 1994. 'The Transition to Post-Fordism and the Schumpeterian Workfare State', in R. Burrows and B. Loader (eds), *Towards a Post-Fordist Welfare State*. Routledge: London.

Kearney, B., G. E. Boyle and J. A. Walsh, 1995. *EU LEADER I Initiative in Ireland:*

Evaluation and Recommendations. Department of Agriculture, Food and Forestry: Dublin.

Kearney Associates, 2000. *Operational Programme for LEADER II Community Initiative: Ex-post Evaluation*. Interim report. Kearney Associates: Dublin.

Keohane, K., 1987. 'Dependent Industrialisation, Crisis Transfer and Crisis Displacement: The Transnational Pharmaceutical Industry and the Irish Republic'. Unpublished MA thesis, University College Cork, Cork.

Kinsella, J., S. Wilson, F. de Jong and H. Renting, 2000. 'Pluriactivity as a Livelihood Strategy in Irish Farm Households and its Role in Rural Development'. *Sociologia Ruralis*, Vol. 40, No. 4, pp. 481–96.

Klausen, J., 1995. 'Social Rights and State Building: T. H. Marshall in the Hands of the Social Reformer'. *World Politic*, Vol. 47, pp. 244–67.

Kooiman, J. (ed.), 1993. *Modern Governance*. Sage: London.

Lange, P. and M. Regini, 1989. *State, Market and Social Regulation: New Perspectives on Italy*. Cambridge University Press: Cambridge.

Lash, S. and J. Urry, 1987. *The End of Organised Capitalism*. Polity: Cambridge.

Laver, M. and K. Shepsle, 1992. 'Election Results and Coalition Possibilities in Ireland'. *Irish Political Studies*, Vol. 7, pp. 57–72.

Leddin, A., 1997. 'Economic Stabilisation, Recovery, and Growth: Ireland 1979–96'. *Irish Banking Review*, summer, pp. 2–17.

Lee, J. J., 1989. *Ireland 1912–1985*. Cambridge University Press: Cambridge.

Leonard, H. J., 1988. *Pollution and the Struggle for the World Product: Multi-national Corporations, Environment and International Comparative Advantage*. Cambridge University Press: Cambridge.

Lowe, P. and S. Ward, 1998. *British Environmental Policy and Europe*. Routledge: London.

LRC (Labour Relations Commission), 1991–7. *Annual Reports*. Stationery Office: Dublin.

McCartney, B. and P. Teague, 1997. 'Workplace Innovation in the Republic of Ireland'. *Economic and Social Review*, Vol. 28, No. 4, pp. 381–99.

McGrath, B. and J. Canavan, 2001. *Researching Rural Youth in the West of Ireland: A Mixed-Methods Approach*. Social Science Research Centre, National University of Ireland: Galway.

MacLean, I., 1994. 'On IPC and Planning, BAT, Monitoring and Enforcement'. *Irish Planning and Environmental Law Journal*, Vol. 1, No. 2, p. 82.

MacSharry R., P. White and J. O'Malley, 2000. *The Making of the Celtic Tiger: The Inside Story of Ireland's Boom Economy*. Mercier Press: Dublin.

Mair, P., 1999. 'Party Competition and the Changing Party System', in J. Coakley and M. Gallagher (eds), *Politics in the Republic of Ireland*. PSAI Press and Routledge: London.

Marsden, T., 1999. 'Rural Futures: The Consumption of the Countryside and its Regulation'. *Sociologia Ruralis*, Vol. 39, No. 4, pp. 500–20.

Marsh, D. and R. A. W. Rhodes, 1992. *Policy Networks in British Government*. Oxford University Press: Oxford.

Meehan, D., 1996. 'The Waste Management Act 1996: The Last Green Bottle'.

Irish Planning and Environmental Law Journal, Vol. 3, No. 2, pp. 59–67.

Metcalfe, L. and S. Richards, 1987. 'Evolving Public Management Cultures', in J. Kooiman and K. A. Eliasman (eds), *Managing Public Organisations: Lessons from Contemporary European Experience*. Sage: London.

Millar, M. and D. McKevitt, 1997. 'The Irish Civil Service'. Paper presented at the Comparative Perspective Conference, Indiana University, 5–8 April.

Morley, M., P. Gunningle and N. Hearty, 1994. 'The Flexibilisation of Work Practices in Ireland: Gradual Incrementalism or Radical Path Breaking Developments'. *Administration*, Vol. 42, No. 1, pp. 92–111.

Murray, M. and J. Greer, 1993. *Rural Development in Ireland: A Challenge for the 1990s*. Avebury Press: Aldershot.

National Pensions Board, 1998. *Securing Retirement Income*. Report of the Pensions Board on the National Pensions Policy Initiative. National Pensions Board: Dublin.

NESC (National Economic and Social Council), 1986. *A Strategy for Development*. Stationery Office: Dublin.

——, 1988a. *The Nature and Functioning of Labour Markets*. NESC: Dublin.

——, 1988b. *Review of Housing Policy*. NESC: Dublin.

——, 1990. *A Strategy for the Nineties*. NESC: Dublin.

——, 1993. *A Strategy for Competitiveness, Growth and Employment*. NESC: Dublin.

——, 1994. *New Approaches to Rural Development*. NESC: Dublin.

——, 1996. *A Strategy for the 21st Century*. NESC: Dublin.

National Income Related Pension Scheme, 1976. Stationery Office: Dublin.

Nolan, B., C. T. Whelan and J. Williams, 1998. *Where are the Poor Households?*. Oak Tree Press: Dublin.

O'Buachalla, S., 1992. 'Self-regulation and the Emergence of the Evaluative State: Trends in Irish Higher Education Policy'. *European Journal of Education*, Vol. 27, Nos. 1/2, pp. 69–79.

O'Connell, P. and F. McGinnity, 1997. *Working Schemes? Active Labour Market Policy in Ireland*. Ashgate: Aldershot.

O'Donnell, R., 1998. 'Social Partnership in Ireland: Principles and Interactions', in R. O'Donnell and J. Larragy (eds), *Negotiated Economic and Social Governance and European Integration*. European Commission. Proceedings of the Cost A7 Workshop, Dublin, 24 and 25 May 1996.

OECD, 1997. *Performance Pay Schemes for Public Sector Managers: An Evaluation of the Impacts*. Paris: OECD.

Offe, C., 1984. *Contradictions of the Welfare State*. Hutchinson: London.

——, 1991. 'Smooth Consolidation in the West German Welfare State: Structural Change, Fiscal Policies, and Populist Politics', in F. F. Piven (ed.), *Labour Parties in Post-Industrial Societies*. Polity: Cambridge.

O'Leary, G., 1999. 'Developing the Pension System in Ireland'. *Administration*, Vol. 47, No. 3, pp. 51–69.

O'Malley, E., 1992. *The Pilot Programme for Integrated Rural Development 1988–90*. Broadsheet 7. ESRI: Dublin.

O'Riordan, M., 1996. 'Towards a European Social Pact: The Irish Experience'.

Paper presented to European Trade Union Institute Conference, Brussels.

O'Riordan, S., 1998. 'Implications of New Organisational Structures: A Trade Union Perspective', in R. Boyle and T. McNamara (eds), *Governance and Accountability: Power and Responsibility in the Public Service*. Institute for Public Administration: Dublin.

Parternship 2000, 1997. Stationery Office: Dublin.

Peace, A., 1993. 'Environmental Protest, Bureaucratic Closure: The Politics of Discourse in Rural Ireland', in K. Milton (ed.), *Environmentalism: The View From Anthropology*. Routledge: London.

Pfaller, A. and I. Gough, 1991. *Can the Welfare State Compete? A Comparative Study of Five Advanced Capitalist Countries*. Macmillan: London.

Pierson, C., 1991. *Beyond the Welfare State?* Polity: Cambridge.

Piore, M. and C. Sabel, 1984. *The Second Industrial Divide: Possibilities for Prosperity*. Basic Books: New York.

Pollert, A., 1988. 'The Flexible Firm: Fixation or Fact?'. *Work, Employment and Society*, Vol. 2, pp. 281–316.

Programme for Competitiveness and Work, 1997. Stationery Office: Dublin.

Programme for Economic and Social Progress, 1991. Stationery Office: Dublin.

Programme for National Economic Recovery, 1987. Stationery Office: Dublin.

Programme for Prosperity and Fairness, 2000. Stationery Office: Dublin.

Purcell, J., 1991. 'The Rediscovery of the Management Prerogative: The Management of Labour Relations in the 1980s'. *Oxford Review of Economic Policy*, Vol. 7, pp. 33–43.

Ray, C., 1996. 'Local Rural Development and the LEADER I Programme', in P. Allison and M. Whitby (eds), *The Rural Economy and the British Countryside*. Earthscan: London.

——, 1999. 'Towards a Meta-framework of Endogenous Development: Repertoires, Paths, Democracy and Rights'. *Sociologia Ruralis*, Vol. 39, No. 4, pp. 521–38.

Regan, S., 1994. 'Advice and Training in Agriculture to Meet the Change in the Direction of Farming', in M. Maloney (ed.), *Agriculture and the Environment: Proceedings of a Conference on the Integration of EC Environmental Objectives with Agricultural Policy*. Royal Dublin Society, Dublin, 9–11 March.

Regini, M., 1996. 'Still Engaging in Corporatism? Some Lessons from the Recent Italian Experience of Concertation'. Paper presented at the 8th International Conference on Socio-Economics, Session on Globalisation and the Future of Corporatism, Geneva, 12–14 July.

Rhodes, M., 1998. 'Globalisation, Labour Markets and Welfare States: A Future of "Competitive Corporatism"?', in M. Rhodes and Y. Meny (eds), *The Future of European Welfare: A New Social Contract?*. Macmillan: London.

Rhodes, R. A. W., 1996. 'The New Governance: Governing Without Government'. *Political Studies*, Vol. 44, No. 4, pp. 652–67.

Richardson, J., 2000. 'Government, Interest Groups and Policy Change'. *Political Studies*, Vol. 48, No. 5, pp. 1006–25.

Richardson, J. J. and G. Jordan, 1982. *Policy Styles in Western Europe*. George Allen and Unwin: London.

Roche, W. K., 1998. 'Public Service Reform and Human Resource Management'. *Administration*, Vol. 46, No. 2, pp. 3–24.

Roche, W. K. and J. F. Geary, 1998. 'Collaborative Production and the Irish Boom: Work Organisation, Partnership and Direct Involvement in Irish Workplaces'. Centre for Employment Relations and Organisational Performance Working Paper. University College Dublin: Dublin.

——, 2000. 'Collaborative Production and the Irish Boom: Work Organisation, Partnership and Direct Involvement in Irish Workplaces'. *Economic and Social Review*, Vol. 31, No. 1, pp. 1–36.

Rose, R., 1991. 'What is Lesson Drawing?'. *Journal of Public Policy*, Vol. 11, pp. 3–30.

Rowthorn, R E., 1992. 'Centralisation, Employment and Wage Dispersion'. *Economic Journal*, Vol. 102, pp. 504–26.

Rubery, J. and F. Wilkinson (eds), 1994. *Employer Strategy and the Labour Market*. Oxford University Press: Oxford.

Rustin, M., 1994. 'Flexibility in Higher Education', in R. Burrows and B. Loader (eds), *Towards a post-Fordist Welfare State*. Routledge: London.

Sabel, C., 1995. *Ireland: Local Partnerships and Social Innovation*. OECD: Paris.

Saward, M., 1997. 'In Search of the Hollow Crown', in P. Weller, H. Bakvis and R. A. W. Rhodes (eds), *The Hollow Crown: Countervailing Trends in Core Executives*. Macmillan: London.

Scannell, Y., 1989. *The Law and Practice Relating to Pollution Control in the Republic of Ireland*. Graham and Trotman: Dublin.

——, 1990. 'Legislation and Toxic Waste Disposal in Ireland', in *Environmental Protection and the Impact of European Community Law: Papers from the Joint Conference with the Incorporated Law Society of Ireland*. Irish Centre for European Law, Trinity College, Dublin: Dublin.

——, 1993. 'Agriculture and Environmental Law', in J. Feehan (ed.), *Environment and Development in Ireland*. Environmental Institute: Dublin.

——, 1995. *Environmental and Planning Law in Ireland*. Round Hall Press: Dublin.

Serving the Country Better, 1985. Stationery Office: Dublin

Sherwood, M., 1994. 'The Role of the EPA in Agriculture', in M. Maloney (ed.), *Agriculture and the Environment: Proceedings of a Conference on the Integration of EC Environmental Objectives with Agricultural Policy*. Royal Dublin Society, Dublin, 9–11 March.

Shortall, S., 1994. 'The Irish Rural Development Paradigm: An Exploratory Analysis'. *Economic and Social Review*, Vol. 25, No. 3, pp. 233–61.

Sinnot, R., 1999. 'The Electoral System', in J. Coakley and M. Gallagher (eds), *Politics in the Republic of Ireland*. PSAI Press and Routledge: London.

Stone, D., 2000. 'Non-Governmental Policy Transfer: The Strategies of Independent Policy Institutions'. *Governance*, Vol. 13, No. 1, pp. 45–71.

Streeck, W., 1988. 'Comment on Ronald Dore, "Rigidities in the Labour Market"'. *Government and Opposition*, Vol. 23, No. 4, pp. 413–23.

——, 1992. *Social Institutions and Economic Performance: Studies of Industrial Rela-*

tions in Advanced Capitalist Economies. Sage: London.

Streeck, W. and P. C. Schmitter, 1991. 'From National Corporatism to Transnational Pluralism: Organised Interests in the Single European Market'. *Politics and Society,* Vol. 19, pp. 133–64.

Tansey, P., 1998. *Ireland at Work.* Oak Tree Press: Dublin.

Taylor, G., 1993. 'In Search of the Elusive Entrepreneur'. *Irish Political Studies,* Vol. 8, pp. 89–105.

——, 1995. 'Marxism', in D. Marsh and G. Stoker, *Theory and Methods in Political Science.* Macmillan: London.

——, 1996a. 'Labour Market Rigidities, Institutional Impediments and Managerial Constraints: Some Reflections on Macro-political Bargaining in Ireland'. *Economic and Social Review,* Vol. 27, No. 3, pp. 253–77.

——, 1996b. 'The Politics of Conviviality: Voluntary Workfare and the Right to Useful Unemployment'. *Administration,* Vol. 43, No. 3, pp. 36–56.

——, 1998a. 'Conserving the Emerald Tiger: The Politics of Environmental Regulation in Ireland'. *Environmental Politics,* Vol. 7, No. 4, pp. 53–74.

——, 1998b. 'Me Thinks thou Do'st Protest Too Much: Oral Hearings, Public Registers and Environmental Democracy in Ireland'. *Irish Planning and Environmental Law Journal,* Vol. 5, No. 4, pp. 143–55.

——, 2001. *Conserving the Emerald Tiger: The Politics of Environmental Regulation in Ireland.* Arlen House Press: Galway.

——(ed.), 2002a. *Issues in Irish Public Policy.* Irish Academic Press: Dublin.

——, 2002b. 'Hailing with an Invisible Hand: A "Cosy" Political Dispute Amid the Rise of Neo-Liberal Politics in Modern Ireland'. *Government and Opposition,* Vol. 37, No. 4, pp. 501–23.

——, 2003. 'Bargaining Celtic Style', in G. Lemhbruch and F. Van Waarden (eds), *Renegotiating the Welfare State: Flexible Adjustment through Corporatist Concertation.* Routledge: London and New York.

——, 2004. If No Risk is Proven, Is There a Risk?: The Reconfiguration of Risk in the Modern State'. Centre for Public Policy working papers. National University of Ireland: Galway.

Taylor, G. and A. Horan, 2001. 'From Cats, Dogs, Parks and Playgrounds to IPC Licensing: Policy Learning and the Evolution of Environmental Policy in Ireland'. *British Journal of Politics and International Relations,* Vol. 3, No. 4, pp. 369–93.

Taylor, G. and M. Millar, forthcoming. 'The Politics of Food Regulation and Reform in Ireland'. *Public Administration.*

Titmuss, R., 1967. 'Choice and the Welfare State', in *Socialism and Affluence.* Fabian Society and Civic Press: Glasgow.

Tovey, H., 1996. 'Rural Poverty: A Political Economy Perspective', in Curtin *et al..*, 1996.

——, 1999. 'Rural Poverty: A Political Economy Approach', in D. Pringle, J. Walsh and M. Hennessy (eds), *Poor People, Poor Places: A Geography of Poverty and Deprivation in Ireland.* Oak Tree Press and Geographical Society of Ireland: Dublin.

Tutty, M. G., 1998. 'Implications of New Organisational Structures', in R. Boyle and T. McNamara (eds), *Governance and Accountability: Power and Responsibility in the Public Service*. Institute for Public Administration: Dublin.

Van der Straaten, J., 1994. 'A Sound European Environmental Policy: Challenges, Possibilities and Barriers'. *Environmental Politics*, Vol. 1, No. 4, pp. 65–81.

Verheijen, T. and M. Millar, 1998. 'Reforming Public Policy Processes and Securing Accountability: Ireland in Comparative Perspective'. *International Review of Administrative Sciences*, Vol. 64, No. 1, pp. 97–119.

Ward, H., 1993. 'State Exploitation, Capital Accumulation and the Evolution of Modes of Regulation: A Defence of Bottom Line Economism'. Paper delivered to the PSA Conference.

Walsh, J., 1993. 'Internalisation v. Decentralisation: An Analysis of Recent Developments in Pay Bargaining'. *British Journal of Industrial Relations*, Vol. 31, No. 3, pp. 409–32.

Walshe, J., 1999. *A New Partnership in Education: From Consultation to Legislation in the Nineties*. Institute for Public Administration: Dublin.

Warde, A., 1994. 'Consumers, Consumption and Post-Fordism', in R. Burrows and B. Loader (eds), *Towards a Post-Fordist Welfare State*. Routledge: London.

Index